Heavenly Treasures

Compiled and Written
By
Rayola Kelley

Hidden Manna Publications

Heavenly Treasures
Inspirational Quotes & Stories

Copyright © 2022 by Rayola Kelley

ISBN: 978-1-7347503-0-0

Cover Design: Pam Wester

Printed in the USA

**Hidden Manna Publications
PO Box 3572
Oldtown, ID 83822**

Facebook:
https://www.facebook.com/HiddenMannaPublications/

**In loving
memory of
my parents:**

Lester & Ramona Kelley

CONTENTS

INTRODUCTION

This is the fifth book in what I call the Nuggets Series. It is a combination of sayings, stories, prayers, and poems that are inspirational and thought provoking. They are meant to cause us to pause, consider, and examine our own life in the Lord, our attitude towards Him and our calling, as well as our walk before others.

There are those who question my reasoning for putting such books together, especially since many of these sayings can be found on the Internet. I must admit, I compiled these books because I want to preserve such nuggets for myself. The idea that the cloud of technology will someday completely crash, dissipating these nuggets into an unseen wasteland to be forever lost is never far from my consideration. That is one reason why I have wanted to put these nuggets into a written record that can be held, opened, and partaken of.

The other reason for putting the Nuggets books together is because of how Christians spiritually feed themselves today. They feed on bits and pieces of truth. After all, they are busy people with many demands nipping at their heels. They have been conditioned on fast food, and do not have time to wade through repetitious mantras, long dissertations, rambling thoughts, brain-numbing nonsense and the indoctrination enveloping the dark days in which we live,

As in previous Nuggets books I have written the stories unless indicated differently, and used just my initials RJK to identify personal sayings. Some of the quotes are from controversial people, some who have fallen from the pinnacle of trustworthiness and godliness to the point that they became hypocrites playing the court jester or fool on the different stages of the world. To my dismay such an event even happened as I was finishing up this book.

This has caused a struggle in my own soul as to whether I need to revamp the book, but I was reminded true wisdom comes from God and God can use any instrument He chooses to declare it, as He did in the case of a donkey setting straight a prophet by the name of Balaam. Jesus also warned the Pharisees that the rocks would even cry out praises to God if human voices remained silent.

I was also reminded that the Lord will never repent or take back a gift He may have given us, but in the end, that servant will be judged with how he or she used that gift and the attitude and spirit in which they operated in it. In fact, the proclamations and teachings of His truth and wisdom will prove to be a greater damnation on those who hide their hypocrisy behind God's wisdom because they knew what was to be, but they didn't fear, believe, love enough, repent, or obey Him to walk in it.

I have known for years that when it comes to truth our test as believers is not whether we can trust the vessel, but whether it is truth or wisdom from God. If it is, we must receive it, assimilate it, and walk in it, regardless of the hypocrites that delivered it.

Each section is highlighted by one of God's banners of truth. My prayer is that these banners will cause the reader to pause, consider where they presently are in their life before following the bits and pieces that hopefully will inspire them to explore greater heights in God, while causing a deeper hunger for His Word.

SALVATION

The Cost of Salvation

What does salvation cost? As believers we know the answer. Salvation cost God His Son, and His Son His life. We can stand in awe of God's amazing love, rejoice over Jesus' great gift of life, and bow before Him because of His grace. However, did the cost of my salvation stop with Jesus' death on the cross?

The truth about the reality of salvation is that it will continue to cost those who dare follow in Jesus' footprints. My salvation not only cost Jesus, but others. The torch of the believer's commission has been handed down from one generation to another. However, each generation presented its own sacrifice in order for the torch of the Gospel to reach into the dark recesses of the world. Lives first always had to be offered up to ensure consecration from above. Such consecration was often followed by tears, watering the hard ground of the lost.

This reality was brought out in the life of a missionary by the name of John G. Paton. He took his young bride with him to the New Hebrides. His call brought him to a distant station on the island of Tanna. However, tragedy struck him with a double blow. It was then that his tears watered the ground. His wife died in childbirth and she was later joined in glory by their infant son seventeen days later.

One must ask how this double blow affected Paton. He described how he had to dig the grave at the end of the house with his own hands and a broken heart for his beloved wife, and later he also placed his child in it. He spoke of how he was never forsaken by the Lord, and that his ever merciful Lord sustained him. He then said this about it, "That spot (grave) became my scared and much frequented shrine during all the following months and years when I labored on for the salvation of these savage islanders amidst difficulties, dangers, and deaths. Whensoever Tanna turns to the Lord and is won for Christ, men in after days will find the memory of that spot still green where, with ceaseless prayers and tears, I claimed that land for God in which I had buried my dead with faith and hope. But for Jesus and the fellowship he vouchsafed me there, I must have gone mad and died beside that lonely grave!" (HA, pgs. 50, 51)

It is easy to assume much about our salvation. We think of Christ and His death on the cross, but we fail to realize that many crosses have been formed through the years. Like Jesus, the cross represents suffering and death. And, whosoever will follow Jesus, must deny self and pick up the cross. Each cross may be different, but each one will produce death, while the ground is being watered with tears for the furtherance of the Gospel.

***

♦ I am only pointing out the absurdity of thinking that one can gain eternal life apart from a real righteousness that is born of repentance and genuine faith.

-David Servant
Happy Endings Magazine

♦ The fact that a method produces decisions or numbers is not measure that it is working. God saves men despite us, not because of us, and some may be saved in spite of the paucity of accurate information. The measure of truth, in the end is not popularity.

-Steve Montgomery
The Berean Call
(October 2013)

***

Wonders of wonders! Vast surprises!
Could bigger wonder be,
That He who built the starry skies
Once bled and died for me?

Amazing, startling sacrifice,
Confounding all our thought!
Stupendous, staggering purchase price
Which our redemption bought!

-Author Unknown

♦ I should not be physically alive at this moment, I should be, were I alive at all, a corrupt or at least an incredibly unhappy, violent, bitter, self-occupied destructive soul, were it not for religion—for its having come and saved me from myself—it, and nothing else; it, in place of everything else; it, in a sense, against everything else.

-Baron von Hugel
(HA, pg. 17)

♦ The Old Testament was all shadow and promise. Jesus brought and gives the reality, *the substance* of things hoped for. In Him the blessings and powers of the eternal life are our actual possession and experience.

-Andrew Murray
(WC, pg. 20)

Heavenly Treasures

♦ What does it mean to receive Jesus Christ? It means to take Christ to be to yourself all that God offers Him to everybody. Jesus Christ is God's gift.

-R. A. Torrey
(BT, pg. 13)

♦ Sin is nearly always symptomatic of a believer's having distanced himself from Christ. All ministering must therefore begin with where a believer is in his relationship with Jesus— and a recognition of where he needs to be.

-T. A. McMahon
The Berean Call

Prayer: *Lord, represent sin to me in it odious colours that I may hate it; ...Teach me to behold my Creator, his ability to save, his arms outstretched, his heart big for me. (VOV, pg. 37)*

♦ A dumb witness is no witness. Confession is one condition of salvation. Your mouth is the damper to your soul. Close the damper, and the fire goes out; open the draft, and the fire burns hotly. Consecration and faith are essential, but testimony opens the soul to God and kindles the holy fire to a Pentecostal glow.

-B. B. Taylor
(SC, pg. 113)

***

Self is the only prison that can ever bind a soul;
Christ is the only Angel that can the gates unroll.
And when He comes to set thee free, arise and follow fast.
His way may lie through darkness but it leads to light at last.

-John Gregory Mantle
(BH, pg. 33)

◆ The Gospel is the death, burial, and resurrection of Jesus. Death was Jesus' work through redemption, His burial the means to silence accusation due to sins, and the resurrection of the body the ultimate victory over death. His death was our victory, His empty grave our witness, and His resurrection our hope. In the Gospel we can possess the seed of life through death, the reality of His life through sanctification, and the expectation of His life through resurrection.

-RJK

◆ His ability to deliver on His promises is tied directly to His omnipotence. If God were not omnipotent, He would be unable to keep His promises. He could not give any of us assurance of salvation.

-A. W. Tozer
(JG, pg. 90)

◆ Though "Grace came by Jesus Christ," it was veiled during His earthly ministry. But when sin reached its climax the only possible alternatives were "the doom of Sodom or the mercy of the Gospel"—judgment unmixed, or grace unlimited. And grace prevailed. God committed all judgment to the Lord Jesus Christ, and He, the only Being in the universe who can judge a sinner, is now seated on the throne of God as *a Saviour.*

-Sir Robert Anderson
(TH, pg. 171)

◆ A spiritual experience should never make you an exception to the rule. Truth is the same for everybody, but not experiences. Regardless of spiritual experiences, one still has to confess that Jesus is Lord and repent of his or her sins to be saved.

-RJK

Prayer: *Lord, let angels sing for the lost who are found, the prodigals that turn back to the Father's house, the wandering heart who is reclaimed by Your love, Satan's captives who are released from their blind, lame, deaf state, broken hearts that are healed by Your touch, those whose robes of self-righteousness have been rip asunder by Your holiness, the formalist who has found no life in dead doctrines, and the ignorant who ceased to hide in darkness, for the saints are perfected in holy faith. Amen.*

♦ We tell people to believe, and certainly they must, but we have soft-pedaled confession. Yet God's Word couples mouth confession with heart belief in an unmistakable and unbreakable connection (Rom. 10:9-10). The Bible demands public mouth confession of Christ as Lord and Savior as emphatically as heart belief for salvation.

-Vance Havner
(RG, pg. 164)

♦ The hand that was pierced by the nails has conquered sin; the hand that was fastened to the wood has fastened up the accusation that was written against us, the hand that bled has brought salvation to us, so that we are Christ's forever.

-Charles Spurgeon
(FJ, pgs. 67-68)

♦ There are not multiple races, just variations within the human race; no people are higher or lower on an "evolutionary scale," but all people are made in the image of God and need Jesus Christ as Savior and Lord.

-Bodie Hodge
(TB, pg. 22)

♦ We have a mistaken notion that God shows mercy because Jesus died. Jesus died because God is showing mercy.

-A.W. Tozer
(MDP, pg. 103)

♦ Sinners are not pelted into Christ with stones of hard provoking language, but wooed into Christ by heart-melting exhortations.

-William Gurnall
(CCA, Vol 1. pg. 507)

♦ How many times should Jesus address our sin? He only had to address it once because the work of redemption took away our sin before the face of God, but as for you and me, we must address old sin by bringing it to the cross, present sin through repentance, and develop a hatred for it to continue to properly address it in the future.

-RJK

♦ A man without Christ is blind and dead. He cannot see or live until he believes and receives the gospel. Light means nothing to a blind man. He must also have sight.

-Vance Havner
(PD, pg. 56)

♦ If there is anything excellent, it is salvation: if there be anything necessary, it is working out salvation; if there be any tool to work with, tis holy fear.

-Thomas Watson
(SWR, pg. 17)

♦ The worst thing that can happen is that Christianity wastes this treasure, her eternal salvation, and throws it away. This has been the case throughout the centuries, and will be till the end of the world.

-Winrich Scheffbuch
Midnight Call
January 2018

Prayer: *Lord, life provides the storms but You provide the way through each storm. The world provides the ways of destruction, but You provide the ways of life eternal. My flesh deserves judgment, but Your mercy allots pardon. In my fallen sinful state, I merit hell, but You have extended grace to me in spite of my treacherous practices towards You. Thank You for doing the impossible and saving my soul. Amen.*

♦ It is only when His people travail in pain that souls are born again. No soul is born without such birth-pangs. And those pangs are temporary—fleeting, for they give place to joy when the soul enters the Kingdom. (PH, pg. 116)

♦ The Gospel brings peace to the sinner, not because it makes light of his sin, or lowers the inexorable claims of Divine perfection, but because it tells how Christ has made it possible for an absolutely righteous and thrice holy God to pardon and save absolutely sinful and evil men.

-Sir Robert Anderson
(RT, pg. 152)

♦ In him the enslaved find redemption, the guilty pardon, the unholy renovation. (VOV, pg. 21)

♦ For it is the new life separated from sin, immorality and indecency that gives us confidence in our salvation.

-Rene` Malgo
Midnight Call
April 2016

♦ Carnality hangs as a fearful incubus in the soul. Full salvation consumes the "old man" (Rom. 6:6) and fills the soul with zeal.

-L. L. Pickett
(SC, pg. 40)

♦ The Lord Jesus wants to live in your heart and in your life through His Holy Spirit. You can't experience His victory at work, in the kitchen, or in the bedroom, if you only open the door of your living room.

-Corrie ten Boom
(MA, Bk. 1, pg. 113)

♦ Shocking as it may seem, God saves those who do *not* work, that is, who do not try to earn or deserve salvation but receive it as a free gift.

-William MacDonald
(NAG, pg. 19)

♦ God's holiness and justice require that sinners be eternally separated from Him. To be cut off completely and eternally from that Love for which one was created will be to burn with a thirst that will only grow ever more unbearable. God, however, graciously and freely offers salvation from that most dreadful condemnation.

-Dave Hunt
The Berean Call

♦ Adam and Christ represent the entire human race—the latter all saints and the former all sinners. The great plan of salvation consists in the infusion of the Christ life into the dead soul, which is regeneration, and the elimination of the sin life, which is sanctification. When the universe shall stand before the great white throne in final judgment all will be identified either with Adam or Christ.

-W. B. Godbey
(SC, pg. 31)

♦ Redemption is not, first, an easy way of salvation for the sinner, and then a display of the character of God. God must be supreme. A man who makes self his chief aim is contemptible, but in the very nature of things God must be first in everything, else He would be no longer God.

-Sir Robert Anderson
(GAM, pg. 31)

♦ Salvation-work cannot be done by the candle-light of a natural understanding, but by the day light of gospel revelation; this sun must rise before man can go forth to this labour.

-William Gurnall
(CCA, Vol. 2, pg. 551)

♦ When we draw our last breath only one thing matters, that our name is written in the Lamb's book of life.

(Internet)

♦ God needs no rescuing, but we do, and we must rescue our concepts from their fallen and frightfully inadequate condition so that boundless confidence in Him can reign once again.

-A.W. Tozer
(MDP, pg. 18)

***

Most of us take note of the lives of actors and actresses. In some cases, we think of them as family; therefore, we root for them, wished we knew them personally, and even almost idolize them.

As believers our desire is to see them saved. For example, I read a story where a Christian shared her faith with John Lennon who was just walking by her house. Just before he died, Rock Hudson's nurse led him through the sinner's prayer.

I read of another incident that involved actor, John Wayne. He always played the honorable hero in his motion pictures. He represented the idea of the "great American," in many ways. The truth is we always want to see the good guy win, but if the "good guy" does not pass from this world into eternity as a blood bought saint by the Lamb of God, he or she will not only be the poorest of all fools and but also the greatest loser.

Some of you might remember the motorcycle accident the daughter of Robert Schuller, Cindy was in when she was a teenager. She lost her leg. According to the account that can be found on the internet, John Wayne heard about it and wrote to her telling her he was sorry to hear about her accident. He told her that he hoped she would be all right and signed his famous name.

The note was delivered to her and Cindy decided she wanted to write him back. Her reply went this way, "Dear Mr. Wayne, I got your note. Thanks for writing to me. I like you very much. I am going to be all right because Jesus is going to help me. Mr. Wayne, do you know Jesus? I sure hope you know Jesus, Mr. Wayne, because I cannot imagine heaven being complete without John Wayne being there. I hope, if you don't know Jesus, that you will give your heart to Jesus right now. See you in heaven."

Cindy signed her name and wrote across the envelope "John Wayne." A visitor came to her room as she was finishing up and asked her what she was doing. She told him that she had just written John Wayne but she did not know where to send it. The visitor's reply was, "That's funny, I am going to have dinner with

John Wayne tonight at the Newport Club down at Newport Beach. Give it to me and I will give it to him."

There were 12 in attendance at the dinner. The group was laughing and cutting up when the man felt the letter in his pocket and remembered that he was to deliver it to the famous actor. The man took the letter out of his pocket and offered a simple explanation, "Hey, Duke, I was in Schuller's daughter's room today and she wrote you a letter and wanted me to give it to you. Here it is."

It was passed down to Wayne and he opened it, while the rest of the table continued on their merry exchange. Someone just happened to look down at John Wayne to see he was not laughing but that tears were present. One of them asked him what was the matter. The inquiry stopped the merriment, especially when the actor stated that he wanted to read the letter to them and preceded to.

When he was through, it was obvious that the letter reached a cord because he was weeping. He folded the letter and put it in his pocket. He then pointed to the man who brought the letter and said, "You go tell that little girl that right now, in this restaurant, right here, John Wayne gives his heart to Jesus Christ and I will see her in heaven." Three weeks later John Wayne passed from this temporary world into eternity.

Regardless of his notoriety, John Wayne was a soul who needed to be saved. As Christians we rejoice over the salvation of famous celebrities, but a more important place rejoices over the lost sheep being found and that is heaven. Our status on earth is insignificant and the only thing that will count is when all is said and done, our name is written in the "Book of Life."

♦ No sin is greater than the sin of unbelief, for if union with Christ is the greatest good, unbelief is the greatest sin. (VOV, pg. 20)

◆ Repentance is a heart deep sorrow over one's sin, and a turning to face the opposite direction with a determination to sin no more.

-Israel Teaching Letter
Bridges for Peace
August 2015

◆ At Calvary, grace and truth kissed. At Calvary, ultimate love was revealed. At Calvary, the holiness of God was eternally propitiated (satisfied).

-Marvin Rosenthal
Zion's Fire Magazine
Jul/Aug. 2015

◆ Some might say that as long as a person believes that Christ died for his sins, was buried and rose the third day he is saved. But that declaration doesn't explain the full gospel....Surely that (message) involves who the biblical God is, who the biblical Christ is, what the biblical problem between God and man is, the biblical and only means of man's forgiveness by God, and the eternal consequences for those who reject the biblical gospel.

-The Berean Call
October 2015

◆ Inward faith and outward confession are necessary to salvation. . .The confession without the experience is hypocrisy. The experience without the confession will soon die.

-W. N. Hirst
(SC, pg. 68)

◆ Our good works will not be the ground of our salvation, but the result of our salvation, and the proof of it. We must be very careful not to mix in our good works at all as the ground of salvation. We are forgiven, not because of Christ's death and our good works, but solely and entirely because of Christ's death.

-R. A. Torrey
(BT, pg. 15)

***

He stooped to one
    by fear oppressed
He gave the weary
    seeker rest.
And came Himself
    to dwell within.

He stopped the flow
    of bitter tears
He stopped the flow
    of wasted years.

He very life
    I receive,
When I cried, "Jesus,
    I believe."

-Cornelius Vanderbegger Jr.

♦ What is the wisdom of the world's greatest scientist or philosopher compared with eternal life? What are the honors of a great general or a mighty ruler of men compared with eternal life? What are the pleasures of the most successful votary of pleasure compared with eternal life?

-R. A. Torrey
(BT, pg. 129)

♦ The propitiation of Christ is the epoch and turning point in the world's history. By the sacrifice of himself, and by this act alone, are we reconciled to God.

-H. A. W. Meyer
(MM, pg. 7)

- In spite of all the philosophies of men, the Cross is still the great *draw*. The word used for the phrase "lifted up" suggests an honorable advancement, "If I be exalted."

  -Herbert Lockyer
  (MM, pg. 22)

***

But none of the ransomed ever knew
How deep were the waters crossed:
Nor how dark was the night the Lord passed through,
Ere He found His sheep that was lost.

-Elizabeth C. Clephane
(MM, pg. 38)

Prayer: *Lord, may I never vex You by my indifference and waywardness, grieve Your Spirit and servant by my cold welcome, and resist Him by my hard rebellion.* (Inspired by personal request—VOV, pg. 29.)

- Redemption has flowed down to mankind from the heart of God through His Son by the Spirit. But salvation, to be effective, must be appropriated and confessed...Redemption is something that took place on the cross, but salvation is something that takes place and becomes known inside of us! Salvation is redemption appropriated by faith.

  -A. W. Tozer
  (JG, pgs. 113, 114)

- There can be no recognition of good works or of amendment of life, and no citizenship with the saints, until after the sinner has, as a sinner, accepted Christ.

  -Sir Robert Anderson
  (RT, pg. 73)

♦ A glance at Christ will save, but it is the gazing at Christ that sanctifies.

-Robert Murray McCheyne
(JJ, pg. 76)

♦ Today, there are many who are enlarging the narrow way to eternal life by erecting their own Jesus. They refuse to let the truths of the Bible align them within the narrow confines of who Jesus really is, and must be in their lives. Since the narrow width of the gate is defined by the God-Man Jesus, many will seek to enter in, but will fail to do so because they will not believe the Word of God concerning Him, preventing them from finding the actual entrance.

-RJK

♦ Ours is a twofold salvation by Christ: a salvation from the guilt and penalty through his death, and a salvation from the government and power of sin through his resurrection.

-Hebert Lockyer
(MM, pg. 144)

♦ If you do not think your sin is big, the Lord cannot save you. If you think your sin is bigger than God, He cannot save you. You must realize that though your sin is big, God is infinite and, therefore, bigger than all your sin. Where sin abounded, the grace of God does much more abound.

-A.W. Tozer
(MDP, pg. 305)

♦ A truly penitent soul is not only conscious of its sin, but it confesses it, abandons it, turns from it. Not a secret purpose to do evil is spared in the heart. The penitent soul makes wrongs right and crooked things straight.

-Seth C. Rees
(SC, pg. 116)

♦ Sin is the disease of the soul that kills, the poison sting of the conscience that will not let us rest, the curse that destroys all hope, the monster that mocks grace, the foe that scoffs at hope, and the jester who dances around the work of redemption with foolish jesting and antics.

-RJK

♦ Pagan mythology had a three-headed monster at the door of hell, but modern Christianity has its *Cerberus* at the gate of heaven. Faith, repentance, and the Spirit's work, by God intended to bring salvation to our very door, are turned by men into a threefold hindrance on the way to life: faith is a rugged mountain, repentance a dreary slough, and the fickle phantom of the Spirit's work.

-Sir Robert Anderson
(GAM, pg.56)

♦ The reason many do not have the assurance they are saved is they are *not* saved. They need *salvation* before they need *assurance.*

-R.A. Torrey
(HSC, pg. 26)

♦ And the gospel is the sacrificing knife in the hand of the Spirit. The word is called 'the sword of the Spirit,' as that which he useth to kill and slay sin within the hearts of his people.

-William Gurnall
(CCA, Vol. 1, pg. 545)

Heavenly Treasures

♦ When the gospel is preached, there will be true and false conversions.

-Ray Comfort
(GWP, pg. 16))

♦ He will save all who trust in Him. But it is only a small crowd today who wants His Son to be revealed in them; only a small crowd who are willing to be the showcase of Jesus, in whom He can reveal His lovely character. If we decide to become His exhibits, it is goodbye to self, and, praise God, no man has yet fathomed the wonders that Jesus can display in an empty showcase.

-Paul Rader
(GBM, pg. 172)

♦ The homerun story? It is Christ crucified, dead, and buried, resurrected, ascended into heaven, where He waits to welcome God's children home.

-Dois I. Rosser Jr.
(GHC, pg. 208)

♦ My soul is often a chariot without wheels, clogged and hindered in sin's miry clay; Mount it on eagle's wings and cause it to soar upward to thyself. (VOV, pg. 90)

♦ But old fallen Judaism, which killed Jesus, did preach salvation by legal obedience, thus inculcating the most fatal heresy, *i.e.*, legalism, which this day ever rings out from the popular pulpits and constitutes Satan's sleekest plank to hell. You never get sanctified by good works, but by faith alone in the cleansing blood.

-W. B. Godbey
(SC, pg. 33)

- Let us work out our salvation in thankful co-operation with Him. The diamond can offer no resistance to the cutter, nor can the clay offer intelligent response to the potter. We can both resist and respond.

  -John Gregory Mantle
  (BH, pg. 145)

- For what constitutes a Christian is not accepting the Christian's creed, but accepting Christ as Saviour and Lord.

  -Sir Robert Anderson
  (RT, pg. 167)

- If the gospel does not change a man, transform him and take the evil out of him, then he does not have the gospel in power. The gospel is a transforming power.

  -A.W. Tozer
  (RCF, pg. 102)

- Conscience is God's officer; and, though the debt be paid in heaven, yet it will not let the soul go free, till a warrant comes from thence to authorize it

  -William Gurnall
  (CCA, Vol. 1, pg. 525)

Assurance

What does it mean to have assurance when it comes to your salvation? I watch many people struggle with this issue. There are a few things that can definitely throw a shadow across the terrain of our soul and mind when it comes to this matter.

This shadow is caused by corruption that is present in the soul, a knowing heart that is found to be divided, and a mind that can't be fooled until it is seared with seduction and indoctrination by darkness about what is right and wrong.

Heavenly Treasures

The shadows come when we compromise with the world, chase after the fleshly desires while trying to hold on to God's promises that remain unmoved, and failing to totally agree with God about matters that pertain to godliness. To cause the shadows to flee, we must turn in repentance towards God to cause them to part with His light, flee the temptation of the flesh, separate from the influences of the world, dissipate the cold environment with humility, and cry out to God for mercy.

It is when the joy of our salvation returns that we can once again walk in assurance that our spirit has been revived, our soul rescued, our mind changed, and our heart single in its love and devotion towards the One who is worthy of all praise and worship.

♦ God's mercy does not make us repent; rather God's mercy paves the way for us to come to that point of repentance. Not all will come, but all can.

-A.W. Tozer
(MDP, pg. 108)

♦ When the saints shall remember, that the waters of wrath he was plunged into, are the wells of salvation from whence they draw all their joy; that they have got the cup of salvation, in exchange of the cup of wrath his Father gave him to drink…how will their hearts leap within them burn with seraphic love, like coals of juniper, and the arch of heaven ring with their songs of salvation.

-Thomas Boston
(SWR, pg. 141)

♦ Some receive Christ as a sin-bearer and thus find pardon, but they do not get beyond that. Thus their life is ongoing of daily failure. Others receive Him as their risen Savior also, and they experience victory over sin.

-R.A. Torrey
(HSC, pg. 13)

♦ Believing there is a god will not save you. Believing God about your spiritual plight will lead you to salvation.

-RJK

♦ I am guilty but pardoned, lost, but saved, wandering, but found sinning, but cleansed. (VOV, pg. 83)

♦ The plan of salvation begins not with Christ but with God and His *holiness*, then *sin* and man's *lost* state. There is much superficial "believing in Jesus" that has never faced sin, that professes but never possesses eternal life.

-Vance Havner
(RG, pg. 194)

♦ …no one has a right to confess himself a Christian who is not seeking to live for the glory of God. If there be not a nature that delights in the will of God, there is every reason to doubt whether one has ever been truly saved.

-H. A. Ironside
(HC, pg. 46)

♦ A rabbi once asked his disciples, "How can you tell when a sin you have committed has been pardoned?" His disciple gave various answers but none of them pleased him. "We can tell", the rabbi said, "by the fact that we no longer commit that sin."

♦ The key word of the false gospel is *Do.* The key word of grace is *Done.* Christ has already finished the work of redemption. So you don't have to.

-William MacDonald
(NAG, pg. 53)

♦ Alienation is exactly what the Bible calls that moral incompatibility between God and man. God is not far away, but He seems to be far away because He is far away in character. Man has sinned, and God is holy. Only Christ's atonement remedies the gap.

-A.W. Tozer
(MDP, pg. 212)

Where Are My Sins?

A little boy once asked his mother, "Mother, where are our sins after they are blotted out?" His mother replied, "My boy, where are those figures that were on your slate yesterday?" He answered, "I rubbed them out." Then she asked, "Where are they now?" He replied, "They are nowhere." "Well," she said, "that is just so with your sins when God has blotted them out. They are nowhere. They have ceased to be."

***

I see the crowd in Pilate's hall,
    I mark their wrathful mien.
Their shouts of "crucify!" appall,
    With blasphemy between.
But of that shouting multitude,
    I feel that I am one.

-Horatius Bonar
(MM, pg. 111)

- It is not that the sinner *believes*, nor yet that he believes the *gospel*, but that he believes GOD.

  -Sir Robert Anderson
  (GAM, pg. 157)

- It is the Christians having assurance and peace and joy who have always been used by God in the propagation and the spreading of the truth. This is the great secret of triumphant living, but it is also the secret of true evangelism.

  -Martyn Lloyd-Jones
  (SFG, pg. 121)

Ever Needing Him

Salvation is not a one-time experience. This miraculous work is ongoing and will be so until we come face to face with Him. It consists of possessing the very life of Christ, which comes through the born-again experience. God has given us the gift and promise of the Spirit to work that life in us. It is only as we obey what is true and right that this incredible life is work worked through us.

We must not forget that without the life of Christ in us, we are wretched through and through, our best is filthy rags before Him and anything that originates from the flesh will be considered perverted and worthless to the Lord.

We must also not forget that even in the household of Christ, it is easy to become a prodigal child that runs to the world, a Noah caught unaware of the danger of change after great judgment, a King David who was in the wrong place at the wrong time because he was not where he needed to be and fell into great sin, a religious Eli who ignored sin in his household, and a backslider who has slid into some cesspool and is being swallowed by the hopelessness of it all.

A puritan asked the Lord to grant him to never lose sight of his great sinfulness, the excellent righteousness attached to salvation, the indescribable glory of Jesus, the beauty of His holiness and the exceeding wonder of grace. May this be our deep desire and prayer as we continue to remember we will always be needful of Him. (VOV, pg. 76)

To Know

If we can have one word to describe the reality of God it would be the word, "Jesus." Jesus was clear in John 14 that if you see Him, you will see the Father. Paul was also clear in Colossians 2:9 that in Jesus all the fullness of the Godhead dwell in bodily form.

In bodily form Jesus became the perfect sacrifice as the Lamb of God and in His humanity, He could serve as the High Priest in the courts of heaven where, as fully man He could stand in the place of intercession where He would represent man to God, and as fully God, He could represent the heart and face of God to mankind.

There are things we can know about God, but to know God we must have a growing relationship with Him. Enoch and Noah walked with God because of grace, Abraham was called a friend of God because of faith, Moses and Job were called servants by Him because of obedience and patience, and Jesus made it clear that He did not want us to accept the status of servant; rather, He wanted us to graduate to that of friendship, for as Lord He may command servants to carry out duties on His behalf, but we only share heart matters with our friends. Jesus wants to share with us the deep matters of the heart (*John 15:12-17; 1 Timothy 2:5; Hebrews 5:1; 10:5*).

♦ It is possible to be worked up over the coming of the Lord without being stirred up about the Lord Who is coming. One is an event, the other is a Person, and it is the Person Who makes the event.

-Vance Havner
(RTR, pg. 65)

♦ Mercy is God's goodness confronting human guilt and suffering, and all men are recipients of this mercy.

-A.W. Tozer
(MDP, pg. 264)

***

When God wants to drill a man
And thrill a man
And skill a man.
When God wants to mold a man
To play the nobliest part:
When He yearns with all His heart
To create so great and bold a man
That all the world shall be amazed,
Watch His methods, watch His ways!
How He ruthlessly perfects
Whom He royally elects!
How He hammers him and hurts him
Into trial shapes of clay which
Only God understands;
While his tortured heart is crying
And he lifts beseeching hand!

31

How He bends but never breaks
When his good He undertakes;
How He uses whom He chooses
And with every purpose fuses him;
By every act induces him
To try His splendor out—
God knows what He's about!

-Author Unknown
(SL, pg. 150)

♦ That truncated Christianity which disregards the pre-incarnation Christ, the Christ of history, and the Christ of the future, and emphasizes on a subjective experience of a Christ Who need not ever have lived at all is as absurd as it is impossible.

-Vance Havner
(RTR, pg. 94)

♦ God is greater than everything. His love is greater than our fear. His help is greater than our need. His hope is greater than our despair. His mercy is greater than our failure. His strength is greater than our helplessness. His consolation is greater than our injuries. His loyalty is greater than our shortcomings.

-Greeting Card

♦ This was why He came—to draw men to Himself. Our Lord Jesus was the face of God looking longingly into men's faces.

-Samuel Dickey Gordon
(QT, pg. 11)

♦ There are three things considered in the nature of a holy righteous life, that are enough to demonstrate it to be the only pleasant life. It is a life from God; it is a life with God; it is the very life of God.

-William Gurnall
(CCA, Vol. 1 pg. 459)

♦ Shadow and sunshine! Jesus for the joy set before Him endured the cross, despising the shame. He reached the sunshine through the shadow. Who follows in His train?

-Vance Havner
(PD, pg. 76)

♦ God wills my holiness. I must not rest until my will is surrendered unconditionally to the will of God.

-Andrew Murray
(TG, #147)

The Essence of His Reality

It is natural in our humanity that we want to comprehend God and understand what He is doing. As a result, we are always looking for ways to bring God down to our understanding so we can control our reality about Him. This means we have to adjust, fit, and dissect aspects of His character and work into a nice little theological box that we can manage.

The Bible simply states "GOD IS," or as the Lord stated to Moses, "I AM THAT I AM." We need to accept God is who He is and that He will never step outside of being who He is—El the ever present that brings the past together with the present to fulfill His great purpose for the future. There is no other explanation of who He is outside of this revelation.

One puritan in his writings stated that Jesus is his refuge, and that he will wash in no other fountain, build on no other foundation, receive the fullness of promises, or find rest in any place of relief but Jesus. (VOV, pg. 23)

The reality of Jesus is that "HE IS ALL IN ALL." Outside of Him, there is nothing of substance that will satisfy, sustain, make sense, or bring about completion in and to our lives but Jesus.

♦ Some people do not quite grasp this God. They get dreamily poetic about the goodness of our heavenly Father who is love. They write, "Love is God, God is love, love is all in all, and everything will be okay." That sums up a lot of teaching today, but it is false teaching.

-A.W. Tozer
(MDP, pg. 172)

♦ What will you do with Jesus? Neutral you cannot be; Someday your heart will be asking, "What will He do with me?"

-A.B Simpson
(1843-1919)
(MDP, pg. 152)

♦ Even when we are in our lowest valleys, the truth remains that God is still on the throne and sovereign over all.

-Ray Comfort
(SWR, pg. 82)

♦ The Lord Jesus was the face of God looking into ours, the voice of God speaking into the ears of our hearts, the hand of God reached down to make a way back and then lead us along the way back again, the heart of God coming in touch to warm ours and make us willing to go back.

-Samuel Dickey Gordon
(QT, pg. 48)

♦ You may know God, but not comprehend Him.

-Richard Baxter
(SWR, pg. 16)

♦ God's compassion reaches into your life as you really are, not as you think you are. A great many people are merciful in their beds, merciful in their lovely living rooms, merciful in their brand-new cars, but they are not actively compassionate. What they see does not move them to actions.

-A.W. Tozer
(MDP, pg. 100)

Only A Pronoun?

The one thing about our present world is that it has been inundated with endless versions of the Bible. You would think that with so many Bibles that most would be Scripturally savvy, but according to statistics, many don't know what they are supposed to believe let alone what the Bible says.

There are some noted reasons for this ignorant state. One is that people read, hear, and study the opinions, beliefs, and ideas that others have about the Bible, but never read, study, or seek out the truths of the Bible for themselves. They have failed to obey 2 Timothy 2:15 that instructs us to study the Word of God to become a workman that needs not be ashamed because we know how to rightly divide the Word; and, 1 Peter 3:15 that tells us we must be able to give an account of the hope in us.

In fact, most people do not even bring their Bibles with them to church. I can remember when I became a Christian that if I didn't have my Bible in hand on Sunday morning, I felt naked, totally undone, and foolish. After all, my main goal for going to church was to become more aware of who God is and acquainted with my spiritual weapon so that I could stand, withstand, and continue to stand in whatever spiritual darkness affronted me.

The second reason is that many people do not want to be bothered with too much information. Most people do things on the run, in their cars, sitting behind some screen of technology, or working hard all day. They grab a bit here to sustain them, quickly graze as they race by to keep the pace, and settle for quick leftovers and do overs to get by. At the end of the day, they are physically tired, emotionally drained, and mentally taxed out from the demands of the world. They do not want to think too hard about something, dig too deep into a matter, or be bothered with too many details that would cause any real inconvenience to their limbo state of nothingness.

The problem with such a state is that it opens people up to be seduced, indoctrinated, and deluded. The Bible is clear we are personally responsible for our spiritual well-being and growth.

The third reason is it appears as if Christianity has become a subculture that fits into the culture of the world, instead of remaining distinct from it to maintain the light of its testimony. Methods of the world have come into many churches where sensationism becomes a point of attraction, entertainment the mode, and tacking Christ on to all that has religious connotations to make the practices legit. The mixture of the world and Christian beliefs causes people to end up in a complacent state where they become less and less stirred up by the matters of God.

Another reason for this state is the many versions of the Bible. Most people think the different Bible translations are naturally the word of God. Granted, they may have godly concepts, principles and truths in them, but if the Spirit of God is not anointing them, then the source that makes His Word living is missing, and the words will remain lifeless and unimpactful. Keep in mind, wherever man mixes his two-cents worth into the things of God, whether it be translations, doctrines, procedures and practices, confusion and strife will be the byproducts.

I have read different versions of the Bible, but the one that I found rhythmically flowing with living revelations, while vibrating with life and joy is the King James Version. Remember God's true Word has been inspired and if inspiration is missing, the power and authority will be missing as well. When inspiration is missing, it means a link is missing, and for me every time I hit an area that is missing a link in some version, I am left empty and disappointed.

Many of these versions not only lack the flow of inspiration but they lack certain parts of the Scriptures as well. Any time you change the intent of God's Word, you defile it, making it strange even to Him, and to offer it to others in His name would be the same as offering strange fire to Him. As we know, offering strange fire did not fare well for Aaron's sons and Romans 1:18 tells us if we mishandle His truth, His wrath abides on us.

This brings me to the different versions. We like and prefer them because they make the Word of God understandable. The problem with making the Word of God familiar or common to our way of thinking is we assume we understand God and we fail to delve into the unseen, eternal realm of what makes God, God, incomprehensible to our mind, shrouded by mystery, and unexplainable when it comes to His sovereign ways. Often times this lack of revelation causes us to become spiritually anemic.

The other aspects of these versions are they strip God of His glory in vulnerable minds, soft-pedal or do away with sin to be tolerable to the unregenerate soul, adjusted to worldly agendas and narratives to fit within the world's flow, and to placate a few. while betraying the righteous. In fact, many of these versions have rendered God into a mere pronoun by taking away those titles that describe Him, such as Son of God, Son of Man, God, the Messiah or Anointed One, and Lord. Like the gender crisis of our day, they simply use some pronoun such as "he" that keeps Him vague.

Since I know the Word of God, my mind puts the right title in the place of the pronoun because the Lord is real and living to me.

37

He is not a "he," an "it," or a vague notion. He has traits that are holy, a face that is unveiled in Jesus, a personality that never changes, and a mission that has turned the world upside down and caused my life to be turned right side up.

We must avoid fitting God into our limited understanding and making His inspired Word nothing more than a common book that can be read like a novel or an informative book that can be put on the self with the rest of our resource books. The Bible is either God's inspired Word or it is not. It is His absolute truth or it is a farce; and not any book called the Bible can be considered the inspired Word of God. It must have the source of inspiration that brings life to it before it can be considered reliable and sure.

♦ Where there are problems in the relationship with God, problems within society will inevitably follow—as it is in our country today… Our society has a God-problem.

-Thomas Lieth
News From Israel
July 2018

♦ Our business is to know Him and to make Him known: anything less is useless, anything more is superfluous.

-Vance Havner
(RTR, pg. 100)

♦ The Lord never gives cheap miracles in order to expose His glorious, mysterious will to please carnal saints. The Lord is willing to do the impossible when His people dare to believe that He is a faithful God and means exactly what he says.

-A.W. Tozer
(MDP, pg. 322)

◆ The Lord did not call us to be successful, he called us to be faithful.

-Bob Glaze

◆ He who waits on God loses no time.

-Vance Havner
(RTR, pg. 2)

God is Able

As believers we take much for granted. The more we assume things about God, His Word, His perfect ways, and abiding faithfulness in and upon our lives, the more we become self-sufficient in our understanding about Him. It often takes a shaking or crisis to cause us to know we are not in control, nor are we self-sufficient. Our very breath is a gift from God, the duration of our lives rests in His Hand, and all that is bestowed upon us comes from above.

There is an incredible story that reveals God's power and intervention in lives of people who did not really know Him, but found Him in a most challenging time. It took place in 1979 in Cambodia. It was when the Khmer Rouge took control of the countryside. This country became a killing field, no one was really safe and lives became dispensable for the insane cause of the tyrannical despots.

When soldiers came to a community, their techniques were the same. These communists would emerge from the jungle and investigate each hut, ordering the villagers out. Those who resisted were killed at once, and many died in the shadow of their huts. Those remaining were marched to a clearing behind the village. Their own farm tools were thrust into their hands and they were ordered to dig their own grave. Those who lost their nerve and tried to save their lives were gunned down like animals and dragged to the edge of the grave that was being dug.

In one village, the villagers had been digging their graves for hours. Sweat and tears mingled with the dirt on the ground. Hopelessness was arising out of the abyss of despair. They were trying to brace themselves as they waited for the killing blows, knowing that the soldiers would not waste their bullets on what they considered to be the refuse of the land. They would instead bludgeon them to death.

The humid air hung heavy upon their bodies and the despair in their souls began to rise up in the form of wailing. Some screamed to Buddha, others to ancestors, and some to demon spirits. A few cried to their mothers. However, there was one woman who began to cry as a faint echo of a story began to take center stage of her mind.

It was from one of her earliest memories. Her mother had told her a story about the God who hung on a cross. She began to call out to that God. Perhaps the One who had so greatly suffered on the behalf of others would somehow show compassion on those who were about to die. Time stopped as the humid air of the jungle lay still. Suddenly the screams around her became one great wail, as the entire village called out as one, crying for their lives to the God who hung on the cross.

Then there was silence that gave way to sobbing as the graves beckoned to them. Again, the blanket of silence rested on the people as hope began to peek around the edges of uncertainty. It was then that the people began to turn around one by one by one to discover that the soldiers were gone.

The God who they did not know had saved them that day. They knew He was real. They waited for 20 years before they discovered the identity of the God who hung on the cross and had saved them. His name was and is Jesus Christ, the Son of the Living God. He had not only saved them but died in their place so they could be redeemed from the tyrannical dictates of the wicked ways of the tyrants and despots of this present world. (GHC, pgs. 35-37)

♦ I can tell you the secret of beauty, men and women, the secret of permanent, indestructible beauty. It is Jesus Christ in the heart.

-R. A. Torrey
(BT, pg. 200)

♦ He was lifted *up on* the earth at his death, lifted *out of* the earth at his resurrection, and lifted up *from* the earth altogether at his ascension. It takes all that which is wrapped up in these three cardinal facts of the Christian faith to complete his drawing power.

-Herbert Lockyer
(MM, pg. 22)

***

Lifted up was He to die,
   "It is finished!" was His cry;
Now in Heaven exalted high:
   Hallelujah! What a Saviour!

-P. P. Bliss
(MM, pg. 27)

♦ They exalt him as the Christ of Galilee, magnificent teacher and social reformer, but they will not own him as the Christ of Golgotha, whose "rich wounds are still visible above." We accept no Christ who does not bear the imprint of nails and a riven side.

-Hebert Lockyer
(MM, pg. 127)

♦ Patience, I told you, is the back on which the Christian's burdens are carried, and hope the pillow between the back and the burden, to make it sit easy.

-William Gurnall
(CCA, Vol, 2, pg. 149)

♦ Every believing man knows that he is perfect master of himself only in the proportion in which Christ is Master of him, and he knows that Christ is Master of him in proportion as he shrinks from sin, and puts Self-seeking and Self-indulgence under his feet.

-John Gregory Mantle
(BH, pg. 127)

♦ When Jesus left the glory all he asked for was a stable to be born in, a Cross on which to die, and a spot to be buried in…Born in another's manger, dining at another man's table, sleeping in another's bed, He is now buried in another's tomb. Rich, for our sakes he became poor that we might be enriched forever by His grace.

-Hebert Lockyer
(MM, pg. 134)

My Hiding Place

Hail, sovereign love, which first began
The scheme to rescue fallen man!
Hail matchless, freed, eternal grace,
Which gave my soul a Hiding Place.

Against the God who built the sky
I fought with hands uplifted high—

Despised the mention of His grace,
Too proud to seek a Hiding Place.

Enrapt in thick Egyptian night,
And fond of darkness more than light,
Madly I ran the sinful race,
Secure—without a Hiding Place.

But thus the eternal counsel run:
Almighty love, arrest that man!
I felt the arrows of distress,
And found I had no Hiding Place.

Indignant Justice stood in view:
To Sinai's fiery mount I flew:
But Justice cried with frowning face,
This mountain is no Hiding Place!

Ere long a heavenly voice I heard,
And mercy's angel soon appeared:
He led me, with a beaming face,
To Jesus as a hiding place.

-Unknown

♦ It was not easy for Him to be our friend. Friendship is sometimes very costly, His reputation went, and then His life. But He never flinched. He was thinking of us. Our need controlled Him. There were two controlling words in our Lord Jesus' life—passion and compassion. He had a passion for His Father. He had compassion for us.

-Samuel Dickey Gordon
(QT, pg. 170)

♦ To do something contrary to God's nature and call it service is sheer ignorance and an affront to God. Get to know God, and then you can serve Him in a way that is pleasing unto Him.

-A.W. Tozer
(MDP, pg.116)

♦ We naively think that the more we grow as Christians, the easier it will be to discern the will of God. But the opposite is often the case. God treats the mature leader as a mature adult, leaving more and more of his or her spiritual discernment, and giving fewer bits of tangible guidance than in earlier years.

-J. Oswald Sanders
(SL, pg. 122)

***

And those Hands hold,
Though pierced with nails
   They hold on still,
Through power and pain.
   And they shall hold
   Till Satan falls
And love comes to its own to reign.

-Author Unknown
(MM, pg. 126)

♦ How often the work of the Holy Spirit has been hindered and even stopped by petty jealousies; someone feeling that he is not having the position he ought to have, or someone has passed an unkind remark of an uncharitable criticism about someone else. (PH, pg. 82)

***

No one's told the daffodils about the pause to Spring
And no one's told the birds to roost and asked them not to sing

No one's asked the lazy bee to cease his bumbling round
No one's stopped the bright green shoots emerging through the
    ground
No one's told the sap to rest, deep within the wood
And stop the sleepy trees from waking, wreathed about in bud
No one's told the sky to douse its brightest shades of blue
And stop the scudding clouds from puffing headlong into view
No one's asked the lambs to still the springs beneath their feet,
To stop their rapid rush and quell each joyful bleat
No one's told the stream to halt its gurgle or its flow
And warned the playful breezes, not to gust and blow
No one's asked the raindrops not to fall upon the earth
And fail to quench the soil in the season of rebirth
No one's locked the sun down, or dimmed the shimmer of the
    moon
And even in the darkest night, the stars are still immune
Remember what you value, remember who is dear
Close the doors to danger and keep your family near
In the quiet all around us, take the time to sit and stare
And wonder at the glory unfurling everywhere
Look towards the future, after the ordeal
And keep faith in our Lord Jesus' power to heal.

                                                    - Unknown

GOD'S WAYS

The Master's Hand

Most Christians have heard the song, *The Touch of the Master's Hand*. It was about a discarded violin. It was overlooked in the midst of worldly stuff and thought to be quite worthless by the

45

auctioneer. In his ignorance, the auctioneer started the bidding out very low until one who understood the value of the instrument took hold of it and begin to play it. The music of angels came out of the battered violin as the violinist revealed that it was a masterpiece. After he played the violin, it became a prized instrument.

This is true for our lives. Each of us start out like that violin, long tarnished by sin and discarded by a world that has no knowledge of our Creator. However, when my life was at its lowest, being completely devalued by Satan and mocked by the world, the Master of my life stepped on the scene to reveal my worth in light of His redemption.

The concept behind the Master's Hand is priceless, but there is also an amazing history behind it. The poem was first anonymously put into the church bulletin by the poet, who surmised that it was a gift from God and did not need her name on it. Therefore, no one knew who wrote it.

However, its popularity spread. It was not until several years later when it was being read at a religious international convention, and noted that the author was unknown, that the identity of the poet was discovered. A young man stood up and declared that he knew the identity of the poet. It was his mother, Myra Welch.

Apparently, after hearing a speaker in 1921, Mrs. Welch became filled with light, and wrote *The Touch of the Master's Hand* in 30 minutes. After she was identified as the writer of this inspirational piece, her name, as well as her other beautiful works of poetry became known worldwide. However, what the world did not see was the rest of the story. Welch no doubt saw herself as the discarded violin in her poem. She loved playing the organ, but due to severe arthritis, her battered body became confined to a wheelchair. Her ability to make music was taken away from her.

However, she did not rage at her plight; rather, she was thankful for it. She recognized that the Master had a glorious opportunity to prove what He can do with a battered life. Due to her love for the Master, her personal violin (her life) would not remain silent. Her music and message came out in her poems, opening a door for many to see into the miraculous touch of the Master's hand.

♦ You can't say God is all you need until He is all you have.

-Leonard Ravenhill

♦ God is good. He never misses what he aims at.

-Pastor Rob Greenslade

♦ The miracle of Christmas is that the infant Jesus learned to walk among us so that we might learn to walk with God.

-Christmas Card

♦ The perfect life was the life of Him who never did His own will, but only and always the will of God. All that is short of this, or different from this, is characterized as sin.

-Sir Robert Anderson
(RT, pg. 15)

♦ We can see that Jesus in His deity is the Rock of our salvation, but in His humanity, He was that cornerstone of the Spiritual building, His Church, a cornerstone that was initially rejected by the religious people of His day.

-RJK

♦ Since God has always "been," therefore His glory has always "been." Since God is infinite, His glory is inexhaustible. Since God is eternal, His glory will never end.

-Marvin J. Rosenthal
Zion's Fire
November-December 2015

♦ The Lord expects complete surrender from us. The potter can't shape clay that is not completely in his hand. Complete surrender means making our life available to God.

-Corrie ten Boom
(MA, Bk.1, pg. 74)

Prayer: *God, Your ways are higher than our ways. It is a grievous offense to think we can improve on Your ways by making them more understandable and manageable according to our way of thinking and doing. When are we going to learn Your ways are perfect and they lead in the ways of righteousness in order to bring us to perfection? Lord, keep me from competing with Your ways and order, and help me by faith learn to walk in them. Amen.*

♦ My relationship with God is part of my relationship with me. Failure in one will cause failure in the other.

-Andrew Murray
(WC, pg. 107)

♦ You cannot stand FOR righteousness unless you are living IN righteousness.

-Jeannette Haley

♦ Cruel disappointments beat upon him (Jesus). The crude ambitions of his disciples and the bigoted opposition of his enemies must have made life incredibly lonely for him, but it could not freeze the stream of his love.

-W. E. Sangster
(HA, pg. 48, 49)

♦ Some commit their work to God, some commit everything. His keeping will be just in proportion to our committing.

-R. A. Torrey
(BT, pg. 157)

♦ We cannot be neutral. Serving God with half of the heart is serving Satan with all the heart; God will accept no half-hearted service.

-C. W. Ruth
(SC, pg. 102)

♦ The birth of Jesus Christ did not leave us with a depotentiated deity. He took upon Himself something that He never before had—humanity. It was incarnation by addition, not incarnation by subtraction.

-Larry Spargimino
Prophetic Observer

♦ God is my end! Everything that does not revolve around Him as its center is doomed to destruction, and will be found to be wood, hay, and stubble in the day when every man's work shall be made manifest – when the fire shall try every man's work of what sort it is.

-John Gregory Mantle
(BH, pg. 39)

♦ I often wonder if we are making it plain enough to our generation that there will be no other revelation from God except as he speaks it through our Lord Jesus Christ.

-A. W. Tozer
(JG, pg. 16)

♦ There is only one explanation of man, and that is God! Man is too big to be explained in human terms. He is more marvelous than the cosmos itself, this little microcosm that we call man.

-Martyn Lloyd-Jones
(SFG, pg. 20)

How Does God Make Himself Known

The Bible is clear we can know God, but in what way? Clearly, He is beyond our comprehension; therefore, we can't really intellectually know Him. Granted, we can know about Him but He is Spirit and truth. Our mind can understand truth, but without being transformed by the Spirit, spiritual matters will seem illogical, silly, or stupid.

The Bible tells us to be able to grasp anything about God other than simply knowing there is a God, it must be revealed from above. We are also told creation declares there is a God but even though He is unseen, creation reveals His great works.

The other way we can know God is through His ways. There is a pattern to His ways because He will not step outside of who He is or His order.

The children of Israel errored in their heart because they did not know the ways of God. Since, they didn't discern His ways, they failed to recognize His order, and error by not walking in the way that was opened to them.

My desire and prayer have been, "Lord show me Your ways and have Your way because I know they are perfect and trustworthy.

***

♦ The Lord Jesus was first made known to shepherds, who represent the working class; to the wise men, who represent the student class; and to Simeon and Anna, who represent the worshipping class. Christ has ever been made known to men in their work, their study, their worship.

-Vance Havner
(RG, pg. 16)

♦ While to a certain extent these offices overlap, yet generally speaking we may say that He (Jesus) was Prophet on earth, He is Priest in heaven, and He will reign as King when He returns in glory. (Parenthesis added.)

-H. A. Ironside
(HC, pg. 52)

♦ We don't believe in Christ the way other religions do, Jesus is the beginning and the end. He is everything. Any view that diminishes His perfect completeness is a false view. Jesus is the one and only true Savior of the world. Nothing you can do will make us deny that truth or water it down.

-Marziyeh Amirizadeth
(Captive In Iran, pg. 244)

♦ Truth is that foundational reality we often resist but that, ultimately, we cannot escape. Nothing is so destructive as running from the truth, even as we know it will always outdistance us.

-Ravi Zacharias
(WJ, pg. 16)

Heavenly Treasures

♦ The fatherhood of God is our guarantee that His sovereignty will never require of us anything that will not in the long run be in our highest interests.

-J. Oswald Sanders
(JJ. pg. 28)

♦ The first coming of Christ is perfect but incomplete without His second coming. And the second coming of Christ is powerless without the first coming.

-Marvin J. Rosenthal
Zion Magazine
May/ June 2015

♦ There is something exceedingly improving to the mind in the contemplation of the Divinity. It is a subject so vast, that all our thoughts are lost in its immensity; so deep, that our pride is drowned in its infinity.

-Charles Spurgeon
(WJ, pg. 265)

♦ The world is looking for mixers, but the Lord Jesus Christ is looking for separators. The world thinks if a man is a good mixer he will come out fine; but if you will look over the records you will find that God's men always come out clean.

-Paul Rader
(GBM, pg. 25)

♦ Clearly, when the true God of heaven is missing from the equation, there is no premise of truth in which to discern a matter, no moral compass in which to make sound judgments, and no sure foundation in which to stand. There is nothing but a vacuum that will be filled with the lies of the age, the practices of the world, and the wicked philosophies of the modern-day heretics, despots, and tyrants.

-RJK

♦ If you take Christ's presence away, all the doctrines and precepts and the invitations of the Gospel would not declare God to this blind-eyed generation, this hard-hearted multitude. But, where Jesus is by His Spirit, there the Father is declared by the Word.

-Charles Spurgeon
(FJ, pg. 44)

♦ When we assume evil, we assume good. When we assume good, we assume a moral law. When we assume a moral law, we assume a moral lawgiver, but that's whom the skeptic or atheist is generally trying to disprove.

-Ravi Zacharias
(WJ, pg. 176)

♦ When Jesus came the first time, it was a manifestation of God's glory in humility – He came as a **lamb** to die. ...When Jesus comes the second time – He will come as a **lion** to rule.

-Marvin J. Rosenthal
Zion's Fire
November-December 2015

♦ We must not fix upon our rapturous experiences as the norm of our Christian lives. Mountaintop experiences come and go, but Christ remains.

-Vance Havner
(RG, pg. 83)

♦ There are two choices. We live our lives in the context of the world, which makes up its own rules as it goes along, or in the context of the Kingdom of God, in which the law is the Lord's.

-Elisabeth Elliot
(TGT, pg. 99)

♦ God is a Substitute for everything, but nothing is a substitute for God.

-Unknown
(HC, pg. 125)

♦ God, although He has loved and saved unholy men, has never stained His holy hands in the act of saving them. He remains the *"holy, holy, holy, Lord God Almighty"* (Revelation 4:8)

-Charles Spurgeon
(FJ, pg. 68)

♦ Satan tempts and seduces the disciple to sin. God tests the disciple to produce the gold of proved character and leads him to greater spiritual maturity.

-J. Oswald Sanders
(JJ, pg. 79)

♦ The spirit of this age is one of personal power; the spirit of Christ is one of humility. The spirit of this age is one of ambitious accomplishment; the spirit of Christ is one of poverty. The spirit of this age is one of self-determination; the spirit of Christ is one of abandonment to Divine Providence.

-Peter Reinhart
(TGT, pg. 122)

***

He only wins who sides with God,
To him no chance is lost;

His Will is sweetest to him when
It triumphs at his cost.

-Faber
(GBM, pg. 125)

♦ Those who see only the meek and gentle side of our Lord should balance that with His fearless attack on the religiousness of His day.

-Vance Havner
(RG, pg. 162)

♦ Who is God? As you can see, the first four words in *Genesis 1:1* reveal that He something of a phenomenon that is beyond our comprehension. To try to understand God would be like trying to take the entire ocean and put it in a small jar. It is not possible, and it is for this reason we must approach the Bible to simply believe what it says about God rather than trying to fit it in the small jar of our understanding. The more people try to fit God into their limited theology, concrete doctrines, and worldly notions, the more apt they are to erect a lifeless idol and succumb to the darkness of unbelief toward the true God of heaven.

-RJK

♦ The heart of the world is breaking under this load of pride and pretenses. There is no release from our burden apart from the meekness of Christ.

-A. W. Tozer

♦ God calls Himself not a force, not a power, not an influence, but "the Living God." He has shown Himself in three ways at least. Through creation, through conscience, and through the revelation of His Spirit. Martha, and Mary, and Lazarus, illustrate these three revelations. Martha, the realm of creation, Mary the realm of conscience, and Lazarus the realm of spirit.

-Paul Rader
(GBM, pg. 162)

♦ What a frozen religion it is that does not have the Godhead of Christ in it!

-Charles Spurgeon
(FJ, pg. 138)

♦ God needs great people whose dominate ambition is to further the glory of God.

-J. Oswald Sanders
(JJ, pg. 64)

♦ You address sin in love, but you never overlook sin in the name of love.

-RJK

♦ There are two rivals for God's voice, namely, yourself and the devil. We have to learn to differentiate between these voices.

-Corrie ten Boom
(MA, Bk. 2, pg. 75)

Prayer: *Lord, our ways seem clean to us but You weigh the spirits behind us. Lord help me to walk in truth in order to discover what is true, right, and acceptable to You in Your holiness. Amen.*

♦ As long as the anger of God is viewed in light of the psychology of passions rather than in the light of the theology of pathos, no adequate understanding will be possible.

-Abraham Heschel
(TP, pg. 362)

- God gives us great quests every day. We don't usually call them quests—that sounds so grand. We call them opportunities. Or often we call them interruptions.

  -Ellen Vaughn
  (GHC, pg. 43)

- Where common sense clearly points out a duty, that is the voice of God. We do not need any other, provided a higher duty is not claiming us.

  -Isobel Kuhn
  (IA, pg. 97, 98)

- And yet the same revolutionary beliefs for which our forebears fought are still at issue around the globe—the belief that the rights of man come not from the generosity of the state, but from the hand of God.

  -President John F. Kennedy
  (AWC, pg. vii)

- We should not separate what God has joined together. He has joined faith and salvation, works and reward. Just remember these two marriages and all will be well.

  -William MacDonald
  (NAG, pg. 64)

- Such a great redemption implies a great Redeemer...A superstitious assent to the dogma of His Deity is so common in Christendom that we need to be reminded that a real heart belief of that supreme truth is the mark of divine spiritual enlightenment.

  -Sir Robert Anderson
  (TH, pg. 21)

♦ Until we have learned that no individual, church, or nation can play tricks with God, that He has His own way and time of doing things, He will *wait,* that He may be gracious; and blessed are they who turn away from Egypt, with their chariots and horsemen, and *wait for Him.*

-John Gregory Mantle
(BH, pg. 11)

♦ Jesus Christ is God's last word to us. There is no other. God has headed up all of our help and forgiveness and blessing in the person of Jesus Christ, the Son.

-A. W. Tozer
(JG, pg. 23)

♦ Justification introduces you into the kingdom of peace and sanctification into the kingdom of power.

-W. B. Godbey
(SC, pg. 36)

♦ Since man is finite, he wrestles with the concept of an infinite God who is not subject to anything or anyone. In his limited understanding, man has a hard time accepting by faith that God never had a beginning because He always has been inclusive (He was) and continues to be who He is (distinct and singular), and will ultimately be what He always has been. In God there is no past that is not part of what is present and there is no future for it already has been established as being so in the realm of eternity.

-RJK

♦ Jesus is the God-man. In theological terms He is **Theanthropos**—one person with two natures.

-Pastor Larry Spargimino
Prophetic Observer
December 2014

- The conscious companionship of God is the great secret of abiding peace…Communion with God rather than scholarship opens to us the mind and thoughts of God.

  -R. A. Torrey
  (BT, pg. 170)

***

Dear dying Lamb! Thy precious blood
  Shall never lose its power
Till all the ransomed church of God
  Be saved to sin no more.

  -William Cowper
  (MM, pg. 102)

- When God took the form of a man, his behavior differed from the patriarchal ideals of both his world and of ours. Instead, acting sometimes as a bold leader, but other times as an emotionally vulnerable friend, he embodied the fruits of the Spirit. Let us all, men or women, do likewise, cultivating the fruits of the Spirit for the benefit of all and for the glory of our Creator.

  -Don Neufeld
  Mutuality Magazine
  Vol. 21, Issue 1

- God is holy and cannot tolerate sin. It is repugnant to His character. He who endorses sin becomes party to it, hence a sinner. God's holiness necessitates the law of holiness, and consequent eternal antagonism to sin.

  -L. L. Pickett
  (SC, pg. 37)

♦ It is not a question of what God *can* do, but what God *will* do.

-Marv Rosenthal

♦ (In regard to John 15) In this chapter Christ recognizes four different kinds of branches in the vine: the no-fruit branch, the some-fruit branch, the more–fruit branch, and one that bore much fruit. The first is taken away, the second purged that it might become the third, while the fourth is just the kind that every keeper and owner of a vineyard would be glad to have abound.

-Beverly Carradine
(SC, pg. 9)

♦ God is not simply available once and for all, to be found whenever man so desires. There is an alternative to God's presence, namely His absence. God may withdraw and detach Himself from history.

-Abraham Heschel
(TP, pg. 552)

♦ The Jews were not content with blows and buffetings and scourgings; these were but the forerunners of death, and we may well beware of attempting to "run with the heart and hunt with the hounds," or, in other language, to make a pretense of crucifixion with Christ, while at the same time we are secretly parleying with the enemy. We shall not parley if we resolutely remember that to do so is to prolong the power of "the old man," and so defeat the purpose of Jesus Christ, who was manifested not to buffet or maim, but to "destroy the works of the devil," and only by that destruction can we fully know what real marriage union with Jesus means.

-John Gregory Mantle
(BH, pg. 45)

♦ Because holiness is God's being, He cannot lie. Because He is God, he cannot violate the holy nature of His being. God does not will to lie. He does not will to cheat. He does not will to deceive. He does not will to be false to His own dear people.

-A. W. Tozer
(JG, pg. 90)

***

Unbelieving talk leads to cowardice and certain defeat.
God wants no cowards in His ranks,
Who from their colors fly;
He calls for noble-hearted men,
Who are not afraid to die.

-M. L. Haney
(SC, pg. 62)

♦ God longs to set us free from that boxed-in thinking. He loves us! And he takes great pleasure, as He always has, in using weak, flawed, eccentric failed human beings to highlight His power. That way onlookers won't mistakenly give anyone else the credit due God alone.

-Ellen Vaughn
(GHC, pg. 68)

♦ If the Lord tarry, there must come, some time, a last platform. Always the flesh would pray that it might be an easy one. But the Lord looks to the eternal weight of glory and so He may choose otherwise sometimes.

-Isobel Kuhn
(IA, pg. 219)

♦ Justification comprehends adoption—making us children of God. Sanctification comprehends the "anointing"—making us kings and priests unto God.

-C. W. Ruth
(SC, pg. 100)

♦ But the Lord's claim to be Son of God was rightly understood by the Jews to be an explicit claim to Deity; and because of it they decreed His death.

-Sir Robert Anderson
(TH, pg. 22)

♦ Jesus is the tree, the Father is the Gardener, the Holy Spirit is the life and sap. Jesus was cut and wounded that we might be grafted in. Repentance cuts us out of the world, and regeneration engrafts us into the true vine, binding us by faith and the Spirit life of Christ begins to flow.

-W. N. Hirst
(SC, pg. 73)

♦ And is this carefulness to please God, even in the smallest trifles, that proves the reality and delicacy of our love, "We do not love perfectly when we neglect small occasions of pleasing the One Whom we love, and when we do not fear to wound Him with trifles. The jealousy of God is infinite; it extends to everything, and every soul that truly loves will try never to give this divine jealousy any cause of offense.

-John Gregory Mantle
(BH, pg. 150)

♦ Yes, our life is like a garden of the Lord, walled by grace, cultivated by love, and weeded by heavenly discipline. Sin comes between us and God, like the weeds that impede the growth of plants and flowers. Heavenly discipline cultivates us by pulling out the weeds. These can be difficult times in one's life.

-Corrie ten Boom
(MA, Bk. 2, pg. 24)

Prayer: *Lord Jesus, my life looks more like a wilderness than a garden. Fill me with Your Holy Spirit so that from now on I can receive power to be a faithful, cheerful witness who bears fruit.*

-Corrie ten Boom
(MA, Bk. 2, pg. 26)

♦ God is indeed very much above man, but at the same time man is very much a reflection of God.

-Abraham Heschel
(MQG, pg. 126)

♦ If we do not walk with God on earth, we are not likely to live with God in heaven. If we do not care to cultivate His society now, we may be sure that He will not take us to be in His society forever.

-R. A. Torrey
(BT, pg. 174)

***

I hear the words of love,
    I gaze upon the blood;
I see the mighty sacrifice,
    And I have peace with God.

-Horatius Bonar
(MM, pg. 79)

Heavenly Treasures

♦ Arriving at his highest understanding, man is reduced to stillness.

-Abraham Heschel
(MQG, pg. 42)

♦ Inadequate people, in fact, are the only people God has to work with.

-Ellen Vaughn
(GHC, pg. 67)

♦ God does the healing; the doctors get the fee!

-Zvi Weichert

♦ If we are saved from wrath by what He (Jesus) has done for us, and what He is to us, our access to the divine presence depends on what He is to God for us.

-Sir Robert Anderson
(TH, pg. 61)

♦ God can be approached through God alone.

-Abraham Heschel
(MQG, pg. 108)

♦ For whether our stories are exciting or not, God gives each of us a walk through life. Along the way He uses us, and He equips us for the pleasure of spending eternity with Him. We can't understand it, but we have been a part of who He is from the beginning of time, and He can make any life a journey, or a quest, of meaning and adventure.

Dois I. Rosser Jr.
(GHC, pg. 50)

♦ A wide stream of human callousness separates us from the realm of holiness.

-Abraham Heschel
(MQG, pg. 112)

♦ He is the *Chief* Shepherd with reference to the under-shepherds. He is the *Good* Shepherd, because He cares for the sheep and gave His life for them. And as brought up again from the dead He is the *Great* Shepherd.

-Sir Robert Anderson
(TH, pg. 146)

♦ To imitate God, to act as He acts in mercy and love, is the way of enhancing our likeness. Man becomes what he worships.

-Abraham Heschel
(MQG, pg. 126, 127)

HOLY SPIRIT

The Holy Spirit is the most controversial person of the Godhead. He is often wrapped up in vague doctrines or notions that leave Him with no real identity other than He is some Spirit who works in the ether waves of nothingness. As a subject He is feared because ignorance about Him is rampant in some religious camps, sadly mocked because His gifts do not fit inside man's way of thinking, and shunned because the very mention of Him and His work is a trigger that often sets people at odds with each other and the Word of God.

The concept of "spirit" points to the breath of life that is associated with the "born again" experience. He is the fulfillment of God's promise that He would give His people a new spirit. Like the wind, the Holy Spirit moves where He will and can't be controlled by man. He is unseen; therefore, man can't logically identify His work or way. In fact, man is told the Holy Spirit can only be discerned.

The Bible is clear that without the Spirit man has no spiritual life because the breath of heaven is missing, no place in which he will fit in the body and in God's kingdom. Such a man will fail to be a lively stone that can be prepared by the Holy Spirit with calling and gifts to be placed in the Body, the Church, as well as absent of any means or connection to interact with God in blessed worship and fellowship.

For the Holy Spirit to be missing from a body of believers leaves the church empty and often the things of the flesh are used to fill it. To be missing among believers means there is no place of unity and fellowship, and to be missing between God and man means there is no communion or worship to be found.

Prayer: *Lord, You gave me the gift of the Spirit to instill the life of Christ in me and the promise of the Holy Spirit to empower me to walk in the life, and the anointing of the Spirit to fulfill my calling. He is my breath, my teacher, my guide, and my counselor. Thank You for the gift and promise that keeps giving and is personal, living, powerful, and heavenly. Amen.*

♦ The witness of the Spirit to sonship is only for the believer. His witness to the person and work of Christ is for every sinner who, as a sinner, hears "the word of the truth of the Gospel."

-Sir Robert Anderson
(RT, pg. 75)

♦ It was not to be life of the Holy Spirit alone, nor of the individual alone, but a combined life. When two gases are united, we have fire and its phenomena. Now God is showing by the fire symbol that when the Holy Spirit unites with the believer there is to be an attending spiritual phenomenon symbolized by fire, which is light and heat. Therefore, it is not only the coming of the Holy Spirit, but fire also.

-Paul Rader
(GBM, pgs. 12-13)

♦ Our lives, as long as they are untouched by the power of God, are simply like a pathless wilderness.

-Martyn Lloyd-Jones
(SFG, pg. 64)

♦ A frequent source of error and fanaticism about the work of the Holy Spirit is the attempt to study and understand His work without, first of all, coming to know Him as a person.

-R. A. Torrey
(BT, pg. 23)

♦ In emotion, we are conscious of its being our emotion; in the state of being filled with spirit, we are conscious of joining, sharing, receiving "spirit from above" (Isa. 32:15). Passion is a movement; spirit is a goal.

Abraham Heschel
(TP, pg. 405)

♦ Caiaphas and Pilate, seeking to examine the Spirit-filled Jesus, were utterly baffled. The Spirit-filled Paul was to Festus a madman. The heritage of every Spirit-filled soul is to be misunderstood and called a fool by the world, because the only way to *know* the teaching of God is to do His will.

-W. N. Hirst
(SC, pg. 70)

♦ Without the Holy Spirit we can't be light, salt, or witnesses. Not in the street where we live nor in the place we work, neither close to home nor far away on the mission field.

-Corrie ten Boom
(MA, Bk. 1, pg. 41)

♦ But the Spirit of God can only anoint in proportion to the willingness He finds in our lives.

-A. W. Tozer
(JG, pg. 64)

♦ We want a formula, a day-today schedule to follow. But following Christ is not a matter of a to-do list, checking off the boxes. It is matter of a relationship with Jesus and obedience to the nudge of His Holy Spirit in all things.

-Dois I. Rosser Jr.
(GHC, pg. 190)

♦ Salvation by works is so deeply ingrained in the human mind that it takes a supernatural work of the Spirit of God to eradicate it...The most deep-seated heresy in the human mind is that salvation is by works; that good people go to heaven.

-William MacDonald
(NAG, pgs. 46, 47. 48)

♦ Some believers react so strongly against the pervasive worldliness of our culture that they lose the ability to communicate with their friends, relatives, and neighbors. Walking in the Spirit doesn't take us out of reality; it allows us to function in reality with optimum effectiveness.

-Chuck Smith

- If we do not confess the Holy Ghost, He will not remain. Experiences must have ventilation. They will breed worms and stink. If not confessed.

  -Seth C. Rees
  (SC, pg. 120)

- Moral character, built up under the guidance and inspiration of the Holy Spirit, partakes of God's immortality, because it is nothing less than the divine nature incarnate, incorporate and made manifest in man.

  -John Gregory Mantle
  (BH, pg. 145)

- What we need is not so much some new organization, some new wheel, but "the Spirit of the living creature in the wheels" we already possess.

  -R. A. Torrey
  (BT, pg. 44)

***

Spirit of grace Thyself reveal,
  And make the Father known;
Upon us set Thy sacred seal,
  Within us crown the Son.

-L. L. Pickett
(SC, pg. 41)

- Grace is boundless, but it is *sovereign*; and if God has brought salvation within the reach of all, it is not by making men independent of Himself, but by giving the Holy Ghost to bear witness to the finished work and glorified person of a Saviour.

  -Sir Robert Anderson
  (GAM, pg. 157)

♦ I believe in the old-fashioned genuine call to ministry by the power of the Holy Spirit—men set apart, picked out by God. You can turn men out of colleges, theological schools and universities as fast as you can turn out carpet-tacks, if you want to; and when you have done it you haven't a preacher, nor a teacher, nor a Christian worker.

-Paul Rader
(GBM, pg. 24)

♦ Shattered dreams are never random. They are always a piece in a larger puzzle, a chapter in a larger story. The Holy Spirit uses the pain of shattered dreams to help us discover our desire for God, to help us begin dreaming the highest dream. They are ordained opportunities for the Spirit to awaken, then to satisfy our highest dream.

-Larry Crabb

Is He Leading?

The Bible tells us there are three responses towards the Spirit of God. We are to WALK AFTER the Spirit. This must be our initial response to the Spirit's prompting because He will lead us away from all condemnation into the ways of righteousness.

The next instruction is to be LED BY the Spirit. This points to Him leading us away from carnal thinking into a relationship as a child of God where we will discover our place in the household, learn about our inheritance, and begin to take on the likeness of Jesus Christ.

The final instruction is to WALK IN the Spirit. If we walk in the Spirit we will not walk according to the flesh. We will be overcomers of the flesh and victorious over the world's influence.

Walking after the Spirit ensures we are walking in the right direction, being led by Him maintains the real integrity and purpose of our life in Christ, and walking in Him enables us to endure the course and finish the race.

♦ If we are consumed with longing for God's gifts, then our life will become a journey of discovery. We are assisted on that journey by the Holy Spirit who is the Owner of those riches.

-Corrie ten Boom
(MA, Bk. 1 pg. 69)

♦ We cannot love honestly without hating dishonesty. We cannot love purity without hating impurity. We cannot love truth without hating lying and deceitfulness…On our human side, it is our imperfection in loving the good and hating the evil that prevents us from receiving the Holy Spirit in complete measure.

-A. W. Tozer
(JG, pg. 65)

♦ The possession of the Spirit commits us irrevocably to separation from sin. For what is holiness but an emancipation of the Spirit of holiness who dwells within us? A sanctified life is, therefore, the print or impression of His seal. He can never own us without His mark, the stamp of holiness.

-Dr. A. J. Gordon
(SC, pg. 19)

♦ In relationship to the difference between the sickly and the healthy Christian life, Andrew Murray stated, "In the former the Christian is content to 'live by the Spirit'; he is satisfied with knowing that he has the new life; but he does not walk by the Spirit. The true believer, on the contrary, is not content without having his whole walk and conversation in the power of the Spirit." (BH, pg. 147)

Heavenly Treasures

♦ The Holy Ghost has come, and now He gives a double testimony. He bears witness against the world's rejection of the Son, and He testifies to the rejected One as now exalted to be a Saviour. It is His mission to convict the world of sin, of righteousness, and of judgment: of sin because the Son of God has been cast out by earth; of righteousness because the Outcast of earth has been welcomed by the Father in heaven; and of judgment, because Satan, who put forth all his power against Him is now himself been judged.

-Sir Robert Anderson
(GAM, pg. 68)

♦ Paul Rader talked about how today's educated men perceive that their thought process can afford them to create their own reality according to their intellectual arrogance. He goes on to say, "We have polished them so much that they have forgotten Jesus, and their dependence on the Holy Spirit." (GBM, pg. 31)

♦ The religion of Jesus Christ is a supernatural religion from start to finish, and we should live our lives in supernatural power, the power of God through Jesus Christ, and we should perform our service with supernatural power, the power of God ministered by the Holy Spirit through Jesus Christ.

-R. A. Torrey
(BT, pgs. 50-51)

♦ We need Christians who are so endued with the fire of the Holy Spirit that people fall prostrate on their knees crying, "Holy, holy, holy!"

-A.W. Tozer
(MDP, pg. 62)

♦ To be filled with the Spirit means simply that the Christian voluntarily surrenders life and will to the Spirit. Through faith, the believer's personality is permeated, mastered, and controlled by the Spirit. The meaning of "filled" is not to "pour into a passive container" but to "take possession of the mind.

-J. Oswald Sanders
(SL, pg. 80)

♦ For mark keenly, the initiative is in human hands. God's action has always waited on human action. The power is only in the Holy Spirit. The most astute and strong leadership amounts to nothing without Him flooding it with His presence. But the power needs a channel.

-Samuel Dickey Gordon
(QT, pg. 72)

♦ The world will never be won by cowards. Before Pentecost the disciples, being yet carnal, were moral cowards. The baptism with the Holy Ghost and fire destroys fear and cowardice out of the heart and endows a man with holy boldness.

-B. S. Taylor
(SC, pg. 107)

♦ Power corrupts, and it is only the acceptance of the spirit of God that saves, that prevents disaster, that ennobles both body and soul. (MQG, pg. xiii)

♦ In regeneration we drink of the Spirit and have life, in sanctification we are flooded with the Spirit and have life more abundant.

-W. N. Hirst
(SC, pg. 72)

♦ A joyless Christian is almost invariably a disobedient Christian. "A life of self-renouncing love is a life of liberty," for where the

Spirit of the Lord is – where He is recognized and obeyed in the minutiae of life –"there is liberty."

-John Gregory Mantle
(BH, pg. 149)

The Fire from Above

W. N. Hirst put forth a powerful description of fire. He related how it was the manifestation at Pentecost, and that it is a most impressive symbol of the Spirit. He pointed out three facts about water.

(1) Fire can be extinguished by water, which can also be related spiritually to the pouring out of cold human authority on the operations of the Spirit and the use of His gifts when it comes to the spiritual realm.

(2) Fire can be snuffed out. Hirst's exhortation was, "Don't blanket your coals of testimony with attempted witticisms, sensations or palpable deviations from the truth."

(3) Finally, fire must be fueled or it will go out from the neglect. Hirst's advice was, "So, let all Timothy's "stir into a flame" the gift of God! With timber from the Word, soaked with oil of prayer and meditation and with the draft of testimony wide open, let us keep the fire blazing in our hearts." (SC, pgs. 74, 75)

♦ Every day we are presented with the options of living after the Spirit or after our own fleshly desires. Our mind is the battleground where we will decide which will have dominion.

-Chuck Smith

***

The heavenly fire now burns within
    Kindling a holy zeal;

74

It stirs the soul to deepest depths
    As at the throne we kneel.

-L. L. Pickett
(SC, pg. 40)

♦ "The works of the flesh" suggest a factory; "the fruit of the Spirit" suggests a garden.

-Paul Rader
(GBM, pg.58)

♦ (In relationship to the ineffectiveness of preaching the Word) No, the trouble is it is not preached with power, "with the Holy Ghost sent down from heaven" (1 Pet. 1:12). The bench-warmers in the pews would sit up and take notice, and hungry souls would be fed and sinners convicted if we recovered that note of authority.

-Vance Havner

♦ When sin or our selfness, at any distance whatever shows itself in our horizon, when we notice something in the wind so that our moral sky, our spiritual atmosphere, is not altogether clear, let us know that it is His grace which signals the danger, His Spirit Who awakens our attention. Let us stop at once; let us hasten to our refuge under the shadow of His wings; let us renewably tighten the bonds that unite us to Him, until the light of His countenance has driven away the last vestige of the cloud, and the atmosphere has again become luminous.

-Pastor Stockmayer
(BH, pg. 151)

♦ A person who understands the language of the Holy Spirit, but who does not understand a word of Greek or Hebrew or Aramaic, will get more out of the Bible than one who knows all about Greek and Hebrew and cognate languages, but is not born again, and, consequently, does not understand the language of the Holy Spirit.

-R. A. Torrey
(BT, pg. 211)

♦ Better a noble Stoic than a man who moans his way through life masquerading as a Christian. But better still a man who has so caught the spirit of Christ that he scorns the luxury of self-compassion and soars above that sub-Christian grace called "resignation," and cordially accepts the discipline of life, believing that God can wrest it to his good.

-W. E. Sangster
(HA, pg. 67)

♦ Sanctification is marriage to the Holy Spirit. Why, then, do some sanctified souls call the Holy Spirit "it?" They have magnified the blessing above the Blesser and fixed their eyes on it instead of Him, failing to cultivate that intense, holy intimacy with Him which discerns His voice in guidance and understands His declarations of things to come.

-W. N. Hirst
(SC, pg. 69)

THE WORD

Where Is the Power?

It seems that much of the church in America is powerless in every avenue. It has its methods of occult like-confessions, fleshly worship that stirs up the senses and emotions, intellectual presentations, and worldly practices, while wondering why its lacks real power, the power that can bring people to the foot of the cross in true repentance and salvation.

Paul Rader, an early 1900's evangelist had been greatly influenced by his father who was a missionary to Wyoming. He traveled by horseback and wagon, in order to evangelize the Indians and lawless cowpokes. He also traveled to the Orient and came back brokenhearted. He told his son that there was so much machinery, institutions, and studying going on. It was then that he asked, "Is this what the sacrificial money has gone for? That they might simply *study* Christianity?"

Rader points out that Christianity is not to be *studied*, but to be *received* by faith for the "just shall live by faith." He points out that the Word of God is to be eaten, assimilated by faith into our thinking and way of walking. He goes on to share how his father stood and looked at him and said, "Son, remember when I am gone, that I protested this thing to the last, that the *world should have the Gospel preached to it*, not educated into it; and remember that you saw raw heathen Indians inside of a few days from the time that they first heard the Gospel, accept it and admit the Lord Jesus into their heart. They did not have to be educated first." (GBM, pgs. 188-189)

It is clear that some of the Church have become so caught up with the world's methods they have lost sight of the simplicity that serves as an avenue for great power to freely flow through. The power of Christianity rests in the simple message of Christ being presented in purity. It is the anointed Word of God that penetrates the darkness of the mind and the Holy Spirit who imparts its liberating truths into the tender, receptive hearts of those who decide to believe. And, it is upon believing that man is endued with power of the Spirit of the Living God from above and given a new life.

♦ The liberating word of God is still able to defeat the devil, but today we stand at the foot of the mountain like the disciples in failure before a devil-possessed world. Our note of authority is gone, and we are not defeating the devil!

-Vance Havner
(RG, pg. 36)

♦ There are no scientific errors in the Bible; it is astrophysically and mathematically perfect, because the Author is the Master Mathematician, the Sustainer of every scientific law.

-Dr. Noah Hutchings
(GMM, pg. 49)

♦ The only source that can bring me back to center in a world that seems like it is going mad and is hell-bent is God's Word. I find so much comfort and hope in His Word. I can edify myself with its truths, encourage myself with its many promises, and rest in the knowledge of God's abiding faithfulness. I can know that in the end it is God's truths that will stand while all other false ways will be cast into the pit of hell.

-RJK

♦ Some people skip and dip in the Bible. They skip what they don't like and dip into what they do like.

-Pastor Rob Greenslade

♦ Christian, never be afraid to speak the truth! TRUTH is a two-edged SWORD, not a popsicle stick.

-Jeannette Haley

♦ The water of purification was, as we have seen, the water of regeneration; and it is by "the word" that the sinner is born again to God.

-Sir Robert Anderson
(RT, pg. 136)

- Men presume to criticize and to sit in judgment on the Word of God, but here (Hebrews 4:12), we are told that the Word itself is the supreme critic of our inmost thoughts and inclinations.

  -H. A. Ironside
  (HC, pg. 49)

- We must quit bending the Word to suit our situation. It is *we* who must be bent to that Word, *our* necks that must bow under the yoke. Love is no pleasing sentiment but a fiery law: *thou shalt love.*

  -Elisabeth Elliot
  (TGT, pg. 94)

- When one begins with a problematic induction, through an inescapable seduction, there is an inevitable reduction and ultimately a false deduction.

  -Ravi Zacharias
  (WJ, pg. 91)

- That Jesus of Nazareth died upon a cross is a mere matter of history; that He who did so die was the Christ, the Son of God is entirely a matter of revelation.

  -Sir Robert Anderson
  (GAM, pg. 166)

- A doctrine, philosophy, or worldview built on any foundation other than that of divine sovereignty will one day crumble and turn to dust.

  -Marvin Rosenthal
  Zion's Fire Magazine
  Jul/Aug 2015

The Priceless Treasure

In America we take the Word of God for granted. In other words, we don't value it. We do not let the Word's precious Scriptures properly interpret and confirm one another. As I have said, truth can stand alone, but Scripture cannot. Scriptures must be compared to one another to ensure the proper intent and message of the Bible.

Today we have so many versions that have been adjusted, compromised, and sacrificed to fit the politically correct environment that there is now a famine of the pure Word of God in the land. Something the prophet Amos warned us about is the sick, sin-laden environment we now live in (Amos 8:11-12.) Sadly, there is no real concern or outcry as many people pick and choose what they believe and how they will interpret God's Word. As a result, many are failing to realize they have been swallowed by the great delusion engulfing our world.

At the core of this problem is the fact that people do not love the truth. They prefer their own twisted reality that blinds them to the narrow way of salvation. They want to merrily travel down the broad path that allows them to walk to the edge of the abyss, fall into it, and face the harsh reality that their soul is doomed and there is no recourse. They have clung to sinking ships of wicked, worldly ideologies, philosophies, and delusions. They have hung on to the debris of false promises, wishful thinking, and liberal insanity, only to find that it, too, will be taken down to the depths of hell.

When you consider that one of the main goals of missionaries, besides bringing the Gospel to those in darkness, is to translate the Bible into the heart language of the people, you begin to realize how priceless it is, and that price includes lives being sacrificed.

The other side of the coin is that God wants people to have His Word in their heart language so they can understand what His truths are. For a man named Hiram Bingham this reality was made apparent by God's miraculous intervention.

Mission work was not foreign to Bingham. He was born in Hawaii where his father had served on the mission field. He had watched his father translate the Bible into the Hawaiian language and had help carry pages of the translation to the printer.

When he received the call to the mission field, Bingham wanted to minister on the Gilbert Islands, which were a thousand miles to the southwest of Hawaii. He and his wife sailed there on the sailing vessel, Morning Star, which would sail from one missionary outpost to another in the vast Pacific. They landed at the Gilbert Islands in 1856.

There had already been seeds planted in this area by missionaries the year before, but the Bingham's had come to not only plants seeds, but cultivate them with the intent of seeing the harvest come to fruition. One of their main goals was to translate the Bible into the people's language.

The Bingham's spent time learning the people's language. Once they learned the language, they had to make an alphabet and then teach the people how to read it. They began to translate the Gospel of Matthew. It was tedious and required patience as they made sure that the people would properly understand God's Word. They managed to translate twelve chapters of Matthew by the time another sailing vessel came their way. They sent the manuscript back with the vessel to Hawaii where it would be printed.

They waited for months for the manuscript to come back in printed form. Meanwhile the missionaries worked with the people, sharing Jesus and even traveled to other islands. They finished translating the rest of the Gospel of Matthew, which was sent to Hawaii when other passing ships came into the harbor.

Heavenly Treasures

One day a ship finally came into harbor. The Bingmans along with the new Christians were anxiously waiting to see the book of Matthew in printed form. Instead of receiving a published book, the printers had sent the manuscript back with a little printing press in a box with type, ink, and paper with a message, "Print the Gospel yourselves!" The problem is that no one knew how to use the small printing press.

As the dust of time settled on the press and manuscript, it seemed hopeless that they would ever see the translation in printed form. However, the Word of God will not be kept from going forth. Granted, it may be hindered by obstacles, slammed by waves of opposition, and buried by godless entities, but God knows how to get around obstacles, calm the waves, and put archenemies on the run.

One day a small boy shouted loudly to Hiram, "Quick! Quick! A boat is coming!" The Bingham's rushed from their house. Across the little lagoon was a tiny rowboat being pulled towards them. When the four weary rowers reached the beach, they were surprised. Hiram asked where their ship was. The answer was that it was wrecked, gone down in the waters and they were the only ones who survived.

As soon as the sailors recovered from their ordeal, they began to help Hiram with his different projects. One of them by the name of Hotchkiss stumbled upon the printing press. He was surprised as he asked if they printed anything on the island. It was discovered that Hotchkiss was a printer. He not only volunteered to print what Hiram already had translated but to show them how to work the press. Hiram realized God's precious work would not be thwarted. Out of tragedy He had delivered the solution right to him.

Hotchkiss not only helped print the translation, but he assisted Hiram and the natives in using the printing press. He also stayed on even when his other shipwrecked crewmembers were taken back to Hawaii by another sailing vessel.

It was in 1892 that Hiram Bingham had finished the translation of the whole Bible. He did not try to print it on the island. The complete manuscript was sent to New York, to the American Bible Society and they printed it.

The Bingham's came to New York for the reading of the proofs and it was finally printed in 1893. The plates of the Gilbertese translation were put in a fireproof vault to ensure that the Society would always have the means to provide the Bible to the people of the Gilbert Islands. (SBB, pgs. 40-45)

♦ The reason so many people haven't any fruit to-day is because the roots of their lives do not run down into the Word of God, and the Holy Spirit cannot draw the Word up into their experience.

-Paul Rader
(GBM, pg. 80)

♦ The root of false theology is belittling God, and the essence of true divinity is enhancing God, magnifying Him, and enlarging our concepts of His majesty and His glory to the utmost.

-Charles Spurgeon
(FJ, pg. 131)

♦ We can relate the principles of Scripture to the details of daily life, remembering that the Bible contains *principles* to guide, *commands* to obey, *warnings* to heed, *examples* to emulate, and *promises* to claim.

-J. Oswald Sanders
(JJ, pg. 81)

♦ Faith that will not depend on His Word would not be convinced by works. If men refuse the Word of God, nothing else will be enough.

-Vance Havner
(RG, pg. 177)

♦ Spoon-feeding the Scriptures is okay for new Christians, but it inhibits real growth and maturity if it continues. Ironically, that is a dilemma even for those excellent teachers and preachers who become popular. Popularity often breeds followers.

-The Berean Call
July 2015

♦ America has loosed herself from the moorings of God's Word and now finds that she is hopelessly adrift in a broken craft with a storm brewing.

-Marvin Rosenthal
Zion's Fire Magazine
Jul/Aug. 2015

♦ How do I know that what I believe is true, and is what I believe in any way relevant to my day-to-day life? The danger here is that we often mistake relevance for truth and make truth so academic that it seems to have become irrelevant.

-Ravi Zacharias
(WJ, pg. XV)

Left Standing

Truth is ever under attack. Some attacks are blatant due to their insanity, others subtle, while there are those which are touted as being special enlightenment that will be understood by only a few, and there are those that prove to be outright lies.

We live in a world where the light of truth has been made hazy with compromise, the shadows have lost any real legitimate outline making it hard to discern what we are seeing, and everything is a matter of optics where people are being jerked around by false narratives that do not have one shred of truth in them. We are being conditioned by foolishness, put to sleep by fantasy and wishful thinking, seduced by a false light, and indoctrinated into an insane reality, leaving many standing on the shores of shifting sand as the waves of judgment move closer to them.

For the last three decades we have been inundated by one heretical movement after another, always promising greater insight when in reality it leads to greater darkness. The one truth I can bank on is that there is only one sure standard of truth--and that is the Word of God. Any deviation, detour, bend, slight change, or dip in it must be rejected up front and not given any audience until its spirit is tested, its pattern examined according to the full Word of God, and it fruits thoroughly inspected to see if it withstands the sword, the fire and hammer of the Word of God.

Keep in mind that after all has been tested, shaken, and judged the one thing that will be left standing is God's truth.

♦ What is left standing when all has been shaken: **TRUTH.** What is left standing when all has been tested by fire: **UNFEIGNED FAITH.** What is left standing when all has failed: **GODLY CHARACTER.**

-RJK

Prayer: *Lord, we get so caught up with the circumstances of this present world, we often forget to lift up Your Rod by faith, knowing that it will overpower and eventually swallow up all the concerns of this age. Amen*

♦ We must make a distinction between personal opinions and biblically-grounded truths that constitute the core doctrines of the Christian faith. If you have ever been in a church business meeting where people are fussing with one another, the Holy Spirit is grieved. And you know it.

-Larry Spargimino
Prophetic Observer
April 2016

♦ Whether a man or a woman believes it or not, the Word of God is one of the greatest of the realities he or she will face in a lifetime. He or she may deny the Word and the presence of God, dismissing them both as unreal. But the living, speaking Word of God cannot be escaped. Neither is it negotiable.

-A. W. Tozer
(JG, pg. 72)

♦ Few words in the New Testament have been more neglected than our Lord's rebuke of bigotry.

-W. E. Sangster
(HA, pg. 189)

♦ Indeed, "scriptural doctrine" contains no lofty speculations nor philosophic reasoning, but only very simple matters, such as could be understood by the slowest intelligence.

-Abraham Heschel
(TP, pgs. 524, 525)

♦ Often we want instant answers so we can charge off to do the next thing. Sometimes we read the Bible as if it's a vending machine—you know, punch a button, claim a verse, and a promise pops out. Only as we are willing to wait on the Lord does the Holy Spirit burn a particular leading from Scripture into our hearts.

-Dois I. Rosser Jr.
(GHC, pg. 190, 191)

♦ "Much," or "quantity," is not the criterion for qualifying something as true to God's Word. The Bible, which is God's inerrant communication to mankind, is a believer's absolute authority in all matters of faith and practice. If only *much of it* were true, then it is neither inerrant nor can it be a believer's authority.

-T. A. McMahon
The Berean Call

Nothing New

In spite of the growing number of people who think that the Bible is inadequate for today, few realize that neither man nor God have changed. Time and culture have not changed the essence of mankind. People are still confronting the same old problems and issues due to their fallen condition.

They are still experiencing the same emotions as King David expressed in Psalms. Their quest to understand life is as real as it was when King Solomon wrote Proverbs and Ecclesiastes. Their desire to experience life is as prevalent as the Israelites in the wilderness.

They still must confront giants (obstacles) as David did, conquer the enemies of the mountains (vain imaginations) and of the valleys (the idols of heart) like the Caleb's and the Joshua's. Their questions about suffering are still as intense as Job's. Their temptations are as alluring as Delilah was to Samson. Their self-pity is still as inexcusable as it was in Cain, and their failure as great as Adam's in the Garden of Eden.

♦ Divine truth can never clash with *reason*, but it may be entirely opposed to experience, and seemingly even to fact.

-Sir Robert Anderson
(TH, pg. 95)

♦ But a text without a context is a pretext for all kinds of mischief.

-Larry Spargimino
Prophetic Observer
April 2015

♦ Let us have *one object* in studying God's Word—that to transfer it into our lives, observing it, not for argument but for action.

-W. N. Hirst
(SC, pg. 76)

♦ Christ represented the Father, and as men treated Christ they revealed their sentiments toward the Father. The Word of Christ represents Christ, and *our sentiments toward Christ are revealed by our treatment of His Word.* How many are laboring to settle the question whether they love Christ or not?

-George Bowen
(BH, pg. 125)

♦ If we have to hide behind a matter to defend our position, rather than stand on it as being so, it is most likely a falsehood.

-RJK

♦ The frank and artless narratives of the bible are so obviously indifferent to the *appearance* of consistency, and show so clearly that irregularity which is the sure mark of honest handwork in the Oriental rug and of spontaneity in human testimony, that they have often lured opponents into attempts at destructive cross-examination which have only brought the Bible's truth and consistency into clearer light.

-Irwin Linton
(A Lawyer Examines the Bible)

Not Returning Void

In the market place in Madagascar, a young child by the name of Birdling, looked into the face of an uncertain future. She had a wonderful home but she had been captured by slave traders while her parents were off hunting. She was to be auctioned off at the market place as a commodity. It seemed almost too unbearable for her tender soul to fathom, but thankfully her childlike curiosity was revived as she watched the various activities of the strange new place.

Perhaps it was her expression that had attracted the rich young lady to purchase her. Although duties were catered to her age, Birdling learned quickly, pleasing her new mistress. Her mistress took an even greater interest in Birdling because she remained cheerful in doing her duties. The mistress even asked questions about her past life. She had never really thought about young slaves like Birdling having a real past, with caring parents. She frowned at the prospect of children and people being captured and forced into slavery.

Birdling faced loneliness that became excruciating to her. However, there was one thing that she managed to carry away with her when she was taken captive. It was a book that had been in her pocket at the time of her capture. Her father had taught her to read it. In her free times she would seek refuge under a tree where she read the book aloud. Without knowing it, some of the other household slaves were secretly listening to the words of the book as well.

One day her mistress was wandering out into the garden. She went down the slope and suddenly heard a low voice speaking but saw no one. Curiosity caused her to follow the direction of the sound. There curled under a tree was Birdling earnestly reading.

The mistress questioned Birdling if she was reciting a story. Birdling admitted that she was reading in the Holy Book. Surprised that a young slave girl could read when she could not, she questioned her, only to discover that her father had taught her to read it.

The other slaves were afraid if their mistress found out that Birdling could read, she might give way to fits of jealousy and make it hard on Birdling. But, instead of being jealous over Birdling's ability to read, she took the opportunity to ask Birdling if she would teach her to read.

Birdling jumped at the chance and began to teach her mistress to read from the New Testament. They started with some of the stories that Jesus had told. The mistress was in awe of the stories she began to hear as well as eventually learned to read.

Then the miraculous happened. Bridling's mistress received Jesus Christ and became one of His committed followers. As a result of her conversion, she set all of her slaves free, allowing Birdling to go back to her father's home. It was as if she was raised from the dead.

However, Birdling knew her real calling and heart was not to remain with her family. She went back to her mistress who was taking measures to make the Gospel of Jesus Christ known in Madagascar. The two of them even traveled to a place where there were missionaries and begged them to come and teach the new Christian about the Christian life. Missionaries did come, but succumbed to disease and death, leaving the mistress to teach the people the Words of Life that had been planted in her open heart by a young slave girl.

Who would have thought that Birdling's captivity was part of God's incredible way of bringing His written Word to a formidable place? He then planted the seeds of life in the heart of one woman who became a type of Lydia in a faraway place called Madagascar. (SBB, pgs. 55-62)

♦ If Christians would only study the Word they would not be misled as they so often are by seducing spirits, or by impulses of any kind, that are not of God but of Satan or of their own deceitful hearts.

-R. A. Torrey
(BT, pg. 137)

♦ The wonder of the Bible is against all human expectations, and if it had not been for the book's apparent spiritual glory and for the inexplicable power of human faith, it would have been rejected as absurd and unlikely.

-Abraham Heschel
(TP, pg. 529)

♦ With regard to the Bible, the plain things are the main things, and the main things are the plain things.

-Alistair Begg
(GHC, pg. 59)

***

The Lord is their portion and joy,
    Who gladly His Word obey,
A fountain of praise and delight
    He turneth their night to day.

-L. L. Pickett
(SC, pg. 39)

♦ Use the sword of the word *purely*. And that in a threefold respect: (1) Pure from error. (2) Pure from passion. (3) Pure from levity and vanity.

-Willian Gurnall
(CCA, Vol. 2, pg. 285)

♦ In regard to this great Book (the Bible), I have but to say it is the best gift God has given to men. All the good the Savior gave to the world was communicated through this Book. But for it we could not know right from wrong. All things most desirable for man's welfare, here and hereafter are portrayed in it.

-Abraham Lincoln

♦ Any doctrine not rooted in the character and nature of God is not a biblical doctrine; or we have not understood the doctrine correctly. Every doctrine begins in the heart of God and then flows into the heart of man, creating godly atmosphere in that man.

-A.W. Tozer
(MDP, pg. 205)

♦ Many are accustomed to think that the question of their personal security is the only question of any moment. That is a great mistake, for by careless living, by giving lodgment to Self in any of its forms, whether hateful or beautiful; by carelessness and unwatchfulness; by neglect of communion; by failing to keep the Master's sayings, we forfeit the highest possible service to the world, that of manifesting, in our life, the loveliness of Jesus Christ.

-John Gregory Mantle
(BH, pg. 126)

♦ Disciples of Christ! While we have been excusing our unanswered prayers with a fancied submission to God's wisdom and will, the real reason has been that our own feeble lives have been the cause of our feeble prayers! Nothing can make men strong but the word coming from God's mouth. By that we must live.

-Andrew Murray
(WC, pg. 166)

♦ Abounding life means abounding hunger for the Word...The reason why many get so little out of their Bible reading is simply because they are not willing to think. Intellectual laziness lies at the bottom of a large per cent of fruitless Bible reading.

-R. A. Torrey
(BT, pg. 212)

♦ There is no sin that cannot be prevented when a believer is walking in obedience to God's Word. Moreover, the increased spiritual growth of the believer is the ultimate prevention program, to resist sin and advance fruitfulness.

-T. A. McMahon
The Berean Call

♦ Perfect obedience to all the word and will of God always ensures success and prosperity. Disobedience must end in failure and defeat. Perfect Love is religion made easy, as "love is the fulfilling of the law."

-C. W. Ruth
(SC, pg. 102)

♦ We must not continue to cherish a theory, just because we have embraced it forty years ago. Faith is not something that we acquire once and for all. Faith is an insight that must be acquired at every single moment.

-Abraham Heschel
(MQG, pg. 89)

♦ A pilot without his chart, a scholar without his book, and a soldier without his sword, are alike ridiculous. But above all these, is it absurd for one to think of being a Christian without knowledge of the word of God and some skill to use this weapon.

-William Gurnall
(CCA, Vol.2, pg. 196)

♦ It cannot be said too often that it takes all of the Word of God to make it the Word of God. To divide it, even rightly, is to run the great risk of misunderstanding. When we divide and categorize Scripture, we run into the danger of misinterpreting the mind and heart of God. Leave this work to the Holy Spirit who breathes truth into our hearts.

-A.W. Tozer
(MDP, pg. 160)

♦ He is a shallow thinker who gives up a well-attested truth because there are some facts which he cannot reconcile with that truth. It is a very shallow Bible scholar who gives up the divine origin and inerrancy of the Bible because there are some supposed facts that he cannot reconcile with that doctrine.

-R.A. Torrey
(HSC, pg. 66)

♦ God's word, rightly interpreted, will produce spiritual heartburn. It penetrates, for it is sharper than a two-edged sword (Hebrews 4:12). Believers do not hunger and thirst after righteousness because they do not read God's Word. They fill up with the lollipops of this world and have no appetite for spiritual things.

-Vance Havner
(RG, pg. 177)

♦ God is Truth and Truth is God.

-Andreil Sakharov

♦ A surrendered will, will do more to make the Bible an open book than a university education.

-R. A. Torrey
(BT, pg. 215)

♦ When any statement is made concerning the oneness of all religions, either meditation, intuition, or textual extrapolations are used, the differing doctrines of each religion are always left unaddressed. But when the mystics are questioned, they resort to falsifying other systems by switching to induction.

-Ravi Zacharias
(WJ, pg. 32)

♦ The Bible is about 30 percent prophecy, and for this reason alone it is absolutely unique. There are no prophecies in the Qur'an, in the Hindu Vedas or the Bhagavad-Gita, in the sayings of Buddha and Confucius, in the Book of Mormon, or anywhere, except the Bible. Nor are there any prophecies concern the coming of Buddha, Krishna, Muhamad, Zoroaster, Confucius, or the founder or leader of any other world's religions. The Jewish Messiah is absolutely unique in this respect. His coming was foretold in dozens of specific prophecies that were fulfilled in minutest detail in the life, death, and resurrection of Jesus Christ.

-Dave Hunt

♦ Facts must never be used to constitute what is truth; rather truth must verify the legitimacy of facts.

-RJK

♦ The problem is not *how much* but *how to* observe. The problem is whether we *obey* or whether we merely *play* with the word of God.

-Abraham Heschel
(MQG, pg. 101)

♦ Error is but a day younger than truth.

-William Gurnall
(CCA, Vol. 2, pg. 556)

♦ It seems to me that nothing short of infinite wisdom could by any possibility have devised and given to man this excellent and perfect moral code (Bible). It is suited to men in all conditions of life, and includes all the duties they owe to their Creator, to themselves, and to their fellow man.

-Abraham Lincoln
(TC, pg. 131)

♦ If a man is known by the company he keeps, so also his character is reflected in the books he reads.

-J. Oswald Sanders
(SL, pg. 104)

♦ The Bible needs no defense. Turn it loose, and like a lion, it will defend itself. I believe that, and I believe the Word of God needs no defense. We only need to preach it.

-Charles H. Spurgeon
(RCF, pg. 40)

♦ Before prayer, God's Word strengthens me by giving my faith its justification and its petition. And after prayer, God's Word prepares me by revealing what the Father wants me to ask. In prayer, God's Word brings me the answer for in it the Spirit allows me to hear the Father's voice.

-Andrew Murray
(WC, pg. 161)

♦ Don't come to the Bible to find out what you can make it mean, but to find out what God intended it to mean.

-R. A. Torrey
(BT, pg. 218)

♦ No proof, no truth, no foundation.

-Jeannette Haley

♦ But the Bible is not a religion of an unknown God. It is built upon a rock of certainty that God has made known His will to His people. To us, the will of *God is neither a metaphor nor a euphemism* but more powerful and more real than our own experience.

-Abraham Heschel
(MQG, pg. 131)

♦ ...I know the sinfulness of my own heart and how much dross is there to be purified by the Refining Fire, how excruciating it is for me to submit to the Word that never permits the least indulgence of self-pity, self-vindication, self-aggrandizement, self-justification, or any other form of the self whatsoever.

-Elisabeth Elliot
(TGT, pg. 94)

♦ The most valuable thing in the world is the truth.

-Winston Churchill

◆ God may withdraw His glory, withhold His blessings, and implement His rod of chastening, but He will never break His word or forget His promises.

-Marvin J. Rosenthal
Zion's Fire
November-December 2015

◆ We all have learned through personal tragedies and mistakes that mixing the truth with untruth creates a toxic environment. None of us are spared. A lie seldom comes in recognizable form. It is usually smuggled in as small grains that poison the whole. That is why Jesus referred to the enemy of our souls as the father of all lies.

-Ravi Zacharias
(WJ. pg. 233)

◆ But in these days the truth costs us nothing, and we are ready to barter it for plausible errors and venerable superstitions, in order to maintain a false peace and the semblance of unity.

-Sir Robert Anderson
(TH, pg. 179)

Facts & Truth

Facts deal with the seen world with its methods, formulas, and proven laws; thereby they can be measured, while truth deals with the unseen aspects of the Spirit and cannot be measured. For this reason, truths are received by faith.

Facts are one dimensional, while truth clarifies and reveals the dimensions of the unseen. Facts inform, while truth verifies a record as being so. Facts feed the intellect, but truth feeds the spiritual man. Facts can lack truth, but truth declares and confirms a fact as being so and will be standing when all else falls because of the testing and judgment that will eventually come on all matters relating to life and godliness.

♦ The truth is sin is a contagious disease of the soul. It invades our perception, making us spiritually dull towards truth. It deceives us about our personal condition, making us indifferent towards its work of death in our lives. It operates within the confines of vain imaginations, creating ignorance and superstition towards God. It makes our hearts hard toward truth, our necks stiff with arrogance, and our knees diseased with independence. As a result, man is forever walking in the ways that seem right to him, but they lead to destruction.

-RJK

♦ Neither is it enough to have truth on our side, if we have not truth in our hearts.

-William Gurnall
(CCA, Vol. 1, pg. 291)

♦ Scripture tells us that *sin* is transgression of the Law (1 John 3:4) *righteousness* is of the Law (Romans 10:5), and *judgment* is by the Law (Romans 2:12; James 2:12).

-Ray Comfort
(GWP, pg. 55)

♦ Jesus Christ exercises absolute authority over the Scriptures written by men who were moved by the Holy Spirit. Every problem in the Church, from the day of Pentecost to this very hour, is addressed in that marvelous book we call the Word of God.

-A.W. Tozer
(RCF, pg. 29)

Prayer: *Oh, God, make me a little child. Empty me of my own notions. Teach me Thine own mind. Make me ready like a little child to receive all that Thou hast to say, no matter how contrary it is to what I have thought hitherto."*

-R. A. Torrey
(BT, pg. 218)

FAITH

Declaration of Genuine Faith

While teaching the book of Job, I wanted to present a statement that would best represent the attitude behind Job's faith. When attending a fellowship for women, the guest speaker shared a statement made by a woman in Africa, facing an uncertain future and possible persecution.

The woman stated, "I have quit saying 'What if," and now I say 'Even if." The "what ifs" of life operate in possibilities that may never happen, but the prospects can create great fear, and even though one might be trying to prepare for such possibilities, there is no assurance that one will stand when the trials come.

Genuine faith never operates within the "What ifs," because there is no real assurance. However, it does declare, "Even if God, slays me, I will trust Him." Regardless of the circumstances of life, faith believes that God is still in control and will stand confident on what He has declared. Such faith brings a person to the assurance and trust that God allows all things for personal growth that will bring Him glory.

It was clear that Job came face to face with the "What ifs," when he confronted his worse fears, but it was his attitude of faith, "Even if," that allowed him to stand on the character of God and trust the details of his life to Him.

♦ A sinner must be *"justified by faith."* *Death* then is the judicial ground of righteousness for a sinner. *Grace* is the principle on which God acts in reckoning him righteous. And it is on the principle of *faith,* as opposed to works or merit, that he receives the blessing.

-Sir Robert Anderson
(GAM, pg. 102)

♦ There is more faith in a quiet dependence upon the indwelling Christ than in an excitable anxiousness that would awaken Him in every storm, as though any real harm could come to us when He is within.

-Vance Havner
(RG, pg. 40)

♦ It has always been true that faith in God's Word, whatever that Word may have been, has alone justified man before Him, and through that Word men have been saved in all ages, thus entering into His spiritual kingdom and recognizing His authority in a world at variance with that divine rule.

-H. A. Ironside
(HC, pg. 98)

♦ A true faith must rest solidly on his character and his Word, not on our particular conceptions of what he ought to do. The word *ought* presupposes an idea of justice. When God's actions do not seem to conform to our idea of justice, we are tempted at least to as *why*, if not actually to charge him with injustice.

-Elisabeth Elliot
(TGT, pg. 9)

> **(Prayer)** *(Lord), Nothing in those dark caverns is mysterious to you. Nor is anything in my life or my friend's life. I trust you with the unfathomables.*
>
> -Elisabeth Elliot
> (TGT, pg. 20)

♦ My struggle is not to fight my troubles; but just to believe God; to be a believer. It is my faith that is being tested all the time.

-Paul Rader
(GBM, pg. 121)

♦ Obedience is evidence of the reality of our repentance and faith. Our obedience does not achieve salvation, but it is evidence of it.

-J. Oswald Sanders
(JJ, pg. 19)

♦ There is nothing, nothing at all, apart from belief in God. Accept this revelation, humble yourself, become like a little child, and believe the truth.

-Martyn Lloyd-Jones
(SFG, pg.167)

♦ The primary battle of life is being certain that one maintains a heart of faithfulness to the Lord God, as evident in a lifestyle of obedience.

-Dr. Ron J. Bigalke
Midnight Call
February 2016

The Assurance of Faith

There are different facets of faith. It begins with choosing to believe that God is all He says He is. Because God is, we can have the confidence to stand and ask God for those things we have need of to withstand the challenges of life.

Once our confidence is established on the Rock, we will have the assurance that He is faithful and trustworthy. From there we can come to a place of complete trust in what He presently does or will be doing in the future.

Faith is clearly all about dependency on God. God gives us stakes along the way to remind us that we have need of and that we can trust Him with those things He has put in our hearts. We have the assurance that along the way we will be given those tokens of remembrance that will continue to enable us to stand. For example:

He gives us promises in hopelessness,

Hope in times of loss,

His Word in times of confusion,

Himself in times of storms.

Faith has an enduring anchor of assurance that God is God and will be God regardless of the circumstances and times we live in.

♦ Christ's compassion was not stillborn; He did something about it. Seeing and feeling are sterile unless we are moved to action.

-J. Oswald Sanders
(JJ, pg. 96)

♦ The very building of the ark was in itself a sermon to the antediluvians. Every tap of Noah's hammer was a part of his preaching of righteousness to that generation. It declared him to be a man of faith, and it manifested their utter unbelief.

-H. A. Ironside
(HC, pg. 101)

♦ Rest is both an *obtainment* and an *attainment*. Positionally we receive His rest when we come to Him. But conditionally, in experience, this rest is ours daily as we *abide* in Him and *learn* of Him. It is not earned, but it is learned.

-Vance Havner
(RG, pg. 53)

♦ As I have written so many times before, the grace that God is offering the world through His Son is not a license to sin. Rather, it is a temporary opportunity to repent of sin, be born again, live righteously, and be saved from God's holy wrath.

-David Servant
Happy Endings Magazine

♦ There is a special grace for a special need. That grace is not given with our anticipations; it is given only with the *event.*

-W. E. Sangster
(HA, pg. 36)

♦ I must have some warrant for my faith, some ground on which to rest my faith, and that the surest of all grounds for faith was the Word of God.

-R. A. Torrey
(BT, pg. 73)

***

Put thou thy trust in God;
In duty's path go on;
Fix on His Word thy steadfast eye;
So shall thy work be done.

-Amanda Smith
(SC, pg. 92)

♦ The faith that "comes by hearing," brings us salvation and the knowledge of salvation. The faith that springs from abiding in Him and acquainting ourselves with Him, is the secret of a peace-ruled heart and a holy life.

-Sir Robert Anderson
(GAM, pg.48)

♦ Religion is a scaffolding for faith, but when it becomes the faith itself, it kills faith. We are often inclined to ignore the beauty of what is beneath and be distracted by the scaffolding. It was no different in Jesus' day; worshipper's attention to their religious ceremonies and customs had become so onerous that they had forgotten the purpose of their worship.

-Ravi Zacharias
(WJ, pg. 235)

♦ To relinquish present things in view of future blessing is to declare openly that one is seeking a country. No one can truly relinquish the world below until he has seen by faith a better and brighter world above.

-H. A. Ironside
(HC, pg. 103)

♦ Faith is nothing but the purpose of the will resting on God's Word and saying, "I must have it." To believe truly is to will firmly.

-Andrew Murray
(WC, pg.78)

♦ The law tells a person what he must do in order to attain a righteous standing. Grace gives him a righteous standing before God, then tells him to walk worthy of it. The law says, "Do and you will live." Grace says, "Live and you will do." The law says, "Try and obey." The language of grace is, "Trust and obey."

-William MacDonald
(NAG, pg. 26)

♦ As you follow Abraham, you will see a man that matured in his faith. His faith started out as a mustard seed in response to God's call, was made simple in its purity through obedience, and materialized in a friendship with God.

-RJK

♦ If we want to grow in faith we must be open to listening to our own stories, perhaps familiar or forgotten, where we have not mined the rich deposit of God's presence. With better eyes and ears, we will sense how God has worked to redeem even our most tragic experiences.

-Dan Allender

♦ And to faith the future and the unseen become present realities. Reason testifies to the existence of God, and therefore none but fools are atheists.

-Sir Robert Anderson
(TH, pg. 91)

***

Pentecostal life gives an overmastering faith.

Faith lends its realizing light;
    The clouds disperse, the shadows fly;
The Invisible appears in sight,
    And God is seen by mortal eye.

-George Hughes
(SC, pg. 55)

- The death of Christ was not only an atonement for sin, but a triumph over sin. By faith we see our sins not only on His head for our pardon, but under His feet for our deliverance.

  -John Gregory Mantle
  (BH, pg. 42)

- The power to believe *a promise* depends entirely on faith in *the promiser*.

  -Andrew Murray
  (WC, pg. 89)

- Our faith is not weights but wings! Coming to Him, rest is ours; as we practice His rest, it becomes our condition as well as our position.

  -Vance Havner
  (RG, pg. 53)

- Man is capable of the firmest and most implicit faith in himself and in the world—aye, and in the devil too, as will be proved one day; but his whole spiritual being is so utterly estranged from God that not only does he not know Him, but, if left to himself, he is incapable of knowing Him.

  -Sir Robert Anderson
  (GAM, pg. 49)

- Inactive faith is nothing more than the sin of unbelief. At the point of unbelief, truth will become stagnant, taking away its sharp edge to ensure discernment and liberty.

  -RJK

- Quietness and confidence go hand in hand. Quietness produces confidence and confidence results in quietness. That is our strength, not necessarily "deliverance" from our present crisis. Strength is the result, and strength is what you need when you are weak.

-Jeannette Haley

♦ We should always live out our faith every moment and never let it be shaken.

-North Korean Believer
(TG, pg. 111)

♦ It is still the duty and privilege of believers *to receive by the holy spirit by a conscious, definite act of appropriating faith,* just as they receive Jesus Christ . . . For it as sinners that we accept Christ for our *justification,* but *it is as sons* that we accept the Spirit (by faith) for our sanctification.

-Dr. A. J. Gordon
(SC, pg. 24)

♦ A strong faith will make a strong will, and a weak faith a weak will.

-John Gregory Mantle
(BH, pg. 130)

♦ ...there is no sweeter fragrance to God than the fragrance of faith.

-R. A. Torrey
(BT, pg. 82)

Prayer: Lord, *we talk about great faith, but there is nothing great about it. In its child-like form it allows You as our great God to move, in its trusting form it stands on what is sure, and in its confidence, it remains fearless because nothing can keep it from moving forward once a person is given their marching orders by You. Amen.*

♦ We often think that the walk of faith is a profound matter that only a few can learn, when really it is a simple matter that few ever reach because they will not *unlearn*—get down to its simplicity.

-Vance Havner
(RG, pg. 126)

♦ You must not keep back part of the price of full obedience to God and expect Him to bless you; and yet I often do find persons doing this very thing and then wondering why they do not get help from the Lord. May He help all to see the truth.

-Amanda Smith
(SC. pg. 94)

♦ In the spiritual world failure has only one cause: lack of faith. Faith is the one condition on which all Divine power can enter man and work through him, it is the sensitivity of man's will yielded to and molded by the will of God.

-Andrew Murray
(WC, pg. 97)

♦ Many well-meaning Christians however, do exactly what Paul avoided, convinced that the gospel and the Holy Spirit need the help of scholarship, psychological persuasion, and modern promotional packaging. Consequently, the faith of many believers today stands upon the wisdom of men instead of in the power of God and can thus be undermined by human arguments.

-Dave Hunt
The Berean Call

♦ We know that the center of our faith is the Lord, the inspiration of faith is the joy that has been set before us, and the expectation of faith is that my life may not be according to some script on earth, but it is according to God's heavenly plan.

-RJK

♦ (In reference to Galatians 3:14) Here are two blessings to be received in Christ Jesus: (1) "The blessing of Abraham," i.e., justification by faith. (2) "The promise of the Spirit" is the second blessing, that is, sanctification by faith. Among the thousands of God's unfailing promises, this, shining like the meridian sun, and eclipsing all the others by its glory, is distinguished as "*the* promise of the Father."

-W. N. Hirst
(SC, pg. 72)

♦ The principle of obedience is one thing, and the application of it is another. The disposition of obedience Jesus possessed before He suffered, but the proof that the disposition existed must be shown in deed, and the progress from the disposition to the deed was the practical learning of the virtue of obedience.

-John Gregory Mantle
(BH, pg. 137)

♦ Obedience and faith must go together. But faith can't simply be added to obedience; it must be revealed in obedience. Faith is obedience at home, looking to the Master; obedience is faith going out to do His will.

-Andrew Murray
(WC, pg. 155)

♦ A person who lives in faith must proceed on incomplete evidence, trusting in advance what will only make sense in reverse.

-Philip Yancey

♦ To the man who doubts, a grasshopper looks like a giant; but to the man who believes God, a giant looks like a grasshopper. To refuse to enter the Canaan of Perfect Love is to die spiritually.

-C. W. Ruth
(SC, pg. 101)

♦ Answers to all my questions: there have been none. If I had answers…then I guess there would be no use for faith and hope! I'm hoping in the unseen. Faith is being sure of what we hope for and certain of what we do not SEE.

-Mary Beth Chapman
(CS, pg. 266)

♦ Distrust of God was the cause of the creature's fall; how fitting it is, then, that faith in God should be the turning-point of his repentance.

-Sir Robert Anderson
(RT, pg. 110)

♦ The key-note is not need, nor service to meet the need, but obedience.

-Samuel Dickey Gordon
(QT, pg. 116)

♦ To think about God is almost impossible, because our thoughts must rise above everything else we might think about. Faith is involved here. We look beyond what we can actually see and experience a vison of God that cannot be explained in human language.

-A.W. Tozer
(MDP, pg. 289)

♦ Unbelief fears Satan as a lion, faith treads on him as a worm.

-William Gurnall
(CCA, Vol. 1, pg.110)

♦ God never allows us to go through a test of faith that is not intended to work in us lasting results.

-RJK

♦ Without faith we are not fit to desire mercy, without humility we are not fit to receive it, without affection we are not fit to value it, without sincerity we are not fit to improve it. Times of extremity contribute to the growth and exercise of these qualifications.

-Stephen Charnock
(SWR, pg. 19)

♦ Faith is the fountain of prayer, and prayer should be nothing else but faith exercised.

-Thomas Manton
(SWR, pg. 20)

♦ Nothing clears the mind like obedience; nothing darkens the mind like disobedience. To obey truth you see prepares you to see other truths. To disobey a truth you see darkens your mind to all truths.

-R.A. Torrey
(HSC, pgs. 57, 58)

♦ Practical holiness is necessary, because a living faith is a question of the heart and the whole being of a person, not just the mind...Faith in the Gospel is inseparable from a life of obedience.

-Rene Malgo
Midnight Call
April 2016

♦ Christians with no faith are a much greater danger than great persecution of Christians.

-Winrich Scheffbuch
Midnight Call
January 2018

♦ Confession of the mouth without faith in the heart is gross hypocrisy. To pretend faith without profession of the mouth, is both hypocrisy and cowardice.

-William Gurnall
(CCA, Vol. 1, pg. 306)

♦ Genuine faith is not based on human senses, but on the unchangeable character of an unseen God.

-RJK

♦ Obedience was the one touchstone of His life (Jesus). And it will be the one touchstone of His true follower's life. We shall run across this same vein of bright yellow gold, again and again, as we work on through "Follow Me" mine.

-Samuel Dickey Gordon
(QT, pg. 33)

♦ The most excellent and heroic acts of faith are those that are most removed from sense and reason; he who allows his reason to usurp his faith will never be an excellent Christian. He who is instructed by his own carnal reason, has a fool for his schoolmaster; and he who allows his faith to be overruled by his reason shall never lack woe.

-Thomas Brooks
(MSR, pgs141-142)

***

+ Faith makes everything possible
  Hope makes everything work
  Love makes everything beautiful.

-Unknown

+ Waiting, however, is one of the disciplines in the spiritual life. Waiting is simply transferring the responsibility to someone else...Waiting on the Lord is simply my way of trusting God for a particular situation.

-A.W. Tozer
(MDP, pgs. 330, 331)

+ A righteous man may make a righteous work, but no work of an unrighteous man can make him righteous. Now we become righteous only by faith, through the righteousness of Christ imputed to us.

-Thomas Boston
(SWR, pg. 21)

+ Faith is the wrestling grace. It comes up close to God; takes hold of God, and will not easily take a denial. It in fires all the affections, and sets them on work.

-William Gurnall
(CCA, Vol. 2, pg. 37)

What Does It Look Like?

What does faith look like? Faith is a noun, an action word, and an adjective. It is a passive word that puts a face to the Christian conviction. It is an active word that speaks of belief in action and an adjective that describes a way of being.

Faith expresses itself in trust towards God, confidence in His Word and ways, and assurance in His promises. It is disciplined to stand still when waiting for instructions, committed enough to withstand as it advances forward in expectation, and continues to stand when all of hell is claiming victory. It accepts no resignation when the way is hard, no settling for comfort zones when being challenged. and will avoid false, temporary contentment when obstacles become overwhelming.

Faith holds on to the Rock in storms, stays the narrow course in challenging times, endures the fiery tests and will cast all unnecessary weight aside to run the race in order to gain the prize.

The reason we know what faith looks like is because it has left a cloud of witnesses behind. Each witness may have been consumed by the cloud but their testimony still remains to speak of the ordinary who by faith became part of the extraordinary and the miraculous.

◆ Weak Christians devour devotional literature, always expecting that the next page will unlock the mystic secret. But here is the key: Faith grows as we exercise such faith as we have. The measure of the life abundant is in proportion to our faith. God's resources are ever available to faith. If we make our check small, we have only ourselves to blame.

-Vance Havner
(RG, pg. 48)

◆ We are living in the day of materialism and naturalism and man has taken the praise, but God is pleading: "*Trust Me and see what I will do.*"

-Paul Rader
(GBM, pg. 181)

◆ Faith never considers personal feats. As Christians it is time to climb down from pinnacles of greatness, jump off of molehills of self-importance, and quit trying to catch, capture, or ride the high waves of personal accomplishments and euphoric sensationalism, and out of faith respond to Jesus' simple call, "Follow Me."

-RJK

♦ Faith is heroic and true; unbelief is cowardly and false.

-M. L. Haney
(SC, pg. 65)

♦ Obedience is the rhythm of two wills, that blends their action into rarest harmony. Some of us need to use His tuning-fork, so as to enjoy the music of the road (of Calvary) (Emphasis added.)

-Samuel Dickey Gordon
(QT, pg. 54)

***

Faith-positional truth
Hope-future promise
Love-present, ongoing.

-Unknown

♦ Is our faith only an act: empty, meaningless actions? Is it a bluff, an appearance, a deception? Or does it have a powerful impact? Personal repentance and then prayer are what is necessary.

-Winrich Scheffbuch
Midnight Call
January 2018

♦ Faith in itself is not valuable, but when it ends up possessing the reality of God, it becomes priceless. It is Christ Jesus in us who serves as the priceless treasure that can only be acquired through faith.

-RJK

- Faith is not only the instrument to receive the righteousness of Christ for our justification, but it is also the great instrument to receive grace from Christ for our sanctification.

  -William Gurnall
  (CCA, Vol 2, pg. 17)

- Obedience, to be perfect, must be submitted to test. You cannot call a child obedient if his obedience has never cost him anything; nor do you know that he will obey when the trial comes unless he has been already put to the test, and so has had an opportunity of applying the principle which existed in his heart. In this progress from the principle of the application, from the disposition to the deed, there is, and must be suffering.

  -John Gregory Mantle
  (BH, pgs. 137, 138)

- As faith cannot exist without a creed, piety cannot subsist without a pattern of deeds; as intelligence cannot be separated from training, religion cannot be divorced from conduct.

  -Abraham Heschel
  (MQG, pg. 110)

- I like comfort and the illusion of being in control. But if I stick with what is familiar, I box my faith. It becomes human enterprise rather than godly exercise.

  -Ellen Vaughn
  (GHC, pg. 29)

- Clear vison and love without obedience is—impossible! Where there is no obedience, or faulty obedience, either the vision has blurred or dimmed, or the love is burning low.

  -Samuel Dickey Gordon
  (QT, pg. 196)

◆ A good conscience is the bottom faith sails in…If faith be the jewel, a good conscience is the cabinet in which it is kept; and if the cabinet be broken, the jewel must needs be in danger of losing.

-William Gurnall
(CCA, Vol. 2, pg. 57)

◆ How very important it is to obey the Lord, *step by step!* We cannot know how much may hinge on one single step. The whole course of a life might be changed by just a step.

-Isobel Kuhn
(IA, pg. 8)

◆ Faith is not something which the sinner gives to God, but merely the receiving what God has got to give him.

-Sir Robert Anderson
(RT, pg. 91)

◆ Sinners miss life here and hereafter because they believe not, and Christians live meager and defeated lives because they believe so little. In the midst of it all stands Jesus, the answer to every problem; but we do not believe like the blind men that He is able to do wonders in our lives or, if we believe it theoretically, we do not believe it practically, so our eyes are not opened.

-Vance Havner
(RG, pg. 46)

◆ What thy faith loseth by every act of unbelief, it recovers again by renewing thy repentance.

-William Gurnall
(CCA, Vol. 2, pg. 58)

♦ It is only unbelief and willful rejection of the testimony of God that makes men stumble at and pervert so wondrous an unfolding of the beginnings of the created heavens and earth. Faith bows in subjection to the witness God has given and glorifies Him for such a marvelous unfolding of the divine wisdom.

-H. A. Ironside
(HC, pg. 99)

♦ Hebrews 6:1 talks about repentance from dead works. If you don't put some life (obedience to what is right) in your repentance (about face), there will be no real conversion.

-RJK

♦ Truth disobeyed destroys the capacity for discovering truth. There must be not only a general surrender of the will, but specific, practical obedience to each new word of God discovered…Truth not lived and stood for flees.

-R. A. Torrey
(BT, pg. 215, 216)

♦ By believing in Jesus, we recognize God, His love, His right, His power. In sealing us with the Holy Spirit, God recognizes us, stamping us as His property.

-W. N. Hirst
(SC, pg. 73)

♦ For the faith that suffers is greater than the faith that can boast an open triumph.

-Sir Robert Anderson
(TH, pg. 103)

♦ Faith only can see God in his greatness; and therefore none but faith can see the promises of their greatness, because the value of promises is according to the worth of him that makes them.

-William Gurnall
(CCA, Vol. 2, pgs. 113, 114)

♦ All men are potentially justified by the death of Christ on the cross, but believers are actually justified by appropriating to themselves what there is of justifying value in the shed blood of Christ by simple faith in Him.

-R. A. Torrey
(BT, pg. 231)

♦ Cause and effect are in God's hands. Is it not the part of faith simply to let them rest there? *God is God.*

-Elisabeth Elliott
(GHC, pg.160)

♦ When a child of God decides to step out in absolute obedience to the will of God, there will be a frantic effort by the powers of darkness to block him. Obstacles will spring up to hinder and discourage that one.

-Isobel Kuhn
(IA, pg. 11)

♦ Faith without a promise, is like a foot without any firm ground to stand upon.

-William Gurnall
(CCA, Vol. 2, pg. 333)

♦ Faith is the opened lattice that lets in the light of heaven to the soul, bringing gladness and blessing with it....so many Christians are hypochondriacs respecting faith...faith not only receives the word of Christ; it reaches on, and lays hold upon the person of Christ. Belief of His word leads to belief in Himself.

-Sir Robert Anderson
(GAM, pg. 46)

♦ God has put enough into this world to make faith in him a most reasonable thing; but he has left enough out to make it impossible to live by reason alone.

-Ravi Zacharias
(WJ, pg. XVI)

♦ Having a spiritual experience gives us an expectation, but if it fails to inspire genuine faith towards God, it will prove to be void of sustaining power. If you have an experience without faith, the elements of genuine hope will not be present.

-RJK

♦ Faith, not feeling, measures the efficacy of prayer.

-W. E. Sangster
(HA, pg. 172)

♦ The only impediments we have, like bowling balls bound to our hiking boots, are our fears and the failure to believe that God is really God. He'll move mountains if need be. Or He'll cut steps so we can climb them. The view from the top is magnificent.

-Ellen Vaughn
(GHC, pg. 183)

♦ A strong faith in a wrong object will never save, but even a weak faith in a right object will. It is not the strength of our faith that saves, but the power of the blood upon which our faith is centered.

-Hebert Lockyer
(MM, pg. 82)

121

♦ Faith may live in a storm, but it will not suffer a storm to live in it.

-William Gurnall
(CCA, Vol. 2, pg. 340)

♦ The greatest challenge posed to our faith in dark times is not whether or not God is capable of saving us, but that there is nothing in our character that would warrant Him to do so.

-RJK

GRACE & HOPE

It Is Complete!

We are saved by grace that flows from above to those who are cringing spiritual beggars before a loving God. We are saved by hope that can lift us up from the miry quagmire of futility associated with this present age to grab a hold of that which is eternal. We are saved through faith that chooses the way of grace and walks according to the hope that has been set before us.

Our salvation is complete because of God's unending grace, that it is sure because such hope is based on immutable promises, and that unfeigned faith is what will receive the promise and blessings of this eternal life as it walks it out in complete assurance and confidence.

♦ And the grace of God is not, as some seem to think, a kind of good influence imparted to the sinner to fit him to receive

Divine blessing. It is the principle on which God blesses sinners in whom He can find no fitness whatsoever.

-Sir Robert Anderson
(RT, pg. 83)

♦ My finite sins compared to His infinite mercy get lost in a shoreless ocean of God's grace...The devil may want me to be an accountant (in regard to personal sins), but God desires me to be a worshiper and leave the numbers with Him. (Parenthesis added).

-A.W. Tozer
(MDP, pg. 281)

♦ Every sin hath its opposite grace, as every poison hath its antidote. He that will walk in the power of holiness, must not only labour to make avoidance of sin, but to get possession of the contrary grace.

-William Gurnall
(CCA, Vol. 1, pg. 430)

♦ The sole ground of our rejoicing is not in our powers or successes, but in the unmerited and undeserved grace of God.

-Vance Havner
(RG, pg. 158)

♦ The depravity of mankind is a miracle of sin; it is as great a miracle, from one point of view, as the grace of God is from another. Jesus Christ neglected! Eternal love slighted! Infinite mercy disregarded! I have to confess, with great shame, that even the preacher of the Gospel is not always affected by it as he ought to be.

-Charles Spurgeon
(FJ, pgs. 74, 75)

♦ Grace means *favour*. But what kind of favour? For favour is of many kinds. Favour shown to the *miserable* we call mercy; favour shown to the *poor* we call pity; favour shown to the *suffering* we call compassion; favour shown to the *obstinate* we call GRACE! This is favour indeed; favour which is truly Divine in its source and in its character.

-E. W. Bullinger
(GMM, pg. 59)

♦ His grace is infinite to the humble and contrite, and to such as tremble at His Word. But ignorance begotten of indolence and willful neglect of His Word, grace will not condone. And ignorance due to sheer contempt of His Word, calls only for judgment.

-Sir Robert Anderson
(RT, pg. 77)

Two Channels

There are two conditions necessary to come into a place where one can be used of the Lord: that of obedience and purity. Obedience means surrendering our will so the Lord's will can be done.

Purity is about making sure we are consecrated vessels clean inward by the sanctifying work of the Holy Spirit, for He can't use an unclean vessel. It is only through clean channels that God can pour forth His grace into our lives.

♦ Some graces thrive best, like some flowers, in the shade, such as humility, dependence on God, and etc.

-William Gurnall
(CCA, Vol. 1, pg. 235)

♦ My hope is not in this coming year but in the one who is coming back.

-Facebook Post

♦ Perhaps, above all, I am concerned that many within the Church are unprepared for the stormy days ahead and will not be watching for His coming; the prospect of which should be the ultimate catalyst for holy living.

-Marvin Rosenthal
Zion's Fire
July-August 2017

♦ Faith makes everything possible. Hope makes everything work. Love makes everything beautiful.

-Facebook Post

♦ Peter's "living" hope is the same as Paul's "blessed" hope...Unlike the uncertainty bound up in our common use of the word "hope," the "hope which Paul and Peter had in mind is hope only in the sense that its realization is still future. But what is this blessed hope which is alive, good, certain, and eternal? It is this: Jesus is coming again—not to a stable and manger, but to a palace and throne—not as a lamb, but as a lion—not in silence, but in roaring—not with humility, but with glory—not to die, but to judge.

-David Rosenthal
& Marvin Rosenthal

***

The sun went down in clouds,
The moon was darkened by a misty doubt,
The stars of heaven were dimmed by earthly fears
And all my little candle-flames burned out:

But while I sat in shadow, wrapped in night
The face of Christ made all the darkness light.

-Annie Johnson Flint
(IA, pg. 110)

♦ The "blessed hope" embodies the fact – no matter how dark the night, how long the journey, how large or many the obstacles – nothing, not even death itself, can separate the believer from his ultimate glorification and eternal presence with God.

-Marvin J. Rosenthal
(Zion's Magazine)

♦ A person's hope is only as good as the object of his or her hope.

-Pastor Rob Greenslade

♦ Facing the end of one's earthly pilgrimage is not a melancholy thing for a Christian. It is like preparation for the most exciting journey of all.

-Isobel Kuhn
(IA. Pg. 229)

♦ Hope waits but does not sit. It strains with eager anticipation to see what may be coming on the horizon. Hope does not pacify; it does not make us docile and mediocre. Instead, it draws us to greater risk and perseverance.

-Dan Allender

♦ Peter could walk on the waves as long as he looked to Jesus. But as soon as he looked at the waves, he sank. If you look to Jesus, the waves in life's storms become like firm ground.

-Corrie ten Boom
(MA, Bk. 1, pg. 29)

◆ For the Christian, death is not the dissolution of life but the *consummation.*

-Isobel Kuhn
(IA, pg. 231)

***

Some day the silver cord will break
    And I no more as now shall sing;
But oh, the joy when I shall wake
    Within the palace of the King!
And I shall see Him face to face. . .

-W. E. Sangster
(HA, pg. 24)

◆ We are thankful for God's grace and forgiveness, but we must understand that His mercy is not a license to sin.

-Israel Teaching Letter
Bridges for Peace
August 2015

◆ The Divine grace which freely justifies a sinner, and then teaches him to live righteously, also sanctifies and teaches him to live holier.

-Sir Robert Anderson
(RT, pg. 87)

In Times Like These

Ruth Caye Jones was the wife of a minister and also the mother of five. While we constantly hear of wars and rumors of wars today, it's sometimes easy to forget that things were much worse in the dark days of World War II. The US casualty count of the war in Afghanistan recently reached 2,000, a number far, far too great.

And yet during World War II, over 400,000 young US soldiers lost their lives. And that number itself was just a small part of the 78 million people who died worldwide.

It was during this time that Mother Jones, as she came to be known, reflected on the words of 2 Timothy 3:1, and took a small notepad from her apron pocket, jotting down the words and music to "In Times Like These", exactly as we sing them today.

As with many great hymns of the era, "In Times Like These" was a popular choice of George Beverly Shea to be sung at Billy Graham Crusades. The first time Jones heard her song sung on television, tears came to her eyes. "I can't believe I had any part in writing this song. I just feel that God gave it to me, and I gave it to the world."

Today, we still live in perilous times. And unlike in the 1940s, we as a society have grown further and further from God. The Solid Rock is still there and always has been, but we as a people have chosen to throw our anchor onto sinking sand.

So, the words that Mother Jones wrote 50 years ago ring truer today than they ever have. In our lives, whether we're talking about us as a society or within our own families, we will encounter storms of life, some which threaten to tear our whole ships apart. But if your anchor grips onto the solid rock, there is no storm that can destroy you.

♦ Grace is the beginning of glory, and glory is the fulness of grace. It is all grace, free unmerited favour.

-Samuel Dickey Gordon
(QT, pg. 168)

♦ We cannot have the benefit of the throne of grace till we quit our legal plea.

-William Gurnall
(CCA, Vol. 2, pg. 416)

***

Wonderful grace of Jesus, greater than all my sin;
How shall my tongue describe it?
Where shall its praise begin?
Taking away my burden, setting my Spirit free,
For the wonderful grace of Jesus reaches me.

-Haldor Lillenas
(1885-1959)

♦ When the Lord comes to look upon a poor soul, He lays His finger upon the scar, upon the infirmity—that He may see nothing but grace, which is the beauty and the glory of the soul.

-Thomas Brooks
(SWR, pg. 66)

♦ Grace is too much neglected where gifts are too highly prized; we are commanded to be clothed with humility. Our garments cover the shame of our bodies, humility the beauty of the soul.

-William Gurnall
(CCA, Bol. 1, pg. 196)

♦ Grace is not a display of Divine weakness; nor does it lead to levity in those whom it blesses. It is the crowning revelation of God's sovereignty, and it trains men for a life of self-control and righteousness and godliness.

-Sir Robert Anderson
(RT, pg. 162)

♦ Grace is the goodness of God confronting human demerit

-A.W. Tozer
(MDP, pg. 159)

♦ The state of grace is the commencing of a war against sin, not the ending of it...

-William Gurnall
(CCA, Vol. 1 pg. 121)

♦ Grace does not place either the Saviour or the Gospel at the bar of human judgment; that is the arrogance of infidelity. As has been already seen, grace is based upon the cross, and assumed that man is guilty and finds him there: it does not brand him as ruined and lost, but it comes to him as thus branded already.

-Sir Robert Anderson
(GAM, pg. 53)

***

Judge not the Lord by feeble sense,
But trust Him for His grace;
Behind a frowning providence
He hides a smiling face.

-Cowper
(FJ, pg. 122)

♦ God's highest glory displays itself in sovereign grace, therefore it is that the gospel of His grace is the gospel of His glory. Let us take heed then that we preach grace. He who preaches a mixed gospel robs God of His glory, and the sinner of his hope.

-Sir Robert Anderson
(GAM, pg. 9)

♦ An **ATHEIST** has a reason, but no hope for his reason.
A **HYPOCRITE** has a hope but no reason for his hope.
A **CHRISTIAN** has a reason for his hope and hope for his reason.

-United Brethren Magazine

♦ It is solid grace in the vessel of the heart that feeds profession in the lamp—holiness in the life.

-William Gurnall
(CCA, Vol 1, pg. 447)

She Now Knows What She Looks Like

The one great reality of God is that His will is none perish. His heart is ever open to the wounded, down-trodden soul, His ears to the cries of the lost, and His grace available for those seeking deliverance from their plight.

The truth is God will reach far and wide for the lost sheep of His fold. His net of grace is wide as many flee into it such as myself to escape the tyrannical, deathly hold and claims of this world on their souls.

In our limited, ineptness, we never know how long the door to the sheepfold will remain open to those who are lost and wandering in the darkness of despair. As I read the Scriptures, I have no doubt it will remain open for all who will come until there is no longer any cry in the darkness.

One day I received a call from a friend who told me her sister was ready to meet with me. Her sister had been on my radar for a couple of years. She had lost both of her beautiful children to a rare disease and she was depressed, angry with God and suicidal. Her sorrow had made her inconsolable, and what she considered unfairness in life caused her to rage against the corridors of heaven, driving her to teeter on the abyss of complete insanity.

I agreed to meet with her but I figured she would be a "no show." I realize it is easy for personal reason or logic to limit God, but praise God, He is not bound to our limitations; rather, He is able to do the impossible. Case in point is my own salvation.

Every blood-bought saint is a miracle of resurrection. Dead in sin, but imbued with new life and raised up with such power that they are indeed a walking testimony of God's greatness and ability to do the impossible.

As my friend and her sister stood at my door, I was reminded of Jesus' words, "Oh ye of little faith." However, as I stood there, I had the assurance that God's grace brought her there in order to do the impossible, and He was allowing me to be a witness of it.

I must say that the two-hour battle that ensued was intense. Her anger would rage, but truth was lifted up to put it in its place. When she spoke of the great loss of her children, she was reminded God so loved that He gave up His Son for her. When she questioned how God could let such a thing happen, she was reminded that her children had great hope in a future where there would be no more suffering because they were believers.

She admitted her daughter had greatly suffered from her disease, which was akin to Brittle Bone Disease. They had conducted at least 26 operations on her face. She told her mother that she didn't even know what she looked like.

Eventually the woman had to acknowledge that her anger was for the most part because of her loss and not her children's suffering. She conceded that the only reason she did not commit suicide is because she knew she would not see her children. It was amazing to me she had that small seed of faith planted there by the faith of others including her offspring.

The Lord did meet this woman, and in the end, she was set free from her anger while her suffering gave way to an inner peace as she grabbed hold of the hope of eternal life. She left with a whole new countenance.

As we were ending our meeting by praying for her, the Lord quietly spoke to my spirit, "She (her daughter) now knows what she looks like." I thought to myself I must share that bit of information with the mother, but by the time she left, it had slipped my mind. I thought to myself God has His timing for everything and that I needed to do follow up later on with her and then I could share it.

A month later our friend called us to inform us that her sister had passed away. I was stunned by the news but comforted as the friend shared how her sister was indeed a new creation.

After the phone call, I reminded God what he showed me about this woman's daughter and that I never got a chance to share it with her. It was then He said, "She now knows what her daughter looks like." I realized that the woman did not need the nugget because she would soon enough be united with her in glory and would see her as she is.

It occurred to me that the nugget was for my benefit. It was a confirmation that God had indeed pulled the woman out of the grips of hell at the right time. Even though this woman had raged against Him for years, He had prepared her to receive His provision, and that by doing so she would realize the desire of her heart as soon as she was reunited with her children in glory.

One day we will see every believer as they are in Christ, but the real satisfaction will come when we see Him, "we will be like Him; for we shall see Him as He is" (1 John 3:2).

Prayer: *Father of Mercies...Thy grace has given me faith in the cross by which thou hast reconciled thyself to me and me to thee, drawing me by thy great love, reckoning me as innocent in Christ though guilty in myself.* (VOV, pg. 169)

♦ I've learned the hard way...if you're tired of the same rotten results, stop making the same dumb decisions.

-Jeannette Haley

The Root of Foolishness

The Bible tells us that a fool says in his heart there is no God. However, there is another type of fool that falls into the same category of unbelief as those who say there is no God: the idolater or whoremonger. This is a person who spiritually fornicates with the idols of this world.

God's Word is clear about fleeing all idolatry and describes such idolatry as a form of worship, where one worships the creation rather than the Creator. The truth is there are many idols from the idea of self-importance to all the things that people pursue and lust after in this world. The problem with much of the idolatry is that it is hidden in secret places such as the heart or in high places which often appears as part of the landscape. In other words, people worship their knowledge about such things, which finds its foundation in the world's liberal, godless education and philosophy.

There is a story about a man named Mahmud Ghazni. Hundreds of years ago, Mahmud conquered a great portion of India. While he was seizing populated areas, he destroyed the idols that had been erected. When he captured the great city of Gujarat, he entered into the costliest shrine of the Brahmans and found a gigantic idol fifteen feet high. Like the other idols, he ordered it to be destroyed, but before any action could be taken, the Brahmans of the temple prostrated themselves at Mahmud's feet and pleaded with him to spare it for the fortunes of the city depended upon it.

After pausing, Mahmud declared that he rather be known as the breaker than the seller of idols, and struck the image with his battle-ax. His soldiers followed, and in an instance the idol was broken to pieces. Like most idols, it proved to be hollow, and had been used as a receptacle for thousands of precious gems, which, as the image was shattered, fell at the conqueror's feet. (BH, pg. 30)

This story reminds us that all idols will one day fall at the feet of our righteous God and Judge. At that time, the foolishness of idolatry will be exposed and the folly of the people who put much investment in their idols, adorning them with devotion and riches, will be brought to the light. Regardless of their pleas with those who would threaten their idol, and their rage against those who expose their idol's fallacy, these idols will not be able to stand against a holy God who will not share His glory with any other god, as well as the truth of His Word that will stand as a witness against the foolishness of all such idolatry.

♦ There is a zeal without knowledge, that is superstition. There is a zeal against knowledge, that is interest or faction; there is a zeal with knowledge, that is religion; and if you will view the countries of cruelty, you will find them superstitious rather than religious. Religion is gentle, it makes men better, more friendly, loving and patient than before.

-William Penn

♦ No rapid growth in Christian maturity will be attained until the first indispensable step of *submission to the lordship* of Christ has been taken.

-J. Oswald Sanders
(JJ, pg. 96)

♦ Clearly, time has wisely taught me my great need for God, while experiences have humbled me to receive His mercy and grace, and age has tempered and disciplined me to walk in them.

-RJK

♦ "Thinkers" on the secular left often cite the musings of eighteenth-century philosopher Immanuel Kant. Kant refers to religion and God as "superstition" and "folly." These "thinkers" believe that true enlightenment and freedom can only come from an atheistic—or at the very least—agnostic society. They ignore the many lessons in history that show, beyond a doubt, that tyranny is only possible without religion, and religion; is the greatest enemy of tyranny.

-Brad O'Leary
(AWC, pgs. viii-ix)

♦ Sin is the root of pride. Self-will and vanity are devil-like. Holiness and humility are twin graces well-pleasing to God.

-L. L. Pickett
(SC, pg. 45)

***

Measure thy life by loss instead of gain,
Not by the wine drunk but by the wine poured forth;
For love's strength standeth in life's sacrifice;
And whoso suffers most hath most to give.

-John Gregory Mantle
(BH, pg. 81)

♦ Then I saw that everything about my burden was borrowed. One part belonged to the following day, one part to the next week. My burden was a huge, stupid mistake. I realized that

136

worrying is carrying tomorrow's burden with today's strength...On a calendar, there is only one day for action, and that is today.

-Corrie ten Boom
(MA, Bk. 2, pg. 37)

♦ God who gave us life gave us liberty. Can the liberties of a nation be secure when we have removed a conviction that theses liberties are the gift of God?

-President Thomas Jefferson
(AWC, pg. 2)

♦ I think there's going to come a time, if we don't draw the line in the sand now, that we will lose the right to practice freely what we believe.

-Rep. Walter Jones
(AWC, pg. 21)

♦ Whoever undermines the twin pillars of religion and morality cannot be called a "Patriot."

-President George Washington
(AWC, pg. 60)

♦ Discernment is both learned and given. To be learned there must be a separation from the holy and profane, and to be given, there must be a willingness to be separated from what is considered acceptable to those of the status quo.

-RJK

♦ The philosophy of the school room in one generation will be the philosophy of government in the next.

-President Abraham Lincoln
(AWC, pg. 62)

***

There are different ways, as a great teacher reminds us, both of knowing and of learning. "A large part of our knowledge is either intuitive and ideal, residing in the pure reason; or speculative – that is, gathered by deduction and mental inference.

Another kind is learned by what we call life – by experience, personal trial, entanglement with events, struggles in doing and suffering; and what we learn in this way we know with a depth and familiarity far beyond other knowledge: it is now part of our living energies and powers, and dwells in our very being. Not only is its stamp imprinted on us, but it so passes into us as to blend with our whole inner nature. We are what we have done and suffered."

-John Gregory Mantle
(BH, pg. 138)

♦ Even the saddest things can become, once we have made peace with them, a source of wisdom and strength for the journey that still lies ahead.

-Frederick Buechner

♦ Unless we are prepared to detach ourselves, not only from things sinful, but also from things inexpedient, we shall never know this experience in all its fullness and glory.

-John Gregory Mantle
(BH, pg. 120)

♦ Do not make your conscience a rule of life for other people. But never yield an inch of principle. Stand firmly behind what you believe. Do it in love, but do it at any cost.

-R.A. Torrey
(HSC, pg. 107)

◆ Man's wisdom may be levelled with folly, but God is never interrupted. All the plots of hell and commotions on earth, have not so much shaken God's hand, to spoil one letter or line that he hath been drawing.

-William Gurnall
(CCA, Vol. 1, pg.110)

◆ Past history is the teacher of wisdom, the present the student of ideas, and the future the witness that will bear record as to what is true. Take away the teacher and you end up with ignorance or indoctrination, pointing to the worst of history always being repeated as the future comes at the unsuspecting like a freight train.

-RJK

The Loudest Silence

Proverbs speaks of silence as exhibiting wisdom, and in some cases, it is true, but silence is also a type of mask that hides unbecoming attitudes and ways. Puritan Thomas Brooks stated that the law of silence is upon man's heart, mind, and tongue. Tongue-service without heart-service is no service in the account of God; therefore, tongue-silence without heart-silence is not silence in the esteem of God. Clearly, God knows what is in all silence. Brooks points out that there is a sevenfold silence. They are:

Stoical silence: This has to do with being indifferent to the reality of others' plight.

Politic silence: This is silence towards policy to avoid taking a stand and paying the price.

Foolish silence: This silence is in reference to fools who can't do well or speak well so they keep quiet.

Sullen silence: These are troubled souls who are oppressed and unable to express themselves.

Forced silence: This silence is forced on others through suffering and tyranny. To cry will not change the situation; therefore, silence becomes the end response.

Despairing silence: This is a tormenting silence due to hell in the heart and horror in the conscience.

Prudent silence: This silence is one that is carefully measured out based on heaven above. It shows wisdom and discretion that is touched by grace from the throne of God. (MSR, pgs. 2-8, 11)

♦ The worth of man must be measured by his life, not by his failure under a singular and peculiar trial.

-James Anthony Froude
(SL, pg. 134)

♦ Quantity is what we think we need, but quality is what we know we need.

-RJK

♦ An ignorant person is a man in shape, and a beast in heart.

-William Gurnall
(CCA, Vol. 1, pg. 161)

♦ The measure of our fullness is our emptiness.

-Vance Havner
(RTR, pg.79)

♦ One leak will sink a ship, and one sin will destroy a sinner.

-John Bunyan
(SWR, pg. 18)

♦ More failure comes from an excess of caution than from bold experiments with new ideas.

-J. Oswald Sanders
(SL, pg. 128)

♦ Heavenly wisdom may be ancient, or even present before the beginning of time, but it will never become obsolete, useless, or outdated.

-RJK

♦ God looks upon the pearl—and not upon the spot that is in it!
-Thomas Brooks
(SWR, pg.66)

***

Knowledge and wisdom, far from being one,
Have ofttimes no connection. Knowledge dwells
In heads replete with thoughts of other men:
Wisdom, in minds attentive to their own.
Knowledge is proud that he has learned so much,
Wisdom is humble that he knows no more.

-Author unknown
(SL, pgs. 58, 59)

♦ Morality always sees further than the intellect.

-Unknown

♦ A stable mind and a double heart seldom meet.

-William Gurnall
(CCA, Vol. 1, pg. 300)

♦ This is the whole secret of the Christian life. The more things go against us, the more they drive us to Christ; and the more we are with Christ, the happier we are. So we turn our valley of Baca into wells and into places of rejoicing.

-Martyn Lloyd-Jones
(SFG, pg. 76)

♦ The more that you ascend positions of leadership and responsibility, the greater you need to develop your character and discipline.

-Dr. Ron J. Bigalke
Midnight Call
March 2016

♦ Never start with your problems. Never! Never start with earth; never start with men. Always start in heaven; always start with God...The one thing with which we must always start is our relationship with God. The whole trouble in the world today is due to the fact that this has been forgotten.

-Martyn Lloyd-Jones
(SFG, pgs. 156, 157)

♦ Knowledge without character is deadly. Solomon knew all the answers. He just did not live them. In the end, Solomon's is a sad story and a grim reminder that even the dispensers of wisdom have a breaking point.

-Ravi Zacharias
(WJ. pg. 245, 246)

Standing Wisdom for the Ages

If you are a father, what kind of advice would you offer your son? Let us take it up a notch. You are a Christian father who is in the ministry, what nuggets of wisdom would you share with your son who is at the crossroads of his life?

Thirty-five years ago, the late Marv Rosenthal penned a letter to his son David, who has followed in his father's footsteps. This letter came after David had completed his first year of Bible College. It was later published in the ministry magazine to edify others. As you read the letter, you can't help but see the heart of Marv as a father who clearly took his position as father seriously. His desire for his son was about spiritual matters and it was clear that he had already had a great impact on the man his son was becoming. His son David thought for himself, had asked pertinent questions, challenged his father along the way and did not flow with the establishment just to get along or get by. I felt that since it was in the magazine, I could share some of the nuggets as well.

- ❖ And through the years, we prayed for many things for you. Above all, we prayed that you would come to know and trust the Savior.
- ❖ It has been our hope that our family lifestyle, values, and teaching will help you along life's journey. We have tried to live before you so that we could say, "Do as we do" as well as, "Do as we say." There were times we failed – but never because we have not been trying.
- ❖ I fear, Son, that in many spheres of the Christian life, it is fashionable today to get as close as possible to the world's value system without crossing some imaginary line. Christian lifestyles, goals, and values are often not very different from those of the unsaved around us.
- ❖ And often Christian young people follow the advice of unregenerate guidance counselors who care little about the cause of Christ and eternal values. As a result, many of the King's children are laboring solely for the perishable riches of this world.
- ❖ If God has called you to be His servant, don't stoop to become a king.
- ❖ The world is no friend to grace. Opposition will be strong, hills will be steep, and obstacles will be large. Christ-

denying, satanically-empowered humanism is on the increase. Things are going to get worse.

❖ Dave, always view satanic opposition as an occasion for God to bare His right arm of power and magnify His name through your life.

❖ When the principles of man conflict with the Word of God, it is man who is wrong.

❖ Today, many are substituting experience for doctrine with disastrous consequences. When right doctrine is missing a lack of spiritual discernment cannot be far behind. Heretical doctrine, cultic organizations and an anemic Church will invariably follow.

❖ Many promising believers have been held back by partners of shallow Christian commitment.

❖ Dave, the Church has a destiny of greatness. When the Lord is done with her, she will be purified and without spot or blemish.

❖ I am reminded that you are half-Jewish and half-Gentile. But what is truly important is that you are a 100-percent Christian.

(Read the whole letter in Zion's Fire, July/August 2021.)

Prayer: *Lord, thank You for your grace. There is much we assume about it, take for granted, and even hide behind it to cover some of our unbecoming ways. It was Your grace that provided a way for faith to obtain life, gave wings to hope in preparation to soar, and sent forth the currents of expectation to raise our despairing soul above this world so we can indeed embrace Your redemption and be positionally seated in high places with You while still physically bound to this world. Amen.*

A Bit of History

In 1863 at a national proclamation of prayer and repentance, President Abraham Lincoln wrote, "We have forgotten God. We have forgotten the gracious hand, which preserved us in peace, and multiplied and enriched and strengthened us; and have vainly imagined, in the deceitfulness of our hearts, that all these blessings were produced by some superior wisdom and virtue of our own.

Intoxicated with unbroken success, we have become too self-sufficient to feel the necessity of redeeming and preserving grace, too proud to pray to the God that made us! It behooves us, then, to humble ourselves before the Offended Power, to confess our national sins, and to pray for clemency and forgiveness" (The Presidential Prayer Team website.)

♦ We do not step out of the world when we pray; we merely see the world in a different setting. The self is not the hub, but the spoke of the revolving wheel. In prayer we shift the center of living from self-consciousness to self-surrender. God is the center toward which all forces tend.

-Abraham Heschel
(MQG, pg. 7)

♦ Consecration to God and His will gives wonderful liberty in prayer for temporal things.

-Andrew Murray
(WC, pg. 35)

♦ (Concerning the word "wrestle" in the New Testament.) It is used in the New Testament of men toiling until they are weary; of the athlete on the track, straining every muscle and nerve, of the soldier battling for his very life, this kind of prayer has been termed "an athletic of the soul."

-J. Oswald Sanders
(JJ, pg. 100)

♦ Prayer often meets such a Divine silence, but few of us press on to an answer as did this needy soul. Too often we take silence to mean refusal.

-Vance Havner
(RG, pg. 74)

♦ You may have plans and methods, ways and means, machinery and committees, lots of information about people, but until the people of God pray, and the Holy Spirit writes the vison on the heart, the young men and women will never go.

-Paul Rader
(GBM, pg. 185)

♦ Preach in order to pray. Preach in order to inspire others to pray. The test of a true sermon is that it can be converted to prayer.

-Abraham Heschel
(MQG, pg. 80)

***

Restraining prayer, we cease to fight,
Prayer makes the Christian's armour bright;
And Satan trembles when he sees
The weakest saint upon his knees.

-William Cowper
(JJ, pg. 98)

♦ Within Christendom, prayer too often has become an attempt to manipulate God. Positive confession, which is basically commanding God to act, is a favored technique among growing numbers of Christians.

-T. A. McMahon
The Berean Call
January 2016

♦ But praying is going to the bank, going to the bank that has the largest capital of any bank in the universe, the Bank of Heaven, a bank whose capital is absolutely unlimited.

-R. A. Torrey
(BT, pg. 78)

♦ It takes great inner power to address a nation; it takes divine strength to address heaven and earth.

-Abraham Heschel
(TP, pg. 556)

♦ It is on prayer that the promises wait for their fulfillment, the Kingdom waits for its coming, and the glory of God waits for its full revelation. How slothful and unfit we are for this blessed work.

-Andrew Murray
(WC, pg. 10)

Prayer: *Lord Jesus! Enroll my name among those who confess that they don't know how to pray as they should, and who especially ask You for a course of teaching in prayer.* (Andrew Murray; WC, pg. 15)

- There are many who labor in the vineyard of oratory; but who knows how to pray, or how to inspire others to pray? There are many who can execute and display magnificent fireworks; but who knows how to kindle a spark in the darkness of a soul?

  -Abraham Heschel
  (MQG, pg. 50)

- Fervent prayer and testimony are the sure weapons of conviction and salvation.

  -W. N. Hirst
  (SC, pg. 70)

- God gives His guidance in three ways. If these three are in agreement, then you know that you are safe: 1) Prayer, 2) God's Word, the Bible, 3) Circumstances. If you know God's hidden companionship, your prayer will become a conversation instead of a soliloquy.

  -Corrie ten Boom
  (MA, Bk. 1 pg. 95)

- No, men and women, you cannot approach God on any other ground than the shed blood, and until you believe in the blood of Jesus Christ as a perfect atonement for your sins, and as the only ground on which you can find forgiveness and justification, real prayer is an impossibility.

  -R. A. Torrey
  (BT, pg. 90)

***

Ask but His grace; lo! It is given;
  Ask and He'll turn your hell to heaven.

Though sin and sorrow wound my soul,
Jesus, Thy balm can make it whole!

-Amanda Smith
(SC, pg. 92)

♦ In prayer we shift the center of living from self-consciousness to self-surrender. God is the center toward which all forces tend. He is the source, and we are the flowing force, the ebb and flow of His tides.

-Abraham Heschel
(TP, pg. 564)

♦ Jesus never taught His disciples how to preach, only how to pray. To know how to speak to God is more than knowing how to speak to man. Power with God is the first thing, not power with men.

-Andrew Murray
(WC, pg. 14)

♦ The Christian's victories are won on his knees. His field of conquest is the closet. Here he receives celestial ammunition and arms which make him invincible. If he neglects this supply house, he is doomed to certain defeat.

-Martin Wells Knapp
(SC. pg. 82)

♦ We need God the Father to pray to; we need Jesus Christ the Son to pray through; and we need the Holy Spirit to pray in. It is the prayer that is to God the Father, through Jesus Christ the Son, under the guidance and in the power of the Holy Spirit, that God the Father answers.

-R. A. Torrey
(BT, pg. 93)

♦ We do not refuse to pray; we abstain from it. We ring the hollow bell of selfishness rather than absorb the stillness that surrounds the world, hovering over all the restlessness and fear of life...

-Abraham Heschel
(MQG, pg. 4)

♦ Prayer is the one hand with which we grasp the invisible. Fasting is the other hand, the one with which we let go of the visible.

-Andrew Murray
(WC, pg. 100)

♦ The people who find their times of communion tedious often regard prayer as nothing more than asking for things.

-W. E. Sangster
(HA, pg. 174)

♦ Of all the sacred acts, first comes prayer. Religion is not "what man does with his solitariness." Religion is what man does with the presence of God.

-Abraham Heschel
(MQG, pg. xiv)

♦ It is meet, my brother, that thou shouldst know that our object in prayer is but the consummation of the soul's longing for God and its humiliation before Him, coupled with its exaltation of the Creator, its bestowal of praise and gratitude upon His name, and its casting of all its burdens upon Him.

-Bahya Ibn Paquda
(MQG, pg. 31, 32)

♦ The disciple who lives only for Jesus' work and kingdom will be given the power to appropriate the promise. Anyone grasping the promise only when he wants something very special for himself will be disappointed, because he is making Jesus the servant of his own comfort. But whoever wants to pray the effective prayer of faith because he needs it for the work of the master will learn it because he has made himself the servant of his Lord's interests.

-Andrew Murray
(WC, pg. 143)

♦ Prayer is a crucible in which time is cast in the likeness of the eternal. Man hands over his time to God in the secrecy of single words. When anointed by prayer, his thoughts and deeds do not sink into nothingness, but merger into the endless knowledge of an all-embracing God.

-Abraham Heschel
(MQG, pgs. 13, 14)

Hitting the Target

Studying the prayer lives of people made me aware it is not the quantity of prayers that count but the quality of prayer. If prayer does not hit the target, then as James 4:3 tells us, we are asking amiss.

Prayer is communication with God. As children of God, He is our Father and we can ask Him what we have need of and speak to Him about the desires of our heart. However, the prayer of the selfish is about wants not needs and the desires of the fickle heart often prove to be foolish and is void of any real touch of heaven that points to such a desire being put there by God as in the case of Samuel's mother Hannah, when she asked for a child.

Hannah made a vow to dedicate the child to God, God gave her a son and she kept her vow. She was later entrusted with five more children. It is clear that all prayers are a matter of God's grace. We do not deserve any blessings from Him, but He desires to bless us so we can bless Him and others in return. To ensure such blessings He puts in our heart the very means that would allow Him to show Himself mighty on our part.

In the midst of popular and preferred choices from having material wealth and success given him, Solomon asked God for wisdom and as a result God gave Him wealth and success along with wisdom to govern, because wisdom applied knows how to handle all matters properly. We are instructed to ask for wisdom in James 1:5. Oh, how we need wisdom to walk in the heavenly life through a base, corrupt world.

There are intercessory prayers as in the case of Abraham for Sodom, David for Jerusalem, and Daniel for Israel. We need intercessors who are willing to stand before God in boldness while mingling their intercession with tears and cries for mercy. We know that at the end of mercy is the throne of grace.

We have the Peters who simply cried out the name of Jesus as he was sinking in the stormy waters, and the Enoch's and the Noah's who walked with God in sweet communion. Once again, we are reminded that at the name of Jesus all of heaven and earth must respond to the incredible grace attached to the One who is all grace, and that God's hand of grace is never too short to be extended to us in the deepest waters to rescue us and the sweetest times, to take our hand and walk with us awhile.

The Pharisees of Jesus' day depended on the quantity and show of their prayers, while the poor publican humbly bowed and spoke the deep-seated concerns and desire of the heart, "God be merciful to me a sinner" (Luke 18:13).

The publican is an example of the prayer that had the necessary quality or substance to it--it hits the target. Jesus said of the publican, "I tell you, this man went down to his house justified" (Luke 18:14)

Prayer: *Lord, I ever want to come to You as a needy child, ready to sit on your lap and share with You my heart. I will humbly hang my head in times of failure, knowing only You can meet me at Your throne of grace. In intercession I will boldly stand before You as I hold onto the horns of Your altar until I know You have had Your way in a matter and that You will be glorified. Lord, I know I can approach You because of Your incredible mercy, grace, and love. Amen.*

♦ The purpose of prayer is not the same as the purpose of speech. The purpose of speech is to inform; the purpose of prayer is to partake.

-Abraham Heschel
(MQG, pg. 16)

♦ All successful prayer ends either with an overwhelming reality of God, or a fragrance that leaves the soul satisfied by the sweetness that comes from the Lord's presence.

-RJK

♦ In prayer, I see myself as nothing. (VOV, pg. 145)

♦ Prayer is not monologue, but dialogue. Its most essential part is God's voice in response to mine. Listening to God's voice is the secret of the assurance that He will listen to mine.

-Andrew Murray
(WC, pg. 161)

♦ Words of prayer do not fade. They remain alive in the holy dimension. Words of prayer are commitments. We stand for what we utter. Prayer is the opposite of pretentiousness.

-Abraham Heschel
(MQG, pg. 26)

♦ In prayer all things here below vanish, and nothing seems important but holiness of heart and the salvation of others. (VOV, pg. 144)

♦ My willingness to accept His words will determine the power my words have with Him. What God's words are to me is the test of what He Himself is to me. It shows the uprightness of my desire to meet Him in prayer.

-Andrew Murray
(WC, pg. 163)

♦ The life of prayer depends not so much upon loyalty to custom as upon inner participation; not so much upon the length as upon the depth of the service.

-Abraham Heschel
(MQG, pg. 34)

♦ Hot-tempered people can make only frigid prayers. If we do not obey our Lord's command and love one another, our prayers are well-nigh worthless.

-Unknown Christian
(KC, pg. 114)

♦ The lower the heart descends, the higher the prayer ascends
-Thomas Watson
(SWR, pg. 17)

♦ All hindrances to prayer arise from ignorance of the teaching of God's Holy Word on the life of holiness He planned for all His children, or from an unwillingness to consecrate ourselves fully to Him.

-Unknown Christian
(KC, pg. 118)

- My prayers are not only wishing and asking but they must be believing and accepting.

  -Andrew Murray
  (TG, #69)

- The dignity of man consists not in his ability to make tools, machines, guns, but primarily in his being endowed with the gift of addressing God.

  -Abraham Heschel
  (MQG, pg. 78)

- In prayer it is better to have a heart without words than words without a heart.

  -John Bunyan
  (SWR, pg. 18)

- Prayer is the moment when heaven and earth kiss each other.

  -Jewish Mystic
  (KC, pg. 52)

- Prayer is not a thought that rambles alone in the world, but an event that starts in man and ends in God.

  -Abraham Heschel
  (MQG, pg. 13)

- The highest result of prayer is not deliverance from evil or the securing of some coveted thing, but knowledge of God.

  -Unknown Christians
  (KC, pg. 53)

- Sometimes prayer changes me more than the circumstances.

  -Andrew Murray
  (TG, #45)

♦ Cry aloud—not with your tongue—but with your eyes; not with your words—but with your tears; for that is the prayer that makes the most forcible entry into the ears of the great God of heaven.

> -Bellarmine
> (MSR, pg. 27)

♦ In moments of prayer, we try to surrender our vanities, to burn our insolence, to abandon bias, cant, envy. We lay all our forces before him. The word is but an altar. We do not sacrifice. We are the sacrifice. During the act of prayer, one must "place himself among those who are ready to sacrifice themselves for the sanctification of God's name.

> -Abraham Heschel
> (MQG, pg. 71)

♦ The glory of God hasn't really been an all-absorbing passion in our lives and our prayers. How little we have lived in the likeness of the Son and in sympathy with Him for God and His glory alone.

> -Andrew Murray
> (WC, pg. 150)

♦ Prayer is a humble appeal from our impotency to God's omnipotence.

> -William Gurnall
> (CCA, Vol. 2, pg. 299)

♦ To live without prayer is to live without God, to live without a soul. No one is able to think of Him unless he has learned how to pray to Him. For this is the way man learns to think of the true God—of the God of Israel. He first is aware of His presence long before he thinks of His essence. And to pray is to sense His presence.

-Abraham Heschel
(MQG, pg. 59)

◆ He who prays as he ought, will endeavor to live as he prays.

-John Owen
(SWR, pg. 15)

◆ Prayer is the key, and faith turns the key and opens the door and claims the blessing. Blessed are the pure in heart, for they shall see God. And to see Him is to pray aright.

-Unknown Christian
(KC, pg. 35)

◆ But the crisis of prayer is not a problem of the text. It is a problem of the soul.

-Abraham Heschel
(MQG, pg. 83)

◆ In every revival there is a Divine side of God's sovereign move upon man and a human side of prayer and repentance.

-Unknown

◆ Spending time with God until I know I desire to serve Him with my whole heart gives me the assurance that God hears my prayer.

-Andrew Murray
(TG, #27)

◆ Someone has wisely said, "Satan laughs at our toiling, mocks our wisdom, but trembles when we pray.

-Unknown Christian
(KC, pg. 18)

♦ We need to be open to Scripture and not allow our preconceived notions and theologies determine what we understand the Bible to say…Sometimes our theologies can interfere with our obedience to the Word. We need to stop putting God in a box created by our own theologies. Man's box is too small.

-Larry Spargimino
Prophetic Observer
July 2018

***

Prayer is:
the needed exercise of breathing in the life of Jesus and
exhaling the promises of God,
the avenue between heaven and earth,
the door between the unknown and the heavenly,
the hidden treasure of the tender heart,
the heavenly mission of consecrated lips,
the excellent fragrance that reaches the throne of God,
the very rhythm that reaches the incredible heights,
to dance according to the crescendo of God's will, heart,
and glory.

-RJK

♦ Nothing less than a spiritual revolution will save prayer from oblivion.

-Abraham Heschel
(MQG, pg. 84)

♦ We are never so high as when we are on our knees.
-Unknown Christian
(KC, pg. 15)

♦ When you are on your knees in prayer that is when you are the strongest and when you are on your face in prayer that is when expectation has the greatest opportunity to rise up out of ashes of despair and hopelessness.

-RJK

♦ Give me a man of God—one man, One mighty prophet of the Lord, And I will give you peace on earth, Bought with a prayer and not a sword.

-George Liddell
(SL, pg. 17)

♦ Prayer is the microcosm of the soul. It is the whole soul in one moment; the quintessence of all our acts; the climax of our thoughts. It rises as high as our thoughts.

-Abraham Heschel
(MQG, pg. 58)

♦ O, if thou couldst pray without wandering, walk without limping, believe without wavering, then thou couldst rejoice and walk cheerfully.

-William Gurnall
(CCA, Vol. 1 pg. 205)

♦ As there are two kinds of antidotes against poison, that is hot and cold; so there are two kinds of antidotes against all the troubles and afflictions of this life, that is, *prayer* and *patience*—the one hot, the other cold—the one quenching the other quickening.

-Thomas Brooks
(MSR, pg. 24)

♦ (In relationship to Christ) Without doubt His whole outer life grew out of His inner secret talking things out with the Father.

-Samuel Dickey Gordon
(QT, pg. 20)

♦ Genuine prayer does not flow out of concepts. It comes out of the awareness of the mystery of God rather than out of information about Him.

-Abraham Heschel
(MQG, pg. 88)

PRAISE & WORSHIP

Ensuring the Message

It is hard to know what God has preserved for the future date. But, when prayers surround a matter, and the integrity of the goal finds its springboard in purity with the desire to worship, God is able to keep, secure, and use such a matter for His honor and glory.

There is a story to bring this important point home. A government finally granted a group of believers the right to build a church. Even though it was in a swampland, the dedicated believers would not let the difficult terrain deter them from their mission. For six months the Christians packed the marshy bog with fill dirt, one wheelbarrow after another one.

However, once they prepared the site, they had to obtain the bricks to construct their building. A local official permitted them to tear down a nearby unused nuclear missile silo that was a relic from the Cold War.

Once again, they used the wheelbarrow to carry each brick to the site as they dismantled the old silo. One day a man happened to spot a fragile slip of paper that was tightly rolled up and stuck between two bricks. As it was being gently unrolled and smoothed flat, others gathered around its unveiling.

Although the ink was faded, the man was able to decipher its message. It read, "These bricks were purchased to build a house of worship. But they were confiscated by the government to build a missile silo. May it please the Lord that these bricks will one day be used to build a house to His glory!"

And so they were. (GHC, pg. 140)

♦ Much that passes for worship today is simply people getting together and having a grand old time, not realizing that the purpose of worship is to honor Christ and lift Him up. This is the work of the Holy Spirit within us.

-A.W. Tozer
(MDP, pg. 28)

♦ God may be of no concern to man, but man is of much concern to God. The only way to discover this is the ultimate way, the way of worship. For worship is a way of living, a way of seeing the world in the light of God. To worship is to rise to a higher level of existence, to see the world from the point of view of God.

-Abraham Heschel
(MQG, pg. xii)

***

By the *mouth of the upright* Thou art praised;
By the *words of the righteous* Thou art blessed;
By the *tongue of the faithful* Thou are extolled.
And within *the holy* Thou art sanctified.

-Talmudic Passage
(MQG, pg. 42)

♦ Do we not today, in our church activities, spend too much time with secondary busyness and not enough at His feet in prayer and worshipful waiting on the Lord?

-Vance Havner
(RG, pg. 160)

***

The dearest idol I have known,
Whate'er that idol be;
Help me to tear it from Thy throne,
And worship only Thee.

-Paul Rader
(GBM, pg. 101)

♦ Unsaved men can "enjoy" a "religious service," but only the regenerated can worship by the Spirit of God.

-H. A. Ironside
(HC, pg. 131)

The "W" In Worship

What is the "W" in worship? Pastor Rob Greenslade brought out what the "W" in worship reminds us to do, and that is to wait on the Lord. Waiting involves patience that is refrained by the endurance that can only come from child-like trust.

Most of us do not want to wait; rather, we want to be doing. Worship comes down to honoring the Lord in all we do but first we must learn to wait on Him. Such waiting must be made evident in our heart through the praise of our lips, upheld by pure motives in all we do, and an attitude that displays true awe, reverence, and fear of the Lord.

Pastor Greenslade spelled out wait in this way:

W: *Worship* in all <u>we</u> do.

A: *Admitting* our <u>weaknesses</u>.

I: *Invite* Him because we are <u>willing</u> to do what He says.

T: *Trust* Him as we manifest <u>watchfulness</u>.

There is only one way to allow God to fine tune our hearing towards His voice, prepare us in these days to stand in the midst of darkness, withstand when the world is against us, and continue to stand when all seems lost, and that is to learn to wait on Him. The Lord is perfect in His ways, timing, and will.

Waiting is a great discipline of the Christian walk. God will never be out of step with His plan, but man often gets either in front of Him or is left behind because he procrastinates in righteousness and fails to walk in step with the Lord, guided by His yoke and disciplined by His burden of love.

♦ The truth is, the neglect of family worship opens a wide flood-gate to let in a deluge of profaneness into the Church.

-William Gurnall
(CCA, Vol. 2, pg. 387)

♦ As I meditated on the fact that the Lord wanted me to enter into a more intimate relationship with Him, I realized I first had to learn to be a faithful servant before I would prove to be a faithful friend that could be entrusted with the matters of His heart and kingdom. It was then that I learned an important lesson—we may be interested in position and placing in His kingdom, but He is interested in positioning us close to His heart so that He can have a more intimate relationship with us.

-RJK

♦ Three things a Christian should labor to maintain—1. the honor of God; 2. the honor of the gospel; 3. the honor of his own name. If once a Christian's good name sets in a cloud, it will be long before it rises again.

-Thomas Brooks
(MSR, pgs. 144-145)

♦ The one who stands before an assembly and leads the worship should be the one who has submitted himself to a fresh work of the Holy Spirit. The best preparation for worship is not rehearsal, but surrender.

-A.W. Tozer
(MDP, pg. 34)

♦ When a soul has a deep sense of God's mercy and begins to magnify Him, there is no end to his worship. It grows by what it feeds upon: the more you magnify God, the more you can magnify Him. The higher you live, the more you can see.

-Charles Spurgeon
(FJ, pg. 130)

♦ It is submission of our will, heart, and purpose to the sovereign will and the person of God who created us and loves us. Worship is a relationship from which all inspiration flows and the relationship through which all of our needs are met. It is knowing even partly the One who knows us fully.

-Ravi Zacharias
(WJ, pg. 173)

♦ Possessing Christ comes out of a growing relationship with God. How much we possess of Him is determined by how much He possesses our heart.

-RJK

♦ Nothing that does not come from God is genuine or authentic. Worship starts with God, pierces the heart of man and then returns to the God who started it all. True worship maintains this divine cycle.

-A.W. Tozer
(MDP, pg. 49)

♦ Adoration is the door to beauty. Unless you appreciate the wonders of the work of Christ on Calvary; and the fact that you have been picked up from the miry clay and have been made a joint-heir with Christ—unless this appreciation comes to your heart and you praise and adore Him, everything will become commonplace to you, and you will know nothing of the beauty of the Lord.

-Paul Rader
(GBM, pgs. 103-104)

♦ One needs understanding, wisdom of the spirit to know what it means to worship God. Or at least one must endeavor to become free of the folly of worshiping the specious glory of mind-made deities, free of unconditional attachment to the false dogmas that populate our minds.

-Abraham Heschel
(MQG, pg. 59)

Unity Of Spirit Required

One day while Russian Christians were worshipping in their church, a group of soldiers broke through the door. With rifles aimed at the parishioners, they demanded they all line up against the wall.

They then told them that they only wanted to deal with real Christians and for those who were willing to deny their faith, they could go without any harm being done to them.

Sadly, there were those who separated from the rest and left the premise. After the last one shut the door behind them, the soldiers put down their guns and stated that they had come to worship God, and that they wanted to ensure worship with those who truly loved the Lord and were one in spirit. It was at that time the rest of the saints joined the soldiers and they had a glorious time of worship.

How important is it to have unity of Spirit in worship? It means the necessary agreement will be present so that the Lord can inhabit the praises of His people and meet them in sweet communion.

♦ First there is the ignorant worship of the Samaritans: "Ye worship that which ye know not." Second is the intelligent worship of the Jew, having the true knowledge of God: "We worship that which we know; for salvation is of the Jews." The new, spiritual worship which He Himself has come to introduce is third: "The hour is coming, and is now, when the true worshipers shall worship the Father in spirit and truth."

-Andrew Murray
(WC, pg. 16, 17)

♦ The purpose of Christ in redemption was not primarily to save us from hell, but to save us unto worship that we might be worshipers of the living God.

-A.W. Tozer
(MDP, pg. 58)

♦ What thinking is to philosophy, prayer is to religion. And prayer can go beyond speculation. The truth of holiness is not a truth of speculation—it is the truth of worship.

-Unknown

***

Rock of my heart and my fortress tower
Dear are Thy thoughts to me.
Like the unfolding of some fair flower
Opening silently.
And on the edge of these Thy ways
Standing in awe as heretofore,
Thee do I worship, Thee do I praise
And adore!

-Amy Carmichael
(IA, pg. 69)

♦ Pentecost abounds in praise-notes. Praise in the heart will burst forth in exultant strains. But, mark you, it is praise "unto God," not unto surrounding spectators, or unto the great congregation, as characterizes our modern artistic music—but praising God gratefully and heartily.

-George Hughes
(SC, pg. 49)

♦ Fellowship is not based upon proximity but upon the character of the heart. We can fellowship with God because we have something within us that responds to the person of God.

-A.W. Tozer
(MDP, pg. 214)

He Is Seeking

One scripture that causes me to pause and consider my own spiritual well-being is found in John 4:23, "But the hour cometh, and now is, when the true worshippers shall worship the Father in spirit and in truth: for the Father seeketh such to worship him." The Father is seeking those who truly know what it means to worship Him. After all, He deserves pure worship from the heart of those who claim they love Him.

I realize that "any old worship" will not do when it comes to the ears of heaven. Scraps of religious left-overs will not properly honor Him, worship out of duty will prove to be nothing more than a formality of indifference, and sizing up and judging others during worship to see if they are doing it right is hypocrisy on display.

There are three types of worshippers: those who worship from a distance, those who separate from the religious activities to truly pay honor to God, and those who draw as close as they can with their hearts to honor Him. Those who worship from a distance lack heart, those who separate to worship feel the drawing of the Spirit, realizing that true worship is personal, and those drawing near are seeking to enter through the veil and truly fellowship with Him.

The Father is seeking true worshippers. My prayer is that I get beyond the religious activities called worship; the fleshly hype that is man-centered and is sensationalism on display; and avoid settling for drawing closer to God in worship. I want to enter into that place of worship, which is the place of communion.

Clearly, this is what the Father desires, that time with His son or daughter, sitting on the "lap of communion," in friendship where hearts meet, and in sweet agreement where there is unity in Spirit and the unveiling of matters that are close to the heart of God.

♦ I hate to enter a place of worship where half a dozen sing to the praise and glory of themselves, while the rest stand and listen.

-Charles Spurgeon
(FJ, pg. 52)

♦ What constitutes a place of worship in this true sense is, not that people use it as a place of meeting, but that God dwells there.

-Sir Robert Anderson
(RT, pg. 44)

♦ Many of us are just "give-me" Christians. That is about all the Lord hears from us; and it must be very disappointing to the angels to see people who have been privileged as we are, living without constant praise in their hearts to God.

-Paul Rader
(GBM, pg. 117)

♦ The god worshiped in many places today in America is simply a god of the imagination. Christianity in this generation is decaying, and plunging into the gutter, because the God of modern Christianity is not the God of the Bible. We have fallen short altogether.

-A.W. Tozer
(MDP, pg. 236)

> **Prayer:** *Lord I want to truly worship You, but I realize You must put the desire in my heart to seek You out, a right spirit within me that will lead me to the place of communion, and consecrate my lips to praise You while preparing my neck to bow and my knees to bend in awe and adoration before You. Amen.*

SUFFERING

What is Your Response?

William Barclay shared a story about a sympathetic woman who, in trying to comfort her friend after losing her husband, made this statement to her, "Sorrow does color life, doesn't it?" Her friend responded, "Yes indeed it does, but I intend to choose the colors."

In the early church there were four attitudes towards suffering. There was the *fatalist* who regarded such matters attached to suffering as inevitable and would not fight against it. The second was the *stoic's* take on suffering. Since you can do nothing about it, you need to harden yourself against it, defy the circumstances, and let them do their worst. The third attitude was that of the *Epicurian,* which was, "Let us eat, drink and be merry, for tomorrow we die."

The final attitude was that of a *mature disciple*. The attitude of the mature disciple went beyond the fatalist who accepts a morbid reality of being a victim of circumstance, the stoic who tries to make him or herself look honorable as he or she aggressively fights against what is, knowing it is a useless battle, and the Epicureans who want to indulge themselves in sensual pleasures until the end comes. The mature disciple will not only accept suffering as the will of God, but embraces it joyously as the Bible instructs, even though it be through tears.

As believers we must remember that nothing gets by the Lord when it comes to His saints. Everything directed at His people must first go through Him. It takes faith to believe and know that the Lord is faithful in keeping His promises, sovereign in what He allows, impartial as to what He has made available to all, and powerful enough to preserve those who are in the fiery ovens of trials and temptations. However, it takes a sincere faith to activate the right response. (JJ, pgs. 78-79)

I have known for years that I cannot control events and circumstances, but I can choose how the challenges of life will ultimately affect me by the attitude I take on towards them. Granted, there are times I want to jump up and down, scream foul, fall on the ground and kick my feet, but such actions never change the present situation. I must choose to implement that attitude of Christ towards a matter, to truly come to a place of rest in Him.

♦ Sharp afflictions are to the soul as a driving rain to the house; we know not that there are such crannies and holes in the house till we see it drop down here and there.

-Willian Gurnall
(CCA, Vol. 1, pgs. 245,246)

♦ Suffering is the great tool of God to bring us to the point of great need which produces a state of humility in us. Without humility we can't receive from God in the right spirit, approach God in the right way, and have the authority to actually stand before Him. Author Mary Danielson pointed out there are only two states we can properly function in before the Lord: the State of Humility, and one called, "Headed for Humility." (HD, pg. 89)

♦ In his book, *The Mute Christian Under The Smarting Rod,* Thomas Brooks made this statement, "The choicest saints are 'born to troubles as the sparks fly upwards'" (Job 5:7). He goes on to point out that it is because of God's infinite wisdom and matchless goodness that He has ordered many troubles upon His saints, but it is at such times when personal crosses are great that our awareness of His mercies are heightened. It is clear mercy brings a sweetness to the cross that will nullify the bitterness, and make it a sweet balm to our soul.

♦ Christians in the West often quote the text, "I can do all things through Christ who strengthens me" (Philippians 4:13), giving it a positive spin. But Paul had just said he had learned to endure *all* things – humiliation, hunger and want, as well as the satisfaction of his needs. Persecuted believers take Paul's words as a promise that Christ will strengthen them to endure suffering, because they know a Christian can't escape tribulation.

-Richard Wurmbrand
The Voice of the Martyrs
October 2020

♦ If affliction were thus intrinsically evil, it could in no respect be the object of our desire, which sometimes it is, and may be. We are to choose affliction rather than sin, yea, the greatest affliction before the least sin.

-William Gurnall
(CCA, Vol. 1, pg. 244)

♦ "Follow Me" meant a radical change of life, constant companionship with Jesus, sharing His life, going to school, getting ready for leadership and service; yes, and for suffering too.

-Samuel Dickey Gordon
(QT, pg. 62)

♦ What if we have more of the rough file, if we have less rust! Afflictions carry away nothing but the dross of sin.

-Thomas Watson
(SWR, pg. 17)

Prayer: *Lord, life has knocked me down, adversity has put me in a headlock, and sorrow has made me depressed and complacent. I know what it means to be humbled, but I also know I must be broken over sin in order to be established in a state of humility. Search me, reveal iniquity, and break me so that You can put me back together as a vessel fit for Your use. Amen.*

♦ Of all Christians, none are so rich in spiritual experiences—as those who have been long in the school of affliction.

-Thomas Brooks
(MSR, pg. 104)

♦ God often uses suffering to draw us near to himself. During difficult times, He is sanctifying and shaping us into the image of his Son. We cannot think that we will have glory without the cross or that we will escape suffering in this present evil age.

-Ray Comfort
(SWR, pg. 60)

♦ It's all for Him!—our friend. Out of this personal relation comes service, suffering because of opposition to Him whom we serve, and joy because we may suffer on His account.

-Samuel Dickey Gordon
(QT, pg. 68)

♦ Too many of us are "fresh" Christians; we must be seasoned and salted so that our speech may be seasoned with salt—and often that takes fiery trail and suffering.

-Vance Havner
(RG, pg. 87)

♦ When we are bereft of all things that we normally have and enjoy--health, strength, wealth, friends, entertainment—when we are suddenly laid down by some serious illness, those things are of no help or value to us. We are left alone, and nothing matters except our knowledge of God's loving kindness.

-Martyn Lloyd-Jones
(SFG, pg.120)

♦ Every sorrow the children of God are permitted to endure is designed by God for blessing. Chastening is not necessarily punishment. It is rather instruction by discipline.

-H. A. Ironside
(HC, pg. 114)

♦ You can't live as a Christian in a sinful world without tribulation. Jesus came to bring not peace but a sword. He described himself as a stone, rejected by the builders.

-Elisabeth Elliot
(TGT, pg. 100)

♦ Pain can often be temporary; but disappointment in pleasure gives rise to emptiness...not just for a moment, but for life... This struggle between pain and pleasure, I believe, gives spirituality a more defined goal.

-Ravi Zacharias
(WJ, pg. 153)

♦ You are waiting for some great big ship to come into port; you are waiting for some spectacular experience and think that is going to be victory. Not, it is just taking the very thing that is rubbing you the wrong way, and saying: "Jesus, I take it from Thee; Thou has planned for me and has put me into this hard place, and Thou art bigger than all my hardships and testings.

-Paul Rader
(GBM, pg. 144)

♦ Suffering is the authentic hallmark of Christianity.

-J. Oswald Sanders
(JJ, pg. 15)

♦ We will encounter trials that will test our resolve, tribulations that will prove our character, and adversities that will establish us spiritually or break us emotionally.

-RJK

♦ Afflictions add to the saint's glory. The more the diamond is cut, the more it sparkles; the heavier the saints' cross is, the heavier will be their crown.

-Thomas Watson
(SWR, pg. 17)

♦ Some have tried to deal with suffering by saying it's an illusion. Others have tried to deal with it by rejecting God. And others still have tried to deal with suffering by redefining God. Affliction is a reality in everyone's life at one time or another....God does not suspend the laws of human nature and physical existence simply because we are redeemed.

-Alistair Begg
(SWR, pg. 117)

♦ Before temptation comes there may be innocence but never virtue. Innocence resisting temptation becomes virtue. The temptation is the intense fire in which the raw iron of innocence changes into the toughened, steel of virtue. It is essential to character that it resists the wrong. It is choice that makes character.

-Samuel Dickey Gordon
(QT, pgs. 126, 127)

♦ In Matthew 20 where James and John wanted to sit in places of honor, J. Oswald Sanders made this observation, "James and John wanted the glory, but not the cup of shame; the crown, but not the cross; the role of master, but not servant." (SL, pg. 22)

♦ Boldness without brokenness makes you a bully and brokenness without boldness makes you a bystander.

-Jason Benham

♦ For God to withdraw from me is merely my affliction—but for me to withdraw from God is my sin. Therefore it were better for me that God should withdraw a thousand times from me—than that I should once withdraw from God.

-Thomas Brooks
(MSR, pg. 137)

♦ Our keenest sufferings often result from contact with false brethren. Connection with those who are without is not half so dangerous as those within. The false professor, who has never been born of God; the backslider, who has crucified his Lord;

worldlings in the church and real hypocrites have always been the greatest enemies to spiritual religion.

-M. L. Haney
(SC, pg. 59)

♦ In times of persecution, those who had an experimental knowledge of this inward crucifixion were able to suffer the most terrible outward inflictions without shrinking or fear, while many of those who knew nothing of this interior Calvary abjured the truth to save their lives.

-John Gregory Mantle
(BH, pg. 43)

Any Volunteers

The Bible is clear those who choose the way of godliness will suffer persecution. They will be affronted from many directions, because suffering for the saint is the clearest manifestation of being identified with Jesus in His death, burial and resurrection.

Because of the great curse brought on by sin in the garden, we will not get through this world without tribulation, affliction, and suffering. The currents of life will bring in the storms that can ravish, the tests that can leave us utterly bankrupted, and the despair that can bury us. Faith is purified in fiery ovens, servants in the crucibles of testing, saints pruned by the great husbandman, soldiers seasoned in battles, and the believer prepared to be a sacrifice in the shadow of the cross.

Anyone in their right mind would not volunteer to walk in the way of suffering, but a believer will offer up his or her life as a living sacrifice. It is when the cross is applied, the Word begins it surgical procedures on the heart, and the believer begins to experience loss of the former to gain the eternal, that they catch glimpses of suffering.

Suffering comes out of loss. There are things we want to lose, and things we don't mind losing, but if something is close to our heart, important to our abilities to function, and serves as our focus and pursuit, we will mind greatly when we lose it. We will as they say, "suffer loss."

Suffering reveals that we are needy and vulnerable. It takes the wind out of prideful sails, buckles the knees of self-sufficiency, and causes the stiff-neckedness of independence to hang in utter despair of it all.

As believers, we need to remember that suffering is one of God's tools that He uses to conform us to the image of His Son. This is what we have been designed for, and it is our highest purpose and calling. Such conformity is what ensures God will be glorified in our lives.

♦ Sympathy is a shallow stream in the souls of those who have not suffered. There is something unheeding and harsh in a man who has known nothing of pain. And sympathy is far too precious in this needy world to begrudge the price at which it must be purchased.

-W. E. Sangster
(HA, pg. 25)

♦ Patience will enable us to bear affliction and calamity with fortitude and calmness, with a ready submission to the will of God.

-Seth C. Rees
(SC, pg. 120)

♦ Difficulties afford a platform upon which He can show Himself. Without them we could never know how tender, faithful, and almighty our God is.

-Hudson Taylor
(IA, pg. vii)

177

♦ Loyal soldiers expect to meet with opposition in a rebel country. The Christian is living in a rebel country, and, if he will not compromise with it but be loyal to the banner of Prince Immanuel, he will suffer persecution.

-Martin Wells Knapp
(SC, pg. 82)

♦ If God's *day* of grace is as a thousand years, there is an *eternity* of suffering in the compressed *three hours* of darkness on the cross. In the daylight we see our Lord's suffering at the hands of men; in the darkness He suffered at the hands of God. In the former it is the injustice of men; in the latter it is the justice of God. It is man's hatred of the Bearer of sin; it is God's hatred of the burden of sin.

-Neil M. Fraser,
The Grandeur of Golgotha

***

"Dying together" with Jesus,
    This is the end of strife!
"Buried together" with Jesus,
    This is the gate of life!
"Quickened together" with Jesus,
    By the touch of God's mighty breath;
"Risen together" with Jesus,
    Where is thy sting, O Death?

"Living together" with Jesus,
    Walking this earth with God;
Telling Him all we are doing,
    Casting on Him every load.

Living His life for others,
    Seeking alone His will,
Resting beneath His shadow,
    With a heart ever glad and still.

"Seated together" with Jesus,
    In the "heavenly place" of love;
Love, unequalled – unending,
    In the heart of the Father above.

"Seated together" with Jesus,
    To *live* out the love of God,
And to win this world unloving,
    By His love so deep and so broad.

-Bessie Porter
1850-1936
(BH, pg. 96)

♦ I have found that even during those times when the path is darkest, he leaves little bits of evidence all along the way— bread crumbs of grace—that can give me what I need to take the next step. But I can only find them if I choose to SEE.

-Mary Beth Chapman
(CS, pg. 26)

♦ Suffering helps toward "the exceeding weight of glory" by sundering the heart of its subject from the things visible and centering it on that which is unseen and eternal. Thus our greatest trials, in the hands of the transforming Holy Spirit, lead to the highest triumphs.

-M. L. Haney
(SC, pg. 58)

♦ Should thorns pierce your feet, remember they first pierced His brow. Should your pathway seem rugged, remember He trod the way before thee. While we have no promise of a smooth path, He does say, "I will go before thee, and make the crooked places straight.

-Amanda Smith
(SC, pgs. 98, 99)

♦ When sorrows come, they come not single spies, But in battalions!

-William Shakespeare
Hamlet
(HA, pg. 62)

***

From vintage of sorrow are deepest joys distilled;
    And the cup outstretched for healing is oft at Marah filled.
God leads to joy through weeping; to quietness through strife;
    Through yielding into conquest; through death to endless life.

-C. W. Ruth
(SC, pg. 104)

♦ There are no heroes of action; only heroes of renunciation and suffering. Of such there are plenty. But few of them are known, and even these not to the crowd.

-Albert Schweitzer
(HA, pg. 89)

♦ Love of God is pure when joy and suffering inspire an equal degree of gratitude.

-Simone Weil

♦ Studdert Kennedy used to say that a man who was undisturbed by the problem of pain was suffering from one of two things—either from a hardening of the heart or a softening of the brain.

-W. E. Sangster
(HA, pg. 18)

♦ Sometimes what brings out the beautiful character is the furnace. And I said, "Oh, Lord, help me to be in thy hands as this clay is the potter's hands; and even when the furnace comes, to submit and not dictate."

-Amanda Smith
(SC, pgs. 93, 94)

♦ No man is ever fully accepted until he has, first of all, been utterly rejected.

-Unknown
(BH, pg. 89)

***

In the furnace God may prove thee,
    Hence to bring thee forth more bright,
But He never will forsake thee,
    God, thine everlasting light.

-M. L. Haney
(SC, pg. 89)

♦ Most storms of life will not only test our resolve to endure, but will test what we perceive to be important and significant.

-RJK

♦ What I've found is that it's in the most unlikely times and places of hurt and chaos that God gives us a profound sense of His presence and the real light of His hope in the dark places.

-Mary Beth Chapman
(CS, pg. 25)

♦ There are three ways in which a man expresses his deep sorrow: the man on the lowest level cries; the man on the second level is silent; the man on the highest level knows how to turn his sorrow into song. True prayer is a song.

-Abraham Heschel
(MQG, pg. 44)

♦ The different trials of us Christians of the twentieth century are like so many platforms in the world's Arena of today. The unbeliever looks on at our struggles and is only impressed or influenced if he sees the power of God working there. The purpose of the Arena experience is not for our punishment; it is that God might be revealed.

-Isobel Kuhn
(IA, pg. vi)

♦ We're not necessarily doubting that God will do the best for us, we are wondering how painful the best will turn out to be.

-C. S. Lewis

♦ The quickest way for anyone to reach the sun and the light of day is not to run west, chasing after the setting sun, but to head east, plunging into the darkness until one comes to the sunrise.

-Jerry Sittser

♦ Do we not often make too much of the little we suffer for Christ? It may be a serious question, whether any of us have had severity of conflict sufficient to tone our moral muscle up to the standard of holy war.

-M. L. Haney
(SC, pg. 59)

♦ Death is not the deepest mystery. We must all die. But pain!

-W. E. Sangster
(HA, pg. 18)

♦ There is nothing we can do with suffering except to suffer it.

-C. S. Lewis

THE CROSS

Did You Know?

The name of Simon of Cyrene should be well known by Christians (Luke 23:26). He was the man forced to carry Jesus' cross. He was from North Africa, simply a bystander, watching events that would sweep him into the greatest story ever played out in history. His name would be recorded in the eternal Word of God.

Simon represents each of us. We all start out as spectators when it comes to the events surrounding Christ carrying the cross. But the question is will we follow in the steps of Simon. Tradition has it that Simon became an avowed Christian after seeing Jesus die on the cross. What is more amazing is that he not only is part of the great legacy of spiritual redemption, but this legacy was passed down through the next generation. Evidently Simon's two sons, Alexander and Rufus, were well-known to the church when Mark came to write his Gospel (Mark 15:21).

♦ The Cross has levelled all distinctions, and shut men up to judgment; this is the dark background on which "the grace of God, salvation-bringing to all men, has been manifest."

-Sir Robert Anderson
(RT, pg. 83)

♦ The whole object of Christ and His death upon the cross, His burial, and His resurrection is to bring us to God. And the ultimate test of our profession of the Christian faith is our thoughts about God, our attitude in His presence, our reverence and godly fear because our God is a consuming fire.

-Martyn Lloyd-Jones
(SFG, pgs. 36, 37)

♦ Only reckon your way, your understanding, your plans your wisdom, your very self, to be dead; and then take all from Him, for all things are yours. This life is not your life, it is His; it is not your yolk, it is His.

-Paul Rader
(GBM, pg. 150)

♦ What did the cross mean to Jesus? It was something He took up voluntarily, not something that was imposed on Him; it involved sacrifice and suffering; it involved Him in costly renunciations; it was symbolic of rejection by the world.

-J. Oswald Sanders
(JJ, pg. 22)

♦ Christianity insists always on the *rights of others*. A Christian lays down his own life to obtain them. If he asks, Have *I* no rights? The answer is "The servant is not greater than his Lord."

-Elisabeth Elliot
(TGT, pg. 97)

Is There A Cost too Great?

The cross reminds us that there is a cost to the Christian life. Believers who live in the midst of abundance are sometimes far from relating to such a thought of paying some price that would be considered too great to bear or a cost that would be too humiliating to endure, but true followers of Christ have been doing it for years. The reason why is because believing, knowing, and possessing Christ is worth whatever cost it requires.

Consider the widow, Sister Yuen of Shanghai. She was arrested many years ago because of her faith in Christ. Her oppressors did everything they could to get her to deny Christ including bringing her young son and daughter right up the bars of her small cell so they could beg her to come home. Her heart broke but she resisted the temptation to give way to her mother's heart and wrote a note and put it in the guards' hands. The note stated JESUS CAN NEVER BE REPLACED! EVEN MY OWN CHILDREN CANNOT REPLACE JESUS! On top of the years she had already spent in prison, 23 more years were added to it and by the time she was released her children were grown.

She found her daughter and was reconciled to her but her son had become a police officer and was loyal to the Communist Party and did not want anything to do with her. There would be those who would be critical of her decision but no doubt the Lord considered her offering as a sweet savor. After all, Abraham was willing to offer his son and God counted his action for righteousness and later called him a friend.

It is natural as believers to want to choose our cross, establish our altar, and have an environment that would indeed inspire unadulterated worship and service to the Lord. Consider the story of Pastor George Chen. For most of 18 years in the Chinese Communist labor camp, you would think he had an incredible pulpit to preach from when it came to other prisoners; instead, he found himself standing in the cesspool of human waste, every day of the week shoveling the excrement of 60,000 prisoners that would be used for fertilizer.

What kind of altar of worship can you establish in such a place where the stench is great and the opportunity to touch others is nil? At first Pastor Chen abhorred the situation, but he realized that he had incredible liberty to worship the Lord because the guards never came around. He prayed and worshipped God in complete privacy and solitude, as well as worshipped with songs such as "In the Garden." In the end that smelly place took on a sweetness in the air as it was transformed by the presence of the Spirit that led the pastor into wonderful, daily communion with Jesus Christ. We must remember that we have been created to worship God, which is the highest form of service, and that only comes through fellowship in the Spirit.

God has called us into various forms of service, but the highest form is what Pastor Chen discovered in the place of great humiliation.

♦ How foolish it would be to conclude that God, the giver of my conscience, will grant me a pardon apart from my repentance. My God-given conscience tells me otherwise. That is why the gospel of Scripture is a call to repentance. And that is why the gospel proclaimed without a call to holiness is a grand delusion.

-David Servant
Happy Endings Magazine

♦ Oh, for the simplicity of the gospel, the simplicity of preaching, the simplicity of Christ!

-Steve Montgomery
The Berean Call
(October 2013)

♦ Let a man be determined to give over his hateful self-life to the death of the Cross; let him but know the reality of that inward dying; and all suffering from without will fail to move him. He will never fear the lesser dying because he has learned experimentally what the greater dying means.

-John Gregory Mantle
(BH, pg. 43)

♦ It is fatherlike love that awakens childlike trust...The Cross of Christ does not *make* God love us. It is the *outcome* of His love to us...We must grasp it as the solid foundation of our religious life, not growing up *into* that love, but growing *up out* of it.

-Andrew Murray
(WC, pgs. 50, 51)

♦ When I survey the wondrous Cross I do not see him as the King of Kings but as the great Physician of souls; not beset with monarchs but surrounded by beaten men and women.

-W. E. Sangster
(HA, pg. 16)

♦ But there is many a supposedly orthodox Christian, and often in these days even supposedly orthodox ministers, who deny the atoning blood. They do not believe that the forgiveness of our sins is solely and entirely on the ground of the shedding of Jesus' blood as an atonement for sin on our behalf on the cross of Calvary, and, therefore, they cannot really pray.

-R. A. Torrey
(BT, pg. 89)

◆ The grace of God, as seen in the cross of Christ, never means a thing to us until it takes our breath away and becomes the greatest thing in life.

-Harold St. John
(NAG, pg. 31, 32)

***

I will say, Yes, to the trials,
   Yes to the pain and the loss,
Yes to the valleys and tunnels,
   Yes to the way of the cross.

-From Tears and Triumphs No. 2
(SC, pg. 62)

◆ "The school of the Cross," said John Bunyan when he was dying, "is the school of light." It is the mirror in which the selfishness, hideousness, and penalty of human sin are reflected. There is no searchlight like that which flashes from the hill of Calvary for discovering to us the plague of our own hearts."

-John Gregory Mantle
(BH, pg. 24)

◆ Preach any Christ but a crucified Christ, and you will not draw men for long. Preach any gospel but a gospel of atoning blood, and it will not draw for long...A theology without a crucified Saviour, without the atoning blood, won't draw. It does not meet the need. No, no, the words of our Lord are still true, "And I, if I be lifted up from the earth, will draw all men unto myself."

-R. A. Torrey
(BT, pg. 110, 111)

♦ A man never comes to enjoy himself truly, in any comfort of his life, till prepared to deny himself readily in it.

-William Gurnall
(CCA, Vol. 1 pg. 569)

♦ Times of afflictions, by God's own injunction, are special times of supplication.

-Thomas Brooks
(MSR, pg. 23)

♦ I have begun with the Gospel, and I am determined not to end with the law.

-Barnado
(HA, pg. 77)

♦ Every religious movement, whether in a single human soul or in a community, which leaves out the Cross, ends like a desert river in a march, slips into a chill and pallid Unitarianism.

-Dr. William Clow
(MM, pg. 8)

***

Three crosses stood grimly side by side
  On the hill of Calvary;
On each a suffering man had died:
  Two for their crimes, the other for me.

Like a lamb they led Him out to die
  From shades of Gethsemane;
He uttered no moan, no bitter cry;
  'Twas love that moved Him to die for me.

Heavenly Treasures

On the central cross they nailed my Friend.
   To languish in agony;
He bore it all to the bitter end—
   O wonderful love, He died for me.

"If Thou art the Christ," they taunting, said,
   "Come down from the cursed tree";
He heeded not jeering words they said,
   But, bowing His head, He died for me.

Like a wandering sheep I had gone astray,
   But all my iniquity
My God laid on Him that awful day,
   When, bearing my sins, He died for me.

Oh, thanks for the love that brought Him down,
   Love, fathomless, like the sea;
His brow was pierced by a thorny crown,
   That a crown of life might be given me.

My brother, behold Him, crucified,
   On the cross of Calvary;
Thy ransom see in that crimson tide;
   Oh freely it flowed for you and me.

-British Weekly
(BH, pg. 10)

♦ A scarlet highway runs through the whole territory of the Bible, which makes it a crimson Book. Threaded all through the rope used by the British Navy is a thin red cord, so that no matter where it is cut into, identity of ownership is immediately established. Thus is it with cord, for it has been sprinkled with blood (Heb. 9:19, 20).

-Herbert Lockyer
(MM, pg. 9)

♦ No man is ever fully accepted until he has, first of all, been utterly rejected.

-J. Oswald Sanders
(SL, pg. 120)

♦ Jesus Christ did not die on the cross to change God. He died to change a moral situation.

-A.W. Tozer
(MDP, pg. 131)

♦ The rejection by the Jewish leaders began at once. It ran through three stages, the silent contemptuous rejection, the active aggressive rejection, then the hardened, murderous rejection running up to the terrible climax of the cross...It was the climax of hate, and the climax of His unspeakable love.

-Samuel Dickey Gordon
(QT, pg. 51, 52)

♦ If the preaching of the cross is to the world foolishness, it follows that preachers of the cross will be the world's fools.

-Vance Havner
(PD, pg. 55)

♦ ...for there is a cross which has become fashionable, and for which all trace of suffering and self-denial has disappeared...for the only place in the wide world in which the soul can find true rest is in taking up the yoke or cross of Christ. In doing our own will there is never rest, but in yielding to the will of Another there is...The way of the Cross is the royal way, and they who tread it are kings and priests unto God. It is always to those who tread it the way of glory as it was to Christ.

-John Gregory Mantle
(BH, pg. 153, 154)

♦ Christ's work on the cross enabled God to fully exercise His love without compromising His justice.

-William MacDonald
(NAG, pg.17)

♦ He came not to a throne, but to a manger. He lived not as a king, but as a servant. He chose not a kingdom, but a cross. He gave not just a little, but everything.

-Holley Gerth

***

For all through life I see a cross,
Where sons of God yield up their breath;
There is no gain except by loss,
There is no life except by death;
There is no vision but by faith,
No glory but in bearing shame,
No justice but in taking blame;
And that Eternal Passion saith
Be emptied of glory and right and name.

-Anon.
(BH, pg. 67)

♦ The Cross is not only possessed of sin-conquering, but of sin-discovering, power.

-John Gregory Mantle
(BH, pg. 24)

◆ Departing from the Cross, religionists quickly separate from each other, for whenever we choose a self-created form, and fight for a self-conceived interpretation of a creed (forgetting to keep our eyes fixed upon the uplifted Lord), we miss the unifying power of the superlative sacrifice of the Cross.

-Herbert Lockyer
(MM, pg. 26)

◆ Many would wear the crown with Christ, who do not care for bearing the cross with Christ.

-Thomas Brooks
(MSR, pg. 108)

◆ Christ bides his disciples to stoop not to take up crowns for their heads, but a cross for their backs; 'If any one will come after me, let him deny himself and take up his cross and follow me.'

-William Gurnall
(CCA, Vol. 2, pg. 218)

◆ Too many of the soldiers of the cross today will never be decorated for extreme courage under fire. They will be known only for extreme caution under cover.

-Vance Havner
(ILT, pg. 94)

◆ But the truth is His Calvary sacrifice faced three ways: upward, inward and outward. It faced toward the Father, for it was carrying out the Father's plan...It faced in toward Himself, for it was the purity and perfection of the life poured out that gave the peculiar meaning to His death...It faced outward, for the love of it was meant to break men's hearts and bend their stubborn wills, and so it did and has.

-Samuel Dickey Gordon
(QT, pgs. 40, 41)

♦ Samuel Zwemer remarked that the only thing Jesus took pains to show after His resurrection were His scars.

-J. Oswald Sanders
(SL, pg. 116)

The Glory of the Cross

The Apostle Paul talked about glorying in the cross of Christ. I love the message of the cross and when I sing, "The Old Rugged Cross," I know I am not alone.

Admittedly, I did not understand what Paul meant about "glorying in the cross." Around Resurrection Sunday, I tend to get a bit sentimental because I am reminded of the great price Jesus paid carrying that cross, then bearing that cross so that I could have eternal life and be made the righteousness of God in Him.

Glory has to do with distinction and there are three distinctions of the cross of Christ. The first one is that it is the line in history that casts a great shadow. On one side of the cross is the darkness that exposes lost souls, but on the other side of the cross is the light that penetrates seeking souls; therefore, it serves as a crossroad for every man that will determine his spiritual destiny because of its message that never grows old.

The second glory of the cross is identification in Jesus' death, burial and resurrection. His death reminds me of being baptized, totally immerged with His life, the grave points to the old being crossed out and left silent, and resurrection reminds me that I have been positioned in high places with Jesus, placing me above the judgment that hangs on the whole world due to sin. By embracing the cross, I can be lifted up in Christ to be hid in the eternal ark of salvation.

The third glory of the cross has to do with suffering with Him so that I can be glorified with Him. There is no glory without the work of the cross, whether it is the work of justification concerning the old, sanctification in regard to the present, and glorification in light of the future.

As I began to understand the glory attached to Christ and His work, I began to appreciate even more how complete and glorious the cross of Christ has proven to be and continues to be.

May I always seek the light, allow its work to identify me to my Savior and Lord, while preparing me to be glorified with Him in the age to come.

Prayer: *Lord, thank You for establishing the message of the cross. It reached through history and reached deep into my heart with hope, faith, and salvation. I stood in its light to only experience forgiveness, walked in light of it to discover freedom, and now I continue forward in hope because of the promise of being glorified with You. Amen.*

♦ Only that appreciation of God's love and grace aroused by the gospel transforms sinners into joyful victorious saints—and continues to keep the saints in joy and victory now, and eternally.

-Dave Hunt
The Berean Call

♦ "Throned upon the awful tree." This is how the death of Christ has been beautifully and truthfully described, see Crucifixion led to the coronation of him who became our Substitute. Through his foes, he reached his throne; and in glory he ever wears the insignia of royalty in his scars.

-Herbert Lockyer
(MM, pg. 69)

♦ It is not that Calvary has failed to quench the love of God to men, but that it is the proof and measure of that love. Not that the death of Christ has failed to shut heaven against the sinner, but that heaven is open to the sinner by virtue of that death.

-Sir Robert Anderson
(GAM, pg. 18)

♦ Reconciliation occurs when two enemies come together in love. God, who is the enemy of sin, and man, who is the enemy of God, were reconciled together in Jesus Christ. And when Jesus, who is God *and* man, He brought the two together through the mystery of reconciliation.

-A.W. Tozer
(RCF, pg. 22)

♦ To create, God had but to speak, and it was done. But to redeem, He had to bleed. And He did so in the Person of His Son, Jesus Christ, whom He sent to take the place of death upon the cross which our sin had so richly deserved.

-Roy Hession

♦ No leader lives a day without criticism, and humility will never be more on trial than when criticism comes.

-J. Oswald Sanders
(SL, pg. 120)

♦ The Cross of Christ condemns me to become a saint! ...God has called us to be saints. Happiness, pardon, and Heaven are subordinate. Holiness is the element in which salvation and Heaven are to be found. Yes, the Cross condemns me to become a saint.

-John Gregory Mantle
(BH, pg. 25)

♦ There is no such person as a crossless Christian even as there is not a crossless Christ. As he is, so are we in this world.

-Herbert Lockyer
(MM, pg. 74)

♦ The obedience of Christ was infinitely precious to God, apart altogether from any results accruing to the sinner; and the cross is the expression of that obedience tried to the utmost. In this light, His death was but the crowning act of a life yielded up to God.

-Sir Robert Anderson
(GAM, pg. 31)

♦ A life that is devoid of victory is an up-side-down life. . .God rent the heavens and came down and died on Calvary for sin because life was upside-down, and men were going to death and to hell…If you are outside of Jesus Christ, and cannot see that life is up-side-down, and that Jesus came to set it right-side-up, you are lost and blind.

-Paul Rader
(GBM, pg. 110)

***

There is a man who often stands
'twixt me and Thy glory.
His name is Self, my carnal Self
Stands 'twist me and Thy glory.

O mortify him! mortify him!
Put him down, my Savior;
Exalt Thyself alone,

Lift high the standard of the cross
And 'neath its folds
Conceal the standard-bearer

-Anonymous
(JJ, pg. 89)

♦ Beloved souls, there are consolations which pass away, but true and abiding consolation ye will not find except in entire abandonment, and in that love which loves the Cross. He who does not welcome the Cross does not welcome God.

-Madame Guyon
(BH, pg. 141)

♦ The way of the Cross is certainly the way of death with Christ. The stoning among the Hebrews, the guillotines of the French, the gallows of the English, and the cross of the old Roman times, as instruments of capital punishment, all mean death.

-John Gregory Mantle
(BH, pg. 45)

♦ So the cross lays bare for all eternity the awful truth that beneath the polite façade of culture and education the heart of man is "deceitful above all things, and desperately wicked" (Jeremiah 17:9), capable of evil beyond comprehension even against the God who created and loves him and patiently provides for him. Does any man doubt the wickedness of his own heart? Let him look at the cross and recoil in revulsion from that self within! No wonder the proud humanist hates the cross.

-David Hunt
The Berean Call

- Calvary calls for the dropping of warm tears from the heart, and not for a sloppy emotionalism...Sympathetic tears are meaningless unless they result in penitential tears.

  -Herbert Lockyer
  (MM, pg. 78)

- Death was the Divine judgment upon the sin-bearer; but "the Cross" speaks also of shame and the contempt of men, poured out without measure upon Him who died. And this is the separating power of Calvary.

  -Sir Robert Anderson
  (RT, pg. 156)

- It is perfectly plain to anyone who wants to do a difficult and worthwhile thing that he's got to deny himself a thousand unimportant and probably a few hundred important things in order to do the one thing that matters most.

  -Elisabeth Elliot
  (TGT, pg.19)

- To the apostle (Paul), the Cross of Christ started from the incarnation on one side, and led up to the ascension and enthronement on the other.

  -John Gregory Mantle
  (BH, pg. 97)

- The Cross is the only shelter from the penalty and power of sin, and we are indeed blessed if we are hiding in the smitten Rock of Ages.

  -Hebert Lockyer
  (MM, pg. 80)

♦ Someone has described this cross-bearing life as a *spread-out surrender,* a surrender which covers our whole sphere of action, and lasts all our days. It is often in little things that Christ asks us to deny ourselves, and it would be far easier for some to take up a great cross and die once upon it than to take up these little crosses day by day and die a *deeper* death upon them. So the word "daily" becomes to some, what Christ's Cross was to the Jews, a stone of stumbling and a rock of offense.

-John Gregory Mantle
(BH, pg. 154)

♦ But we must not lower the standard of the Gospel. The remedy is not to veil the truth that God is love, but to proclaim anew the truth that God is light. Not to make less of the truth that Christ is Saviour, but to make more of the truth that He is Lord.

-Sir Robert Anderson
(RT, pg. 151)

♦ There were the soldiers, who only administered the wounds which all the sin of all the world cause. They sat and watched Him, and they gambled for His robe—and so do men today idly face Calvary and gamble away their gospel opportunity. If you are not a soldier *of* the cross, you are a soldier *at* the cross.

-Vance Havner
(RG, pg. 98)

***

Jesus, I my cross have taken,
All to leave and follow Thee;
Destitute, despised, forsaken,
Thou, from hence, my all shalt be:
I will follow Thee, my Saviour
Thou didst shed Thy blood for me,

And though all the world forsake Thee,
By Thy grace I'll follow Thee.

-H. F. Lyte
(JJ, pg. 23)

♦ Some folks are Christian, but not tried Christians.

-Paul Rader
(GBM, pg. 85)

♦ Here is the crux of the issue. The gospel is designed to do to self what the cross did to those who hung upon it: put it utterly to death. This is the good news in which Paul exulted: "I am crucified with Christ!" The cross is not a fire escape from hell to heaven but a place where we die in Christ. ONLY then can we experience "the power of His resurrection (Phil. 3:10).

-David Hunt
The Berean Call

♦ Our altar is not the altar in old Jerusalem. Our altar is Calvary, where Jesus offered Himself without spot to God through the eternal Spirit. Our Holy of Holies is not that section of a temple made with hands, secluded behind a protective veil. Our Holy of Holies is in heaven, where the exalted Jesus sits at the right hand of the Majesty on high.

-A. W. Tozer
(JG, pg. 98)

♦ ...the cross was not the cause of God's love, but the effect of his love. Jesus did not die to make God love us, but because he did love us.

-Hebert Lockyer
(MM, pg. 80)

♦ Let us beware of self-made crosses.

-John Gregory Mantle
(BH, pg. 156)

Prayer: *Lord cut, Lord carve, Lord wound, Lord do anything that may perfect my Father's image in us and make us meet for glory.*
-John Gregory Mantle
(BH, pg. 156)

♦ Justification is an act of God's grace toward the sinner who believes. Reconciliation is a work accomplished on the cross of Christ.

-Sir Robert Anderson
(GAM, pg. 140)

♦ It is not a doctrine, not a set of rules, it is a Person who died for us, who rose for us, who sits in the glory for us, who puts His Spirit in our hearts and causes us to walk in His statutes.

-Paul Rader
(GBM, pg. 114)

♦ What a mixed, diverse crowd formed the Calvary Tableau! Friend and foe alike saw him die, and his death impressed its varying effect upon those who gazed at his agony, for the Cross distinguishes man from man and is the acid estimate of character, as well as the test of personal attitude toward truth.

-Hebert Lockyer
(MM, pg. 110)

♦ It was not the hammer and the nails, as Manning says, which crucified Him; not the Roman soldiers who wielded the weapons of His passion; nor the arm and the hand which smote the sharp iron into the wood – these were but the blind material instruments of His agony. His true crucifiers were our sins – and we, ourselves – the sinners, for whom He died.

-John Gregory Mantle
(BH, pg. 27)

Power of His Life

Vise Grips

Life brings its own elements with it that set up circumstances that can serve as vise grips against our person. It can bring tremendous heat and fire along with great winds, as well as stormy waters.

However, we need to remember that God will use such times to form in us the life of His Son. He has the means to hammer out hardness, chisel away the excess, cut away the profane, construct the impossible, form the incredible, and bring forth the extraordinary.

♦ I have nothing unless I receive it from Jesus. Absolute dependence on God is the secret for power in my work.

-Andrew Murray
(TG, #104)

♦ The thing to draw God to us is His image in us. Sin has destroyed it. Regeneration puts it back in. Now that new man in Christ can have communion and fellowship with the Father of whose image He is.

-A.W. Tozer
(MDP, pg. 188)

♦ Much secret prayer means much public power. Yet is it not a fact that while our organizing is nearly perfect, our agonizing in prayer is well nigh lost?

-Unknown Christian
(KC, pg. 25)

♦ A sickly fear of making mistakes has kept many a Christian from living in the spirit of power.

-Vance Havner
(RTR, pg. 87)

Prayer: *And in Thee is all power and goodness. Give me a pure heart that I may see Thee, a heart of love that I may serve Thee, a heart of faith that I may abide in Thee.*

-Dag Hammarskjold
(TC, pg. 26)

***

Jesus Christ is God creating.
Jesus Christ is God redeeming.
Jesus Christ is God completing and harmonizing,
Jesus Christ is God bringing together all things after the counsel of His own will.

-A. W. Tozer
(JG, pg. 28)

The Christian life is the outliving of the inliving Christ.

-C. H. Scofield
(MM, pg. 50)

***

Thou knowest my soul doest dearly love
   The place of thine abode;
No music drops so sweet a sound
   As these two words—MY GOD.

-Author Unknown

♦ The Christian walk is associated with every letter in every alphabet. It covers it all by reaching heaven, embraces all on earth and extends to the deepest known parts. It is eternal, glorious, and in the end INDESCRIBABLE!

-RJK

♦ The scene of the Cross does its blessed inward work. The wounds which pierced the Redeemer's flesh and spirit now pierce our consciences. It is through crucifixion with Christ the soul enters into communion with its risen Saviour, and learns to live His life. Nor is its sanctification complete till it is 'formed into the likeness of His death.'

-John Gregory Mantle
(BH, pg. 52)

♦ I am persuaded that our Lord Jesus, while He was on earth, did not accomplish His powerful deeds in the strength of His deity. I believe He did them in the strength and authority of His Spirit-anointed humanity.

-A. W. Tozer
(JG, pg. 60)

♦ Christ's soon return should be our greatest catalyst for holy living. If we truly believe Jesus can come in our lifetime, then we will strive to live for Him every moment of our lives.

-Marv Rosenthal
(Zion Magazine)

♦ His was an innocent holiness he never lost in spite of fierce satanic temptation. His life remained unsoiled, just as sunbeams never contact the dirt they shine through. Living and laboring in a sinful world, he remained holy, harmless, and undefiled, and separate from sinners in respect to sin. True, he became sin for us, but he never became a sinner.

-Herbert Lockyer
(MM, pg. 97)

♦ Love may taste good, while faith may sound good, but truth will put the cutting edge in both virtues. Truth will never allow us to accept the mediocre presentation of the Christian life. It will always cause godly love to desire the best and unfeigned faith to pursue what is excellent.

-RJK

♦ The natural loyalty of living, fertilized by faith saved through a lifetime, is the soil on which prayer can grow.

-Abraham Heschel
(MQG, pg. 9)

***

For His sake: I am but one, but I am one.
I cannot do everything, but I can do something.
What I can do, I ought to do.
What I ought to do, by the grace of God I will do.
   Lord, what will you have me do?

-Helen Keller
(GHC, pg. 187)

♦ Excellence cannot occur until people cease to be slaves to the ways of the world and become mountain climbers in relationship to discovering the heights of God in all of His glory.

-RJK

♦ Christians seem more comfortable defining masculine identity, and then, based on that, prescribing feminine identity…This is not so with Jesus. An identity modeled after Jesus is mutually enhancing not mutually exclusive.

-W. Tali Hairston
Mutuality
Vol. 21, Issue 1

***

Like a watered garden,
    Full of fragrance rare;
Lingering in Thy presence,
    Let my life appear.

-E. May Grimes
(MM, pg. 68)

♦ The vocation of every believer is this: to be a revelator of the love of Christ. The believer is an epistle of Christ – and epistle of His love.

-John Gregory Mantle
(BH, pg. 113)

♦ The more I realize that Christ must be everything to me and in me, that everything in Christ is indeed for me, the more I learn to live the real life of faith. This life dies to self and lives wholly in Christ. The Christian life is no longer a vain struggle to live *right*, but a resting in Christ to find strength in Him *as life.* He helps us fight and gain the victory of faith!

-Andrew Murray
(WC, pg. 192)

♦ You never get relief from worry until you confess it as sin. Worry doubts the goodness of God; it says He doesn't know what he's doing. Worry doubts the power of God; it says He cannot deliver me from the thing that's causing me to worry.

-William MacDonald

***

Apart from Thee

I am not only naught, but worse than naught,
A wretched monster, horrible of mien!
And when I work my works in self's vain strength,
However good and holy they may seem,
These works are hateful – nay, The pure sight
Are criminal and fiendish, since thereby
I seek, and please, and magnify myself
In subtle pride of goodness, and ascribe
To *Self* the glory that is Thine alone.
So dark, corrupt, so vile a thing is self.
Seen in the presence of Thy purity
It turns my soul to loathing and disgust;
Yea, all the virtues that it boasts to own
Are foul and worthless when I look on Thee,
Oh that there might be no more *I* or *mine*!
That in myself I might no longer own
As mine, my life, my thinking, or my choice,
Or any other motion, but in me
That Thou, my God, my Jesus, might be all,
And work the all in all! Let that, O Lord,
Be dumb, forever, die, and cease to be,
Which Thou dost not Thyself in me inspire,
And speak and work.

-Gerhard Tersteegen
(BH, pgs. 32-33)

♦ Unless the outer life expresses the inner world, piety stagnates and intention decays.

-Abraham Heschel
(MQG, pg. 93)

♦ God is not the God of the dead, but of the *living*, and the newness of life is the crowning joy of union with the risen Jesus.

-John Gregory Mantle
(BH, pg. 101, 102)

♦ Patience is a daughter of humility, the most beautiful, fundamental and important of all the Christian graces. It is the antithesis of pride, the meanest of all sins. When humility is perfect, patience is also perfect.

-W. B. Godbey
(SC, pg. 29)

***

Look not for a true living strength,
    in the life of the *Me* and the *I*,
With nothing to love but its selfhood,
    and fearing to suffer and die,
As Thou seekest the fruit from the seed –planted grain,
    Seek life that is *living,* from life that is slain.

-Professor T.C. Upham
(BH, pg. 82)

♦ The innermost chamber must be guarded at the uttermost outposts.

-Abraham Heschel
(MQG, pg. 110)

Out of This Life

Out of this life I shall never take
  Things of silver and gold I make.
All that I cherish and hoard away
  After I leave, on this earth must stay.

Tho' I have toiled for a painting rare
  To hang on the wall, I must leave it there.
Though I called it mine, and boast its worth,
  I must give it up when I leave this earth.

All that I gather, and all that I keep,
  I must leave behind when I fall asleep.
And I often wonder what I shall own
  In that other life, when I pass alone.

What shall they find, and what
  Shall they see, in the soul that
Answers the call for me?

Shall the Great Judge learn,
  When my task is through
That my spirit has gained some riches, too?
  That all I'd worked for I'd left behind?

-Author Unknown

♦ The important thing is—how must you live and work under such circumstances? Or are you asking to be conformed to His image, seeking fellowship with Him in this human suffering, watching for His resurrection power to be manifested, confident that you will know Him better when the discipline is past, and to be satisfied with that? The circumstance will pass in time, but the revelation you will receive of Himself, His love, and His power will enrich you forever.

-Isobel Kuhn
(IA, pg. 25)

♦ Humility is as essential to victory as air is to breath. Hence only those who are willing to die to reputation and position and worldly honors can be accounted victors on life's battlefield. If Jesus had not become the Lily of the Valley he never could have blossomed into the Rose of Sharon. Christ's soldiers must be lambs before they can be lions.

-Martin Wells Knapp
(SC, pg. 83)

Prayer: *But with Thy hand, O Jesus,* **break** *me, As mortars crush the hardest rock, As hammers breaks the stony block, As millstones bruise the finest wheat, As nuts are broken for their meat, So with Thy mighty hand, O* **break** *me.*

-W.T. Sleeper
(BH. Pg. 88)

♦ The true character of the loveliness that tells for God is always unconscious. Conscious influence is priggish and un-Christian. If I say—"I wonder if I am of any use" I instantly lose the bloom of the touch of the Lord.

-Oswald Chambers
(IA, pg. 42)

♦ "*Fruit*" is the spontaneous natural manifestation of the life within...Flowers that are bent on perfecting themselves by becoming double, end in barrenness. This mysterious union of our nature with Jesus means marvelous development; but it means also *reproduction*, for the latter, and not the former, is the goal of matured beings.

-John Gregory Mantle
(BH, pg. 113)

♦ Platforms do not make us stronger Christians or better Christians but they do make us *richer* Christians. Rich in our inner fellowship with Him. Rich in our confidence that He will be our rock and our Deliverer in the future. Rich in the relaxation of the little child who leans back on his father's breast, confident, secure, and satisfied.

-Isobel Kuhn
(IA, pg. 194)

♦ The humble, meek, merciful, just, pious, and devout souls everywhere are of one religion and when death has taken off the mask, they will know one another, though the diverse liveries they wore here make them strangers.

-William Penn

***

O love of unexampled kind!
That leaves all thought so far behind:
Where length, and breadth, and depth,
    And height,
Are lost to my astonished sight:
Lord shed abroad that love of Thine
In this poor sinful soul of mine.

-Author Unknown

CREATION

The Indisputable

When I first became a Christian, I was introduced to Scientific Creationism. As the facts were presented from the perspective of the Word of God, history, and the makeup and functions of creation, there was no doubt that evolution was a big hoax. A theory at best, a lie on steroids, and the wicked demonic attempt to strip people of their calling and potential to reflect the glory of the Creator by rendering them into mere beasts that have no spirit to quicken or a soul that can be reasoned with about sin and salvation.

Through the years I have studied such things as DNA to realize more and more how foolish evolution is. Sadly, it's the fools that are running wild with it to justify their unbelief towards God, along with their wicked practices and their evil ways.

I have stated there are three things that declare there is a God and just who He is: the Word of God, creation, and man. God's word is His written record, creation is the visible evidence of both the seen and unseen, and man is the voice or instrument that verbally declares it is so.

Three witnesses confirm a matter is so and when you put all of the evidence together, it becomes indisputable that behind all we see is a Creator Who works in perfect order, according to a perfect plan, and will one day restore His creation back to a perfect garden of fellowship where all is at peace, especially man with his Creator.

♦ Creation exists to show forth His glory. Everything that doesn't glorify Him is sinful, dark, and dead. It is only in the glorifying of God that creatures can find glory.

-Andrew Murray
(WC, pg. 148)

♦ The trees stand like guards of the Everlasting; the flowers like signposts of His goodness--only *we* have failed to be testimonies to His presence, tokens of His trust. How could we have lived in the shadow of greatness and defied it?

-Abraham Heschel
(MQG, pg. 5)

♦ When a spider spins a web, its silk is made up of chains of amino acids. Spider silk is about five times stronger than steel and twice as strong as Kevlar of the same weight. (Kevlar is the material used to make bulletproof vests.) Arachnologists say that a single strand of spider silk, thick as a pencil, could stop a 747 in flight. For its weight, it is the toughest material on the planet. (GHC, pg. 150)

***

The glorious universe around,
  The heavens with all their train,
Sun, moon and stars are firmly bound
  In one mysterious chain.
The earth, the ocean and the sky
  To form one world agree;
Where all that walk or swim or fly
  Compose one family.
God in creation must display
  His wisdom and His might;

Where all His works with all His ways
  Harmoniously unite.

-James Montgomery
Scottish Moravian

♦ Mount Everest. The highest point on the planet. Its peak pierces the roaring winds of the jet stream five miles above the earth. It casts a shadow that stretches for 250 miles. I saw it once from an airplane. Its magnificence—its absolute otherness—made my hair stand on end for a week.

-Ellen Vaughn
(GHC, pg. 172)

♦ We are the kind of people for whom Christ died. What makes it all the more remarkable is that we are so insignificant. We are scarcely visible when viewed form an altitude of 10,000 feet. How much more infinitesimal we appear when seen from billions of light years away. And yet he loved us!

-William MacDonald
(NAG, pg. 34, 35)

♦ Our delight, however, must not be in the creature, but in the Creator. In true holiness God becomes the object of chief affection, and His presence a source of unbounded delight.

-L. L. Pickett
(SC, pg. 39)

♦ Dr. Francis Crick received a Nobel Prize in science work in genetics. He concluded that chromosomes, DNA, and the double helix—units of life involved in reproduction—were so miraculous that they could not have been developed by evolution. (GMM, pg. 65)

♦ Assimilating all the data relating to life originated by natural processes on Planet Earth, two atheists calculated that for that to happen it would be ten to the 40,000[th] power. The probability for this to happen was illustrated by a whirlwind sweeping through a junkyard and assembling a Boeing 747 jet in flight at the other end. The two atheists naturally changed their mind about their philosophy. (FST, pgs. 8-9)

♦ From Adam and Eve, men and woman have received 46 chromosomes in each cell, with some three million genes. Over one hundred thousand of these genes have been catalogued. Genetically, Adam and Eve are represented in everyone' genes today, regardless of race. (GMM, pg. 66)

♦ All creation praises him all the time—the winds, the tides; the oceans, the rivers, move in obedience; the song sparrow and the wonderful burrowing wombat, the molecules in their cells, the stars in their course, the singing whales and the burning seraphim do without protest or slovenliness exactly what their Maker intended, and thus praise him.

-Elisabeth Elliot
(TGT, pg. 127)

♦ Did you know our sun is shrinking at five feet per hour? If this is true evolution would indeed prove to be a fabricated theory. After all, if the earth was as old as the evolutionists claimed and the sun was shrinking at such a rate, it would have been too big and consumed the earth or it would have burned out long ago. Either way none of us would be here to even have this debate about Creationism and evolution. (FST, pg. 58)

♦ The stars furnish heat enough in the course of the year to melt a great crust of ice, almost as much as is supplied by the sun.

-John Gregory Mantle
(BH, pg. 150)

- We are moons, not suns. The moon only reflects the light of the sun. We need only to reflect light; when we live to His glory.
  -Corrie ten Boom
  (MA, Bk.1, pg. 29)

- Our sun is a medium-sized star with a diameter of 864,000 miles, approximately one hundred times that of earth. The mass of the sun is 332,000 times that of earth...The earth makes a circuit around the sun every 365.25 days, while the sun is traveling 700,000 miles per hour around the center of our galaxy, taking its nine planets along for the ride. (GMM, pgs. 49-50)

- The mountain that Noah's ark landed on was calculated to be 10,000 feet high. If the water covered every mountain, we have a slight idea as to the immensity of the global flood that consumed the earth. It was not only immense, but it was sudden, leaving clues behind as to its power and devastation. For example, they discovered a fossil of a 20-foot Theropod that had been condensed to about eight inches. Although there are those who would like to debate the historical event, it is a story that is instituted in the legends of various people and civilization along with there being geological evidence. (FST, pgs. 21, 105)

- The moon is a satellite of earth with a diameter of approximately one-fourth that of earth, and with mass and gravity only a fraction of our planet...The distance of the moon from the earth ranges from 238,000 miles to 221,000 miles. (GMM, pg. 50)

- God also predetermined the numerical ratio of all living things. It has been proposed that if the fly had no enemy, within a few months flies would stack up across the world ten feet high. (GMM, pg. 56)

♦   The fact is, the concept of evolution has never got beyond the hypothesis stage; it is a religious commitment; it is not a true scientific theory.

-Dr. Clifford Wilson
(FST, pg. 6)

♦   Bible Scholars have debated about what the gopher wood was that was used to build the ark. According to modern day rabbis, gopher wood is being made this very day. Apparently, the word, "gopher," means to "house in," and has to do with the process and not a particular kind of wood. The wood used would have to be seasoned as in compressed and crystallized or laminated, which is much stronger than steel. The wood would be fitted together and then a strong resin (pitch) that could penetrate the pores of the cells was used to seal it. A good description of it would be, "Parallel Stranded Lumber." (FST, pgs.13-18)

♦   Fossils show us at least sixty percent of the life forms were larger before the flood than they are today. For example, the modern dragonflies presently have a four-inch wing span, but pre-flood fossils show that dragonflies had a forty-inch wing span. They also discovered a fossil of a rhinoceros in Germany that was 17 feet tall. There is evidence that man and dinosaurs existed at the same time. We must remember before the flood, the oldest man known to live was Methuselah and he lived to be 969 years old. That would indicate that creatures had time to develop to immense sizes. (FST, pgs. 30, 41)

- God attends the funeral of every sparrow.

  -H. A. Ironside

- The power of God's Word holds all things together in an orderly fashion. Consider this: All matter is made of atoms, which consist of negatively charged electrons orbiting around a nucleus composed of positively charged protons and neutrally charged neutrons. The negatively charged electrons are held in orbit by the positively charged protons because of the electro-magnetic attraction between positive and negative charges. But since different charges can repel one another, what holds the nucleus together? As believers, we go back to the first statement—that God's power holds all things together.

- Did you know there are seven million species of plants and animals on earth and if you count the fungi and bacteria, it reaches over 11 million. There are also 220 species of owls and 20,000 species of butterflies with a variety of sizes and colors (HD, pg. 130). God's creation not only declares His existence, His power, and His intervention in all matters, but His glory.

JUDGMENT

Beating the Odds

It is natural to always try to beat the odds when it comes to the law and its principles. We push the line here and there and brag or mock when we think we have got away with something after cheating or robbing at some point. Sadly, when we get caught, we do not mourn over our wrongs; rather, we cry over being caught and paying the consequences.

That is the way of human nature, we know the odds eventually will catch up to us, but we have a way of turning everything upside down in our thinking, especially when it comes to God. We think we can sin or offend His Law on one hand while doing good things on the hand to outweigh the fact that we have broken the law of God. We hide our wrongdoings and ways behind grace and love while highlighting our morsels of "good works."

Such actions may make us feel good about our standing before God, but before God we are still a lawbreaker, one who has shown contempt towards both Him and His perfect law. Author Mary Danielsen put such a concept in this challenging perspective, "There isn't a court on Earth that would allow a good works defense to free a lawbreaker as it would make a total mockery of the law—and yet the great Judge of all the earth is expected to abide by this ridiculous human expectation that 'my good stuff cancels out my bad stuff.'" (HD, pg. 12)

♦ What makes heaven what it is? The unhindered and unsullied presence of God. What makes hell what it is? The absence of a consciousness of the presence of God. That is the difference between a prayer meeting and the dance hall.

-A.W. Tozer
(MDP, pg. 226)

♦ Great gifts are beautiful as Rachel, but pride makes them also barren like her. Either we must lay self aside, or God will lay us aside.

-William Gurnall
(CCA, Vol 1, pg. 193)

- Lazarus had his hell first, his heaven last; but Dives had his heaven first, and his hell at last.

  -Thomas Brooks
  (MSR, pg. 163)

- There is plenty of self-justification these days but not much self-judgment.

  -Vance Havner
  (PD, pg. 50)

- Discernment is about classifying between such things as a duck and a goose in order to make a proper judgment call. To discern you must know what you are looking for before you can discern, or properly classify, what you are looking at.

  -RJK

- Hell is the place where those whose motto is *My will be done* will finally and forever get what they want. Hell is agony and blankness and torture and the absence of all that humanity was originally destined to be. The glory has terminally departed. It is the heat of flames (not of passion—that will long since have burned out) and the appalling lifelessness of solid ice, an everlasting burning and an irreversible freezing.

  -Elisabeth Elliot
  (TGT, pg. 108)

- Due to the judgment executed at the Tower of Babel, there are 6,900 spoken languages in the world today. These almost 7,000 languages came out of at least 94-120 languages based on the descendants of Noah. (TB, pgs. 65, 68)

♦ The truest test of a man is not conduct, but character; not what he does, but what he is…Man judges character by conduct; God judges conduct by character.

-Sir Robert Anderson
(RT, pg. 16)

♦ Whenever justice is applied to a moral situation, you have judgment… When a judge pronounces a judgment, he is pronouncing on a moral situation.

-A.W. Tozer
(MDP, pg. 274)

♦ Self-examination is the setting up a court in conscience and keeping a register there, that by strict scrutiny a man may know how things stand between God and his own soul. Self-examination is a spiritual inquisition, a bringing one's self to trial. A good Christian doth as it were the day of Judgment here in his own soul. Self-searching is a heart-anatomy.

-Thomas Watson
(SWR, pg. 96)

♦ If we drift away from our personal relationship with Jesus, whether individually, or collectively as a church, for whatever supposedly good work that person or church does, will eventually cease to reflect the light and true love of Christ. Their "candlestick" will be removed.

-T.A. McMahon
The Berean Call
June 2018

♦ When you sincerely believe you possess the truth, all disagreement looks like apostasy. For the greater good, it must be silenced. It's distressing when academics take this view. It's terrifying when prosecutors do.

-Tucker Carlson
(SOF, pg. 132)

The Essence of Judgment

It seems people are confused about what constitutes judgment. We make judgment calls all the time. In other words, we are making judgments about the matters of life along with our works and activities. Some judgments we are more aware of because we must stand back and calculate a matter, and others we make without really thinking about them because they are either based on past experiences or prejudices and biases we have been conditioned and indoctrinated with through the years.

What is the main purpose of judgment? It is to separate facts from exaggeration, common sense from ridiculousness, the best from the substandard, the easiest way from the hardest, the shortcuts from the detours, and the most constructive means from the destructive.

God has three forms of judgment and they result in some type of separation: 1) the work of holiness (separation from the unholy to the holy for His purpose and glory), 2) chastisement (separation from the unbecoming behavior to the acceptable,) 3) wrath (separating the wicked for the ultimate judgment).

There are three judgments that will occur: 1) judgment begins in the house of God. This is where fire will be put to the works of a believer to see if they will stand (1 Corinthians 3:11-15; 1 Peter 4:17). 2) There is the judgment of nations where God separates the sheep from the goats. This judgment is in relationship to the treatment of Israel. The goats will have their excuses for why they mistreated Jesus' biological brethren, the Jewish nation, while the sheep know that curses and blessings are attached to the covenant that God made with Abraham about his descendants. The goats will be separated to everlasting punishment while the sheep will enter into eternal bliss (Genesis 12:1-3; Matthew 25:31-46). 3) The third judgment is that of the wicked and that will be done at the great white throne described in Revelation 20:11-15.

It is easy for man to blame his foul attitudes and ways on others but when the matters of this world are revealed by heaven, each of us must recognize that it always has been our judgment call as to how we faced, responded, and handled a matter.

♦ Faith sees the world and all the pleasures of sin sinking; there is a leak in them which the wit of man cannot stop. Now is it not better to swim by faith through a sea of trouble and get safe to heaven at least, than to sit in the lap of sinful pleasures till we drown in hell's gulf?

-William Gurnall
(CCA, Vol. 2, pg. 79)

♦ A man who is not morally bound to what is right and good, will not be morally bound to be just in what he does or the judgment calls that he makes in regard to others.

-RJK

♦ Christ calls us, and we do not heed the Spirit's pleading. One day He will come in judgment. Ah, that we knew the thing which belong unto peace! Pharisaism stands by and scoffs at the believer's joy. Sadduccism criticizes in its skepticism. A wild world hurtles onward to ruin. But He will come again to reign, and woe unto His enemies in that day!

-Vance Havner
(RG, pg. 90)

- To apostatize either from the truth as to His person or His finished work, means eternal ruin.

  -H. A. Ironside
  (HC, pg. 92)

- Our natural life, and all the faculties with which it is endowed, must be sacrificed, immolated, renounced. Otherwise, after having flourished for a moment with more or less of satisfaction, it perishes and withers forever.

  -Frederic Godet
  (BH, pg. 51)

- Wrath is but a last resource with power, and judgment must wait on grace.

  -Sir Robert Anderson
  (GAM, pg. 147)

What Am I Looking At?

Years ago I had this vision from God. I had been fasting and praying for several days, and was caught up in the Spirit, and saw a man. It looked like he was in liquid fire. He was running, and looked like he had been running forever.

Ever so often he would reach down into that boiling fire and pull up a human. I couldn't hear a sound, but it looked like he would curse, and then throw him back. He would run on and pull up another, and throw him back.

In my heart I asked, 'What am I looking at?' The Holy Spirit answered, 'You're looking at a man in hell, who is looking for a preacher that lied to him." (B. H. Clendennen, "The Road to Discipleship")

♦ God will never remove the guilt so long as thou entertainest the sin.

-William Gurnall
(CCA, Vol. 2, pg. 433)

♦ It's either/or. It's self-death and eternal life, or its self-life and eternal death.

-Elisabeth Elliot
(TGT, pgs. 101)

The Way the Sail Is Set

I stood beside the open sea;
The ships went sailing by.
The wind blew softly o'er the lea;
The sun had cloudless sky.

Some ships sail eastward, some sailed west,
Some north, some southward trend.
How can ships sail this way and that,
But one way blows the wind?

An old sea-captain made reply
(His locks with salt-spray wet):
"Tis not the wind decides the course:
Tis way the sails are set."

I stand beside the sea of life:
The ships go sailing by.
The winds blow fair from heaven's land;
No clouds bedim the sky.

But one sails eastward, one sails west,
One north, one southward goes.

How can ships sail this way and that,
With selfsame wind that blows?

A voice made answer to my soul:
"Tis not how blows the gale.
Each voyager decides the goal,
By way he sets the sail."

-Selected

♦ Death is not His coming again to us, but our going to Him. And while, for the Christian, death has no terrors—for sin is gone, and therefore it has lost its sting—it is none the less an outrage bringing home to us the fact of our still unrepaired ruin as fallen creatures.

-Sir Robert Anderson
(RT, pg. 165)

♦ "Judge not that ye be not judged" has come to mean that if you never call anything sin nobody can ever call you a sinner. You do your thing and let me do mine and let's accept everybody and never mind what they're up to...The key to the matter of judgment is meekness.

-Elisabeth Elliot
(TGT, pg. 71, 72)

♦ The problem with religious belief is that nobody wants anyone to preach a destiny that excludes anyone else, and so we reserve the description of evil for only the most heinous. And now some New Spiritualists would not even want that separation.

-Ravi Zacharias
(WJ, pg. 254)

♦ (In relationship to Jesus' description of hell in Luke 16.) Here He plainly shows that those in torment have sight, they suffer, they speak, they have memory, they have concern for others. And there is a great gulf fixed! Critics have done their utmost to tone down this picture, but our Lord here, as well as elsewhere, held the very opposite of present-day sentimental ideas about hell.

-Vance Havner
(RG, pg. 176)

***

Unresting, unhasting, and silent as light,
Nor wanting, nor wasting, Thou rulest in might;
Thy justice, like mountains, high soaring above
Thy clouds, which are fountains of goodness and love.

-Walter C. Smith
(1824-1908)

♦ The world lies a dreary waste. Countless millions are pouring down a steady stream into hell. Rescuers are needed. Time is short; what is done must be done quickly. Weaklings to the rear! Stalwarts to the front! The baptism of the Spirit fills the soul with heavenly dynamite and sends it forth to the work of rescue.

-Unknown

♦ When we think we have discovered a short and easy road to success, and have forsaken the Fountain of living waters to hew out to ourselves cisterns, we shall always find that our hewing has been labor lost, and that our cisterns are broken and will hold no water.

-John Gregory Mantle
(BH, pgs. 11, 12)

♦ In the last days the new light which men seek for to dispel "the deepening gloom" will not be wanting; but it will prove a wrecker's fire, though seemingly accredited as the beacon light of truth.

-Sir Robert Anderson
(GAM, Preface)

♦ When we indulge in pleasure to the point that it destroys the value within us, the ends to which we will go, both spiritually and pragmatically, lead us into the quicksand.

-Ravi Zacharias
(WJ, pg. 154)

♦ If a wicked man should go to heaven without being converted, heaven would be no heaven to him. Heaven is not adapted for sinners. It is not a place for them.

-Charles Spurgeon
(FJ, pg. 31)

♦ Our only safety lies in having our whole life judged in the light of the Cross, appropriating continually the cleansing which the Cross has provided from all defilement both of flesh and spirit.

-John Gregory Mantle
(BH, pg. 27)

***

Did we believe a final Reckoning and Judgment; or did we think enough of what we do believe, we would allow more Love in Religion than we do; since Religion itself is nothing else but Love to God and Man.

Love is indeed Heaven upon Earth; since Heaven above would not be Heaven without it: For where this is not Love; there is Fear: But perfect Love casts out fear. Love is above all; and when it prevails in us all, we shall be Lovely, and in Love with God and one with another.

-William Penn

Prayer: *I see You, Lord Jesus, with Your foot upon the Dragon's neck. I see You with death and hell beneath Your feet. I see the glory that adorns Your triumphant brow as You wait until the whole earth will acknowledge You as King.*

-Charles Spurgeon
(FJ, pg. 96)

CONSECRATED LIFE

Going the Extra Mile

How does one measure the Christian life? It comes down to how much we are willing to consecrate to the Lord. We want to delve deep in God without rowing out to the deep part of the ocean and casting ourselves into the current of the Spirit. We want to experience the heights of God without having to climb the mountain of excellence. We want to become identified with the Lord, but we don't want to walk through the valleys of drudgery where our faithfulness will be tested. We want to follow Christ into greatness without first denying self and picking up our personal cross in order to die to the old life to experience the new life.

Vance Havner makes various references to this very fact in relationship to faith. He states, "We want more faith when even exercises of little will do the impossible." It is clear that we want big things without starting from the premise of small beginnings. We want to experience the heights of glory without first experiencing the depths of brokenness. We want Christianity to be served up to us much like the food at a fast-food eatery.

We want a Christianity that costs us nothing, but bestows on us that which we are not prepared to rightly handle. However,

Christianity is about the life of Christ being worked in us through obedience, forged in us by the way of trials, and firmly established through us by going beyond reasonable service to true sacrifice that serves as a sweet fragrance to the Lord.

To a Christian, going beyond reasonable service, means going the extra mile. It is not just an indication as to the type of quality and commitment of a believer; rather it is about doing something that is not just sensible, but unexpected. Vance Havner asked how many believers go the extra mile in prayer, Bible reading, giving, church attendance, and in forgiving others. Then he made this statement, "How many in trouble only bear and endure it and go not the second mile of victory? How many in temptation merely suppress and do not surpass? How many will not go the way of consecration and separation? Some will give money, but will not give self."

As believers we want the glory for being noble about our Christian duty, but in doing so, we fail to realize what all service must ultimately do and that is bring glory to the Lord. Havner ended his thought about this matter in this way, "We have unduly gloried duty and have failed to see that only Christ within us is true righteousness—that all else is but legalism, though it may profess His name." (RG, pg. 179).

The natural way of the old man is to choose the path of least resistance and sacrifice, but those who go the extra mile in their walk do so because they see it as the least they can do because it is about bringing glory to the One that left heaven and gave it all so that each of us might have everlasting life.

Are you an "extra mile" Christian that consecrates all in order to reach the heights of excellence or are you just getting by in the name of duty? This question will determine the spiritual impact and legacy that is left behind.

♦ Christ, the strong man, must take the devil's place in our hearts. The Christian life is not a mere cleaning-up, it is the possessing and filling of the life by Christ Himself. Otherwise it ends worse than it began.

-Vance Havner
(RG, pg. 118)

♦ God knew that what I really needed was not explanations but sanctification, *purifying*. My notions about myself, my work, and my God needed to be put through the fire. My heart needed deep and painful scouring. "Blessed are the pure in heart, for they shall see God."

-Elisabeth Elliot
(TGT, pg. 140)

♦ I love to have Christ as the absolute Monarch in my heart. I do not want to have a doubt about it. I want to give up all my liberty to Him, because I feel that I will never be free until I abdicate the throne to Him, and that I will never have my will truly free until it is bound in the golden fetters of His sweet love.

-Charles Spurgeon
(FJ, pg. 26)

♦ There is no such thing as short-term discipleship.

-J. Oswald Sanders
(JJ, pg. 8)

♦ I am a channel through which the highest love can reach its aim. I will begin to intercede for those around me.

-Andrew Murray
(TG, #41)

♦ During an outbreak of the bubonic plague in Wittenberg, Germany, Martin Luther weighed in on it even after his wife and him had been sick and his daughter, Elizabeth died from it. Here is what he said, "We die at our posts. Christian doctors cannot flee their districts. Christian pastors cannot abandon their congregations. The plague does not dissolve our duties: It turns them to crosses, on which we must be prepared to die."

♦ Ordinary men separated unto the Lord have always been a riddle to this world, and men are bewildered trying to account for the secret of their power.

-Vance Havner
(RTR, pg. 74)

♦ In her book, *Home Before Dark,* Mary Danielsen talked about totally consecrating her life to Christ. She admitted she did not understand the cost of it, but not any us do in the beginning. In a sense we must first be prepared to pay the cost. She made this statement, "But not only would I never turn back, I also make sure I never soft-pedal the realities of the Christian life to others; they need to know that a desire to live godly will mean sacrifice, difficulty, battles with the flesh, and a certain amount of pain. (pg. 11)

***

The persecuted Huguenots hid away in the rocks and caves of France and they would sing their favorite hymn,

"I have a friend so precious,
   So very dear to me,
He loves me with such tender love,
   He loves so faithfully.

I could not live apart from Him,
   I love to feel Him nigh,
And so we dwell together
   My Lord and I"

Heavenly Treasures

♦ We cannot enjoy fair Rachel—heaven and happiness, except first we embrace tender-eyed Leah—holiness, with all her severe duties of repentance and mortification.

-William Gurnall
(CCA, Vol. 1, pg. 220)

♦ Self must not only be dead, but buried out of sight, for the stench of the unburied self-life will frighten souls away from Jesus.

-John Hyde
(PH, pg. 39)

♦ We experience the question, "Am I willing to pay the price of faithfulness to Christ?" as a daily choice. Our Lord told us to deny ourselves and take up our cross daily (Luke 9:23) because discipleship is not one commitment or action, but rather a repeated action we choose to make—or not—each day of our lives.

-Cole Richards
The Voice of the Martyrs
May 2020

♦ Every Christian has one reason to approach God's Word, and that is to believe it. Every saint has one motivation for seeking God's will, and that is to obey it. Every believer has one purpose for serving the Lord, and that is to bring glory to Him.

-RJK

♦ And, what is holiness, but the creature restored to his right temper, in which God created him.

-William Gurnall
(CCA, Vol. 1. pg. 227)

♦ A vision without a task makes a visionary.
  A task without a vision is drudgery.
  A vision with a task makes a missionary.

(SL, pg. 58)

Prayer: *Lord, I have encountered the hard-hearted in the harvest field, the stiff-necked in the courts of the world, and the half-hearted riding the waves on the ocean of life. However, the hard-hearted will be broken, the stiff-necked brought low to the ground in humility, and the half-hearted crashing on the shorelines of reality. Lord, keep my heart pure, my mind open, and my neck flexible before You and Your Word. Amen.*

♦ All other sentiments have to be discarded when loyalty toward Christ is at stake.

-Richard Wurmbrand
The Voice of the Martyrs
Magazine

♦ The seed must die if a harvest is to spring from it. That is the law for all moral and spiritual transformations. No man can be fruit-bearing unless he sacrifices himself. We shall not "quicken" our fellows unless we "die" either literally or by the not less real martyrdom of rigid self-crucifixion. Self-renunciation guards the way to the "tree of life."

-John Gregory Mantle
(BH, pg. 67)

♦ The Lord may discipline outward actions, but true character ensures the integrity of such actions.

-RJK

♦ May you lose nothing in the furnace but your dross. The Lord will preserve everything else for us.

-Samuel Rutherford
(IA, pg. 215)

♦ The center of man's love must be either in himself, in other creatures, or in God. He may love all, but he cannot love more than one supremely. If this love *centers* in self, if the I is the center of the man's thinking, feeling, willing and doing, the man is of course a selfish being and cannot be a holy being, for holiness is the antithesis of selfishness. Pure love is not inordinate.

-John Gregory Mantle
(BH, pg. 38)

♦ Endurance is not just the ability to bear a hard thing, but to turn it into glory.

-William Barclay

♦ The secret of our boldness is to be found in a false estimate of the dignity of man, and still less does it depend on ignoring what is due to the majesty of God. Our confidence is based on knowing our glorious Saviour, and the eternal redemption He has brought us.

-Sir Robert Anderson
(TH, pgs. 72, 73)

♦ He who would win the crown should strive to be rooted in holiness.

-L. L. Pickett
(SC, pg. 42)

♦ The miracle of Christmas is that the infant Jesus learned to walk among us so that we might learn to walk with God.

-Morgan Weistling

- As it is contrary to His law to allow a creature to prefer self to God as a center, and as it is contrary to His nature not to hate sin, He must hate self-love, which is the very soul of sin, and the plague spot from which all other sins proceed.

  -John Gregory Mantle
  (BH, pg. 38)

- He (steward) cannot despise money because he knows the precious things that it can do, but he cannot praise it. It is a "thing"; it is meant to serve life. He holds it lightly, but uses it wisely and generously, and always as God directs.

  -W. E. Sangster
  (HA, pg. 104)

- If we believe in a crucified Savior, it is imperative that we live a crucified life.

  -Herbert Lockyer
  (MM, pg. 16)

- Whatever is given must be spoken in God's voice. And you only learn to discern His voice by experience. If you want to be able to hear it in the crises of life you must first seek it in the common places of life. It is not suddenly acquired.

  -Isobel Kuhn
  (IA, pg. 191)

- The stairway of self-oblation leads men ever upward and onward, from the life of Christ to the likeness of Christ, the fellowship of Christ, the throne of Christ, and the glory of Christ.

  -John Gregory Mantle
  (BH, pg. 80)

♦ Earth allows preparation in light of the heavenly for eternity possesses the expectation of unhindered glory, and glory reminds us of the glorious face of glory: Jesus Christ.

-RJK

♦ Christ *made* us, *redeemed* us, and has a right to us. The act of consecration is to recognize Christ's ownership and to accept it. It is not an act of feeling but of *will*. It must be *complete* and *eternal.*

-Beverly Carradine
(SC, pg. 23)

A Higher Purpose

When we, as believers in America, think of a consecrated life, we do not understand the cost of such a life. For those who lack vision beyond this world, there can be what they would consider to be a great loss to them. The consecrated life operates in a different dimension. It is not subject to the ways of this world. It possesses a higher calling, and must be willing to give way to that which will prove to be excellent.

We can see this type of consecration in a life of a certain woman. In 1924, Miss Marjorie Harrison had one goal: to be a missionary to China. Marjorie had worked towards this goal most of her life. She had saved her earnings so that she might be able to pay for her own outfit and passage. However, due to her delicate medical condition, she was turned down by the mission's board.

How would this Christian woman who had worked towards such an honorable cause take the news? Even though it was no doubt a great loss to her, she took it like a trooper. When she was alone in her bedroom with the news about not going to China, she knelt down and made a further renunciation to the Lord, whom she loved and served. "Oh Lord, this money I have saved for my outfit and passage—I dare not take it back. Will you help me to find someone to go to China in my place? I will use it for that one."

No one knew about Marjorie's prayer, but the Lord knew. He knew she could be entrusted to not become embittered by her great loss; rather, she would embrace her vision by giving it to another missionary who would end up fulfilling it. Sure enough, Marjorie learned about the aspiring missionary Isobel Kuhn who needed the money for passage to China and ended up giving it to her. Isobel not only became a devoted missionary to China until Communism took over, but wrote valuable books about her many experiences on the mission field. (IA, pg. 5-8)

Sometimes we may be heading in one direction, when, for some unknown reason, the providential hand of God changes our direction. Can we trust Him to use our lives and talents in ways that might serve as a platform for others to fulfill the vision He has given them? Are we willing to regress in order for others to progress to ensure the furtherance of the kingdom of God? This is what a consecrated life looks like. It will always give way to that which is worthy of all consideration to ensure that the matters of the kingdom of heaven will advance forward and bring honor and glory to God.

♦ Sin is a burden. Holiness is an imparted power. The one begets friction, eliminates fear, banishes gloom, irradiates life. Sin causes worry and anxiety. Holiness cleanses the heart, inspires faith, kindles devotion, makes prayer easy as breathing, praise natural, and enables ones to hide away in Christ from earth's fret and care.

-L. L. Pickett
(SC, pg. 45)

♦ Holiness is not getting up so high that there is no danger of falling. It is in getting very low. We are on our faces when it

239

comes to us, and if we stay always prostrate and humble, God will keep us, and we will not fall.

-Seth C. Rees
(SC. pg. 122)

♦ God will give us opportunities to try our consecration, whether it be a true one or not. No man can be wholly the Lord's unless he is wholly consecrated to the Lord; and no man can know whether he is thus wholly consecrated except by tribulation.

-Madame Guyon
(BH, pg. 141)

♦ In the eyes of society everywhere any person who refuses ever to compromise with mediocrity, commonplace, self-approval, is considered mentally awry, half-crazy, a crackpot or monomaniac.

-Abraham Heschel
(TP, pg. 514)

♦ Many fail because they shrink back from this entire surrender. They wish to serve Jesus with half their heart, part of themselves, and part of their possessions. To hold back anything from Jesus means a wretched life of stumbling and failure.

-R.A. Torrey
(HSC, pg. 15)

♦ The half-and-half Christian is of very little use either to God or man. God cannot use him, and man has no use for him but considers him a hypocrite. One sin allowed in the life wrecks at once our usefulness and our joy and robs prayer of its power.

-Unknown Christians
(KC, pg. 71)

♦ Knowing Christ and becoming increasingly like Him is authentic Christian spirituality.

-K. P. Yohannan
GFA World
July 2018

♦ True greatness, true leadership, is found in giving yourself in service to others, not in coaxing or inducing others to serve you. True service is never without cost.

-J. Oswald Sanders
(SL, pg. 13)

♦ We should live each day as if Christ had died yesterday, rose again this morning, and is coming again tomorrow.

-Dr. Maclaren of Manchester
(PH, pg. 139)

♦ The reality of greatness will be based on the type of witness it will leave behind. Often such a legacy of greatness is riddled with what appears to be failure. However, it is in times of what appears to be utter failure, that the forging of character takes place. True character is what lasting legacies are made of.

-RJK

♦ A complete conversion, first in ourselves and then in our preaching, is what is needed. We do not need a religious lecture, but a passionate call to repentance in our churches. Our hearts are darkened, defiant and despondent—deceived by so much evil and deception.

-Winrich Scheffbuch
Midnight Call
January 2018

Prayer: *Lord, we often envision ourselves living a distinct life that stands out, not only among others of this world but in heaven. I know that only a life consecrated to You and sanctified by Your Spirit will have such distinction. Lord, purge me with fire, cleanse me with water, and anoint me as Your vessel to carry out Your purpose. Amen.*

A HIGHER CALLING

What does it mean to have a higher calling? It depends on what it is being compared to. For example, is the Christian calling based on a worldly or heavenly perspective? Clearly, when the world comes into play, the heavenly calling will prove to be higher, but also challenging. It can be in your face where it blatantly declares you need to put action to what you are claiming about your life in Christ.

The second consideration has to be vision. Calling is based on how large and far-reaching your vision is. It is not unusual to start from a worldly perspective as to what it means to fulfill a calling in the kingdom of God, but as believers our calling is not of this world. If we do not walk according to that which is heavenly and eternal, our calling will never catch the wind of the Spirit and be brought to high places.

The third thing that must be considered is what kind of value you put on your calling. The value we put on our calling will be based on how much we value Jesus. Our call should become as great as the One who is calling, but if we do not see Jesus high and lifted up in glory, we will see no need to strive to reach great heights.

The idea of calling can initially make us zealous about the possibilities of what it would mean to be a somebody in His kingdom. It is also natural to define our "high calling" according to our high opinions of self that swings on the limbs of arrogance. High calling in Christianity never starts from the high pinnacles of self-importance but from the low places of humility, brokenness, repentance, and total submission to the will of God.

The final aspect of calling has to do with character. Without character or integrity to demand that we line up to that which is right and excellent, calling will never reach places where it is being fulfilled. Sadly, people stop at feelings about their calling and fail to go on to discover the heights of spiritual growth it brings us to. Some begin with zeal that tends to swing upwards, but it will never climb high enough to reach heights of excellence. Others have the best intentions to walk the walk, but they settle for soothing their religious notions by getting by with "good deeds." However, without walking through the rough places of life, character will never be established to endure the rigors of obtaining that which is excellent.

As believers, we all have a high calling in life, which is to be conformed to the image of Jesus. This high calling may vary as to how it is worked in and out of our lives and how we impart it to others, but we all start out with the same commission to plant the seeds or impart Jesus' life to others and that is to preach the Gospel (planting seeds) and to teach (watering) others as true disciples to observe all that Jesus established in His Word.

♦ We cannot state too emphatically, in these days when self-sacrifice is so little understood, that it is the very salt of the

Christian character, and that without self-sacrifice the Christian life is salt without the savor.

-John Gregory Mantle
(BH, pg. 70)

♦ If you are a wholly *given-up* wick, He will light you, but remember it is the burning oil of His holy presence which alone gives the light. Learn to rest quietly in Him and He will tend the flame.

-Paul Rader
(GBM, pg. v)

♦ All other interests must come second if one is to be a true disciple. He must learn—and so must we—that where there is clash of interests, Christ can be divisive.

-J. Oswald Sanders
(JJ, pg. 36)

♦ "God disciplines us for our good *that we may share his holiness.*" That is a strong clue to the explanation we are always seeking. God's purpose for us is holiness—his own holiness which we are to share—and the sole route to that end is discipline.

-Elisabeth Elliot
(TGT, pg. 18)

♦ Keep your treasures on the *open* palm of your hand. If you hold something tightly clenched in your fist, God may have to hurt you in order to open your fingers and take it from you. But if it is offered on the *open palm* of your hand, you will hardly know when it is gone.

-Alice Macfarlane
(IA, pg. 111)

♦ I expect to pass through this world but once. Any good therefore that I can do, or any kindness or abilities that I can show to any fellow creature, let me do it now. Let me not defer it or neglect it, for I shall not pass this way again.

-William Penn

The Sacrifice

When you think about the consecrated life or our high-calling, we can avoid the subject of sacrifice. However, unfeigned consecration and adhering to the high calling will entail some type of sacrifice. After all, the consecrated life separates us from the old life in preparation for the new, and the high-calling must separate us from the worldly in order to walk out the new life.

When you consecrate all to God, it is for the purpose of being available to offer the best in order to walk the excellent path of victory and glory. I remember the story of a missionary whose mission field became the slaves that worked in the fields. He reached out to them but they were unreceptive because he was a free man who was not indebted to an earthly master and could never understand the life of such slavery.

The missionary realized he had to become identified with those he was called to, in order to take the Gospel to the indebted to fulfill his calling. This meant giving up not only the old, but possible dreams of a family or the normal life. It would mean he would walk away from a life of luxury and indebt himself to an earthly master in order to live and work among the slaves. He would have to count the cost, but there is only one measuring gauge and that is Christ giving up the heavenly glories to become identified to us. As His servants could any of us do any less?

The missionary chose the high road of complete consecration to the Lord, and became indebted to an earthly master. Only eternity will unveil his accomplishments, but no doubt what he

245

considered to be his reasonable service to his Lord became a sacrifice emitting a sweet fragrance coming from a life that became an ongoing sacrifice for God's pleasure, purpose and glory.

♦ It is far harder to live for Christ moment by moment than it is to die once for Him; and if we wait for great occasions in which to display our fidelity, we shall find that our life has slipped away, and with it the opportunities which each hour has brought of proving our love to our Lord, by being faithful in that which is least.

-John Gregory Mantle
(BH, pg. 150)

♦ Is there any person more miserable than the person who has just enough Christianity to make him miserable and to spoil everything the world has? How awful! But many are like that. They have no joy of salvation; they have no joy in the Lord; they know nothing about these great blessings of the Christ life.

-Martyn Lloyd-Jones
(SFG, pg. 97)

♦ As long as you have the tiniest bit of spiritual impertinence, it will always reveal itself in the fact that you are expecting God to tell you to do a big thing, and all He is telling you to do is to "come."

-Oswald Chambers

♦ The defining mark of the Christian is not activity but identity. The redeemed are to be identified with the Redeemer.

-Jerry Benjamin

***

Make me a captive, Lord,
And then I shall be free;
Force me to render up my sword,
And I shall conqueror be.
I sink in life's alarms
When by myself I stand;
Imprison me within Thine Arms,
And strong shall be my hand.

-George Matheson

- ◆ When it comes time for us to leave this world, as we all will, He will not ask us what we have done in life or whether we were important people or not. Writer or carpenter—it will mean nothing when we stand before God. Your relationship to the Lord is what will count at that time. Then you will answer for how you have invested your life—what you have done for Him and other people. This is the most important thing in life, because to live here and not know the Lord is to be lost forever when you die.

-Zvi Weichert

- ◆ A man who is free from the manifold motives of self will move like the sun – steady, majestic, and with no variableness, neither shadow of turning. His course can be calculated.

-John Gregory Mantle
(BH, pg. 100)

Victory Cries in the Light of Tragedy

When you read the history of the church, it is not unusual to run across the name Allen Francis Gardiner. He was a missionary. He journeyed with six companions to Picton Island at the extreme south of South America.

These seven brave souls journeyed to their death. Instead of cries for lost souls, his diary speaks of beseeching prayers about their pitiful plight of facing starvation while waiting for a belated relief ship. Gardiner's death is recognized as taking place on September 6, 1851, and the ship finally arrived on October 21, 1851 to find their unburied bodies lying upon the shore.

In the face of tragedy, Gardiner wrote of victory in his diary, "Great and marvelous are the loving-kindnesses of my gracious God to me. He has preserved me hitherto, and for four days, although without bodily food, without any feelings of hunger or thirst."

On commenting on Gardiner's words, W. E. Sangster made this statement, "In the same simple and unshaken trust, we dare believe, he languished into life."

We can look at this incident and shake our heads that God did not situate the timing where these men could be spared from their ordeal and live to tell of God's abiding care and deliverance, but because of Gardiner's ordeal, he left a greater testimony that did not speak of death but victory.

For Christians, the hope we have in Christ makes the unbearable an opportunity to look up, knowing that one day we will look into the beautiful face of our Lord and Savior. What hope, what promise, and what victory we have as believers of the Most High God.

♦ If it is to be his service, it must be where he appoints, and to the vast majority of his disciples the appointment is to humdrum ordinary tasks...To long for the limelight and fret for notice is a very immature stage in the life of service and quite often leads to desertion when the notice is denied. Disciples must be above that.

-W. E. Sangster
(HA, pg. 90)

- The three great lines of self-surrender are – to be anything the Lord wants us to *be*; to do anything He wants us to *do*; to suffer anything He wants us to *suffer*. These embrace the subjective, the active, and the passive forms of our existence, and every point in each line must be yielded, however severe the struggle may be.

  -John Gregory Mantle
  (BH, pg. 131)

- The private life of the disciple can neutralize the effectiveness of his or her public ministry.

  -J. Oswald Sanders

- Our Lord must need to go through Samaria. Our byway ministries often are more fruitful than our service on the main road.

  -Vance Havner
  (RG, pg. 202)

GOD AND I

What God claims, I yield;
What I yield, the Lord accepts;
What He accepts, He cleanses;
What He cleanses, He fills;
What He fills, He controls;
What He controls, He uses;
What He uses, He blesses.

-Bridge Builders
September 2015

Beware of wolves whose Creed is "Get used to different" & "Binge Jesus." The real Jesus is the same, yesterday, today and forever.

-Jeannette Haley

THE CHURCH

What Was in His Heart?

When you say the word "church," you find it means different things to different people. To some, it is a building where you go once or maybe twice a week to participate in some religious exercise. Once such individuals leave their two cents or form of crumbs at the altar or in the offering plate, they now can go and live any way they want until the next time they put on their best pious front to carry out their religious exercise.

There are those who affiliate church to doctrine. They often give the impression that their particular doctrine alone saves and that if one does not agree with them, they certainly are condemned and can't belong to their particular group. Such a biased attitude reeks with a cult mentality They can take on the pose of spiritual elitism that turns into unmerciful judgmentalism towards those who dare operate outside of their camp.

Then there are those who see it as a social club where they can meet with possible business perspectives or supporters of their particular cause. They have no problem with God or religion, but they keep everything in nice compartments to avoid confusion.

They often judge others based on whether they jump on their bandwagon and will deem those who do not go along with them as being stupid or foolish because they can't see the good deal presented to them.

There are those who go to church because they want to do business with God. They want to be kept sharp by cutting-edge preaching that will not allow them to sleep in a pew, be comfortable straddling some compromising fence, be let off the hook when it comes to sin, or be understanding or tolerant about adhering to devilish ways.

If you are like me, you probably guessed that the ones that bring some legitimacy to the true church is the last group, but what was in the heart of God when it came to the church?

The church is the body of Christ. It is a body of many living members that are united by one head, spirit, and faith. They have been redeemed by the blood of Jesus and sealed as adopted children of God in a relationship. Although callings and talents vary with each member of the body, they are equally important for the function of the whole body.

Each member is an heir with Christ when it comes to the promises, and joint heirs when it comes to being glorified with Him. They have been set apart and are being prepared as the bride for Christ. They are being cleansed by the Word, purified by trials, sanctified by the Spirit, and the wrinkles of deviation ironed out by making right choices, preparing them to be clothed in white linens of righteousness for the great day of the wedding supper of the Lamb.

The question is not what building you attend, what doctrine you are affiliated with or if your association with it has a worldly agenda. The key is if you belong to the one living, true body of Jesus Christ.

♦ When God promises anything, you may be sure God expects to do exactly that. I am afraid the church has come to the place where we scarcely expect anything from God.

-A.W. Tozer
(MDP, pg. 320)

♦ In Europe, Christianity was abused when it was used for political power; in America it has been abused by using it for economic power. And today it is abused by its detractors who deny its power and remove it from any position of moral authority. These detractors live under the illusion that it is the only belief that claims absolutes.

-Ravi Zacharias
(WJ, pg. 102)

♦ There is a pleasant preaching today that tries to prescribe the remedy before people are made to realize that they are sick; tries leading to the light people who do not know they are in the dark! Men will never be convicted until they are made to see themselves as *sinners,* and to do that, sin must be condemned and exposed, and it must be made personal.

-Vance Havner
(RG, pg. 200-201)

♦ Many forget that Christ died not only for the world, but for the church as well. He died for the world that he might offer it pardon, and for the church, that he might sanctify it—wash every spot and iron out every wrinkle.

-Seth C. Rees
(SC, pg. 124)

♦ We are guilty of deception when we deal with our sins in a heap. Let us bring them into the light of the Cross and treat them singly, for each one, taken alone, contains the whole principle of rebellion against God and made Calvary, with its awful anguish and loneliness, a terrible necessity.

-John Gregory Mantle
(BH, pg. 27)

♦ I believe that the kingdom of God is obstructed more by indifferent Christians than by the vigorous marching of the antichrist. A Vietnamese boy once said to me, "Sometimes churches are mousetraps for Christians. They meet there, enjoy the Word and fellowship with the Lord and each other; but they forget that they have been called to spread the Gospel message over the whole world.

-Corrie ten Boom
(MA, Bk. 1 pg. 42)

♦ In regard to the happenings taking place in many churches, Vance Havner made this statement, "It is a performance not an experience...No wonder we meet at eleven o'clock sharp and end at twelve o'clock dull." (PD. pg. 36)

♦ Might it be that because we are so interested in getting people off the earth into Heaven, that we have ignored the possibility of teaching them how to live a Christ-honoring life on the earth?

-Larry Spargimino
Prophetic Observer
July 2018

♦ We have sold out to carnal methods, carnal philosophies, carnal viewpoints, carnal gadgets and have lost the glory of God in our midst. We're a starved generation that's never seen the glory of God.

-A.W. Tozer
(RCF, pg. 12)

♦ Neither strident nor flamboyant, God's servant conducts a ministry that appears almost self-effacing. What a contrast to the arrogant self-advertising of so many hipsters today, both in and out of the church.

-J. Oswald Sanders
(SL, pg. 24)

♦ God owes a debt both to the first Adam and to the second. To the first he owes the wages of his sin, to the second the reward of his sufferings.

-William Gurnall
(CCA, Vol. 1, pg. 247)

♦ It does not speak too well for our Christian testimony when God tells us that He has sent His Son to be His final revelation in this world—and we act bored about it!

-A. W. Tozer
(JG, pg. 13)

♦ Beloved fellow-believer! Let us confess that because we do not abide in Christ as He would like us to, the Church is impotent in the face of infidelity, worldliness, and heathendom. In the midst of such enemies, the Lord could make her more than a conqueror.

-Andrew Murray
(WC, pg. 157)

♦ The evangelist from the Old Spirituality pleaded with his audiences to "invite Jesus into your heart"; the apostles of the New Spirituality tell you to invite yourself into your heart, to feel your own breath.

-Ravi Zacharias
(WJ, pgs. 53-54)

♦ Sin, as we have seen, has a relation both to righteousness and to holiness, but, essentially, it is *lawlessness*: lawlessness and sin are synonymous terms. The answer to the guilt of sin is justification, and to its defilement, sanctification.

-Sir Robert Anderson
(GAM, pg. 180)

♦ Too many Christians sing hymns on Sunday but all week they are out in the world helping the dead to bury their dead.

-Vance Havner
(RG, pg. 155)

♦ The trick of the devil in the modern Church is that he has got us to do a thousand things that are good in our Church work; but they are not *the* things we should be seeking after. He has persuaded us to do a thousand things that do not contribute to the evangelization of the world. Many good things in their way, but they are not *the* things that God has called us to do. When will the Church learn to give up these good things for the best things?

-Paul Rader
(GBM, pg. 102)

♦ Now the church is so weak and the culture so pagan, Muslims come touting their high morality of the Sharia, vowing to conquer and clean up the corruption in the west. But where they gain control, freedom of speech dies along with most other freedoms.

-Battle Cry
Jan/Feb 2015

♦ But beware. Some of the world's greatest bluffers are not poker players and politicians, but preachers. And there is no fog so thick as theological fog.

-David Servant
Happy Endings Publication
Jan. 2014

♦ An emotional religion of sympathy is more compatible with his mentality than a self-detached religion of obedience. Man is expected to love his God with all of his heart, with all his soul, with all his might.

-Abraham Heschel
(TP, pg. 394)

♦ A soft and sheltered Christianity, afraid to be lean and lone, unwilling to face the storms and brave the heights will end up fat and foul in the cages of conformity.

-Vance Havner
(ILT, pg. 31)

♦ The Trojan horse that has been allowed in the church is psychology. This godless, perverted philosophy has undermined the wise and effective counseling of the Word of God, replaced its truth with a bunch of secular terminology and psycho-babble nonsense, made a mockery of God's healing and restoration, and caused people to become more entangled with this world's lies and dependent on Satan's house of cards that will fall when the sands of deception are challenged by the waves of judgment.

-RJK

♦ My heart is to see what was desired for the 20th century by some of the saints: a Church holy in life, triumphant in faith, self-sacrificing in service, with one aim, to preach Christ crucified 'unto the uttermost part of the earth.' (PH, pg. 131)

♦ The most dangerous aspect about heresy is that in many regards what they believe is right. It is not what one believes, but rather, it is what one refuses to believe that makes heretics very dangerous.

-A.W. Tozer
(MDP, pg. 44)

♦ The size of our churches mean nothing if they prove to be full of false converts. May each of us give an account with joy, and not with grief.

-Ray Comfort
(GWP, pg. 108)

What is the Commission?

When I talk to certain church-goers, I get the impression that the main commission of Christians is to go to church, pay tithes, and/or volunteer for some service or work in the church. The concept that by serving the church, pastor, or religious leaders Christians are fulfilling their commission, is erroneous. Sadly, it seems some pulpits either encourage such conclusions or remain silent because it ultimately serves their purpose or agenda.

Matthew 28:18-20 and Mark 16:15-16 are clear that our commission is two-fold. It is evangelistic because we are to preach the Gospel in whatever harvest field we are involved with and the second is to make converts into the followers of Jesus Christ. It is called discipleship.

One great evangelist stated that churches should have revolving doors in them. It is where the lost come in and get saved, healed, and trained and then sent out to do the bidding of the Lord by fulfilling their commission.

I learned long ago that to be evangelistic you must have a heart for the lost, a vision for the prize of eternity, and a burning message that makes a believer a fire-brand who will not compromise the urgency of the message. In some cases, their cry is simple as it warns, contends, and almost pleas with the lost to flee the wrath of God upon all rebellion by receiving the antidote of Jesus Christ.

Discipleship is the second part of the two-fold commission. It is where followers of Christ are taught to observe all things that were declared, taught, and upheld in Scripture. Discipleship may start out in a classroom, but it will often lead to personal investment. Sometimes it requires a minister to get in the trenches with immature soldiers, tread where others refuse to go to challenge the spiritual vagabonds taking detours or walking in the broad way, and stand, ready to wrestle and pull out vulnerable, perishing souls from the very grips and claims of hell upon their souls.

To fail to be open and prepared to fulfill the commission is the sin of omission. Granted, not all saints will be visible in the furtherance of the Gospel because the prayer closet will become the altar to the intercessor where supplication and tears give wings to others who are laboring in the harvest field while others will offer up other gifts so those called can fulfill their calling.

As the church, the harvest fields of the world are our burden and they must not be cast aside, ignored, or left up to a few. Each member of the body must get under the burden of the commission, ever seeking God's perspective and will as to what their part is in fulfilling the great commission.

♦ Generally speaking, evangelism without discipleship does not go deep enough to root and nurture believers in Christian maturity.

-Dois I. Rosser Jr.
(GHC, pg. 106)

♦ Either through ignorance or unwillingness, the vast majority of those who profess to be fellow-workers with God in the regeneration of the world have never definitely hated and renounced the self-life, and it is because they are so much alive to self that they are so little alive to God.

-John Gregory Mantle
(BH, pg. 71)

♦ No Islamic nation in the world operates with a belief in the inalienable right of liberty. Naturalism does not acknowledge a Creator who could endow us with inalienable rights. And pantheism, with its karmic bequest, does not see us as being created equal.

-Ravi Zacharias
(WJ, pg. 39)

♦ (Concerning the woman who anointed Jesus' feet in Luke 7:36-50) Our smug and pale Christianity today shows little of the broken and humble gratitude for sins forgiven that marked this woman. Few alabaster boxes are broken in tearful joy over forgiveness.

-Vance Havner
(RG, pg. 153)

♦ A Christian is double-minded when, after becoming a Christian, with his heart he wants to serve God, and with his flesh he wants to serve himself. He has a wobble and a wiggle in his life. He is double-minded.

-Paul Rader
(GBM, pg. 47)

♦ No sin is little, but the least sin amounts to blasphemy when thou committest it on a Scripture pretense.

-William Gurnall
(CCA, Vol. 2, pg. 235)

♦ Relationship always precedes behavior...The farther God is removed from our consciousness, the more we are strongly drawn to the things that feed and please our fallen nature. When we stumble and fall, we may point to many external factors to explain our behavior, but the root of our problem is failure to keep God's presence in mind.

-Chuck Smith

♦ In all ages spiritual truth has met it bitterest foes in false professors of the true religion.

M. L. Haney
(SC, pg. 63)

♦ Religion, if not made practicable in our several places and callings, become ridiculous and vanisheth into an empty notion that is next to nothing.

-William Gurnall
(CCA, Vol. 1, pg. 280)

♦ Most of our church membership today is an untrained, undiscipline, mixed multitude with no knowledge of the Bible and no clear convictions on creed or conduct.

-Vance Havner
(PD, pg. 51)

♦ Worship is the missing jewel in evangelicalism today. The church today has decked herself with everything to amuse and entertain. Entertainment, I contend, is the curse of the church. It is the devils' replacement of worship.

-A.W. Tozer
(MDP, pg. 60)

♦ While there is growing darkness in our world God, doesn't expect us to deal with it by flashlight, or a flickering candle.

-Larry Spargimino
Prophetic Observer
July 2018

♦ Delays are a Christian touchstone—which will try what metal men are made of, whether they are gold or dross, silver or tin, whether they are sincere or unsound; whether they are real or rotten Christians.

-Thomas Brooks
(MSR, pg. 157)

♦ We have lost the loftiness and have become coarse and shallow. We have lost the substance and have become entertainers. Lost, in our preaching is the sense of lifting up Jesus. We are lifting up everything else but Jesus…When a person nourishes his soul on the high and lofty thoughts of God, he loses his appetite for the watered-down modern-day religion.

-A.W. Tozer
(MDP, pgs. 90, 91)

♦ The 'new creature' is not still-born; true holiness is not a dull habit, that sleeps away the time with doing nothing.

-William Gurnall
(CCA, Vol 1, pg. 409)

♦ The concerns I read the most about the church is the fact that it has been rendered into some organization or club that is often void of spirituality and the activities have been reduced to religious duties, acceptable hobbies, or sacred activities where we blend into the world instead of stand distinct from it. It has been adapted to the culture instead of the believer being conformed by the life of Christ in him or her to manifest His image to a dying world.

-RJK

♦ The great fault in our missions is that no one likes to be second.

-Robert Morrison
(SL, pg. 63)

♦ Many churches focus on cultural topics so they can be culturally relevant.

-A.W. Tozer
(MDP, pg. 146)

♦ Oh, for teachers among us; leaders who know how to read, hear and apply truth to the needs of the people, as a good physician reads patients and applies remedies to their ills. There are soul-sicknesses open and obscure, acute and chronic, superficial and deep-seated that the truth in Jesus will heal.

-Samuel Brengle
(SL, pg. 42)

♦ We are in a battle and we must avoid becoming philosophers about what to do and theologians about what not to do, and as good soldiers do what the Word of God instructs us to do.

-RJK

♦ It is amazing how nominal faith, nominal belief, can weave texts into garments, cloaks and curtains for the church. We have so many of these all around the church, and I must admit that for the most part they are beautiful. But they serve no function in our spiritual walk.

-A.W. Tozer
(MDP, pg. 137)

♦ Without the foundation of Jesus, the religious landscape will constantly change according to the whims of man's foolish doctrines. Without the leadership of Moses and Joshua, the church will dance before the altars of Baal, without the holiness of God as the standard, man will become foolish in his way of thinking, and without the fear of God, man will become an utter fool in his way of doing.

-RJK

♦ Never can we truly recover our courage, till we recover our holiness.

-William Gurnall
(CCA, Vol. 1, pg. 411)

♦ The preachers of our generation are failing us...Too many preachers are satisfied to dwell primarily on the escape element in Christianity...But if we continue to emphasize that truth to the exclusion of all else, Christian believers will never fully grasp what the Scriptures are teaching us about all of the eternal purposes of God.

-A. W. Tozer
(JG, pg. 26)

♦ There is a danger in our evangelical religion of looking too much at what it offers from one side, as a certain experience obtained in prayer and faith. There is another side which God's Word puts very strongly, that of obedience as the only path to blessing.

-Andrew Murray
(WC, pg. 170)

♦ How incongruous it is for a holy Christ to be leading a company of unholy Christians; or a Cross-bearing Christ, a band of self-indulgent Christians, whose hearts are often toward Egypt, and who shrink from the least suffering and self-denial!

-John Gregory Mantle
(BH, pg. 43)

♦ G. K. Chesterton was right. The problem with Christianity is not that it has been tried and found wanting, but that it has been found difficult and left untried. The message of Jesus is beautiful and magnificent and life-changing. If you have not already discovered that for yourself, may you discover it now. Spirituality is not good enough.

-Ravi Zacharias
(WJ, pg. 269)

♦ The devil will have men join the church and become theologically orthodox if only they do *not touch* Christ. And one may come *almost* to Christ! Jostle Him in the crowd but never touch Him and feel His virtue: this is *almost*. Be sure you get through to Jesus.

-Vance Havner
(RG, pg. 133)

An Exception?

Back in the mid 1980's the church I attended hosted a South Korean singing group. Their voices were pure and their songs were powerful to such a point even my father followed them from place to place to hear them.

Their leader made a statement, "We thank you for sending missionaries to our country, now we send them to your country." It was strange to think that America needed missionaries. In some communities there is a church on almost every other street corner.

In 1991, my co-laborer, Jeannette, and I attended a missionary school that was sending temporary missionaries to the third world countries that had been under the Communist regime for at least 50 years. The stories that came back from these different countries of hungry sheep seeking the true God of heaven, and God coming down in powerful ways to save, heal, and restore souls, were inspiring and incredible.

Jeannette and I were both excited at the prospect of being part of and witnessing the powerful move of God to bring in the harvest in those countries. However, the Lord showed us we were not being called to a place such as Russia, but He was calling us to America, and it was not to the highways and byways but to the church.

I struggled with the concept of being a missionary in America--but to the church? I became quite confused. I later learned the third largest mission field was America and that the call to minister to the church was one of discipleship and not evangelism.

Later we would attend a church where the preacher believed in sending out missionaries, but he was clear that America had no need for such missionaries. I don't know if he was making an impulsive statement or whether he was trying to put us in "our place" as far as our work in the harvest field of America. I don't know if he was being smug, unrealistic, limited in his definition, or

265

unthinking when making such a statement, but needless to say, we left that church soon after his declaration.

First of all, no man determines or sends out missionaries. They are called and commissioned by God. No man can determine the calling of another, and no man can look at any harvest field, whether here or abroad and declare there is no need for missionaries.

Every place where souls are, is a field that will eventually be harvested by the great Husbandman. Every parent holds a missionary status in the home, every Christian should be a missionary in the workplace or society, every believer must be ready to serve in any capacity, place, or field among souls. The truth is the whole world is a harvest field and we are to work in whatever harvest field we are in at the present. Is America in need of missionaries or is it an exception that it has no need for people to labor in its harvest fields? You bet it is in need of missionaries whether they are from abroad or local! At one time America sent out the most missionaries, but according to the latest information I have read, now the persecuted church of China is sending out the most missionaries around the world.

All that is left to say is, "God have mercy on us and send us the missionaries that have a love for souls, a vision for their calling, and are not afraid to plough up even the dry, lifeless ground of religion so that dormant seeds can be revived, cultivated, and brought to maturity with Your Living Water."

♦ It is no wonder that the Gospel seems to have lost its power, when men keep preaching another Gospel; and fooling men about their goodness and greatness, until the real Gospel has lost its essence.

-Paul Rader
(GBM, pg. 41)

♦ "I have a dream," proclaimed Martin Luther King. Jr., in his most famous speech as the leader of the civil rights movement. As a servant of God, I too have a dream! It is to see the Body of Christ changed and revolutionized in such a way that we no longer go to church to be entertained and get what we want. Rather, we meet the Living God and understand the purpose He has for our lives and pursue it.

-K.P. Yohannan
Send Magazine
November 2013

♦ The apostaisian ruin of the churches is the departure of the Holy Ghost, who is grieved away by sin, folly, disobedience, and all sorts of worldliness. The reason why all churches multiply human machinery as the years go by is to supply the deficiency of the Holy Ghost in this way, thus leading the people into idolatry and damnation.

-W. B. Godbey
(SC, pg. 26)

♦ We have been doing in our churches all those churchly things that we do. We have done them with our own understanding and in our own energy. But without a bright and conscious confirmation of God's presence, a church service can be very deadly and dull.

-A. W. Tozer
(JG, pg. 14)

♦ Until we have *learned* the great doctrine of the crucifixion of the flesh with its passions and lusts, we shall find it impossible to bring ourselves within the limits of God's appointment and law.

-John Gregory Mantle
(BH, pg. 59)

♦ If we want to get gender relations correct in a biblical way, we need to start by praying for hearts that can be humble and grateful, eyes that are touched by God's gift of sight to see who is truly laboring hard for the Lord around us, and then the courage to speak out and celebrate these often unsung leaders among us.

-William David Spencer
Priscilla Papers
(Summer 2014)

♦ Pentecostal preaching always "pricks" people "in their *hearts*" Much that is *called* preaching only reaches the head. It is head preaching, prepared by a head for another head. . . There is a lamentable lack of deep, pungent conviction, that will make souls cry out in anguish. Men must be harpooned. Cold statements of truth will not suffice. We need *hot messages.* They come by devotion rather than by thinking, by prayer rather than by study. Souls well-convicted give hopeful promise of sound conversion.

-Seth C. Rees
(SC, pg. 116)

♦ Either we make it an altar for God or it is invaded by demons. There can be no neutrality. Either we are ministers of the sacred or slaves of the evil. Let the blasphemy of our time not become an eternal scandal. Let future generations not loathe us for having failed to preserve what prophets and saints, martyrs and scholars have created in thousands of years.

-Abraham Heschel
(MQG, pg. 151)

♦ Our problem is that we keep or allow our churches to stay dingy gray instead of pleading for holy whiteness. We are willing to accept something off-color as long as it does not offend anybody.

-A.W. Tozer
(MDP, pg. 156)

♦ Winter providences kill the weeds of lusts, and summer providence ripen and mellow the fruits of righteousness. When he afflicts it is for our profit to make us partakers of his holiness.

-William Gurnall
(CCA, Vol1, pg. 417)

♦ You are told there are no absolutes, but if you run afoul of the relativist, the castigation that follows knows no boundaries and the bigotry vented knows no limits.

-Ravi Zacharias
(WJ, pg. 99)

♦ …people are not given the message of sin, righteousness, and judgment with the command to repent and flee from the wrath to come.

-Ray Comfort
(GWP, pg. 53)

♦ As believers, we must behold the Son in greater measure to close any gap in our relationship with God. After all Jesus is the bridge that connects us to our life, worship, and service in His kingdom.

-RJK

***

There is a story about a certain person taking down the clock in the Metropolitan Tabernacle when Charles Spurgeon was pastor. In the place of the clock was a note which read, "Since the pastor

is more interested in eternity than time, he will not miss this clock"
(MDP, pg. 146).

As a church we should be more interested in preparing for
eternity instead of making time in the world.

♦ The Christian church in America, over the last several
generations, has made God almost a God of grace and nothing
else. So we have a god who cannot see moral distinction and
because he cannot see moral distinctions, His church has
been unable to see moral distinction...the reason is that grace
has been preached to the exclusion of everything else.

-A.W. Tozer
(MDP, pg. 315)

♦ Soul-fishing is the Christian's business. We are not to uplift,
reform, cultivate them, but to bring them to know the Lord. We
have forgotten our commission and are out proselyting, calling
the righteous to repentance, instead of bringing men to Christ.

-Vance Havner
(RG, pg. 103)

♦ Eventually we will learn that no matter how much money, effort
or innovation the church possesses, it will never be as cool as
the culture. Relevance is a race it cannot win, but in our
misguided attempts to compete with the culture, we risk losing
sight of the only thing of value the church can offer the world—
Jesus Christ.

-How Churches Became Cruise Ships
(Excerpt: SKYJETHANI.COM, 6/19/14)

♦ When a Christian stands in a compromising place it will not be
long before he slips into sin.

-Paul Rader
(GBM, pgs. 33-34)

- Most Christians want to simply experience the mountain tops and avoid the deep places that can bring one to utter despair and hopelessness. They may want to know the deep things about God, but they avoid being brought into deep places to gain a type of dependency on Him that allows them to know Him. They want to know great things about God, but they are unwilling to become disciplined spiritual mountain climbers to experience His greatness.

  -RJK

- If we will admit our inadequacy, we can have God's adequacy.... The greatest problem in the church is trying to do God's work with man's strength.... The key to Christian sufficiency is realizing that everything comes from God and nothing comes from me.

  -Ray Stedman
  (GHC, pg. 69)

- Those who believe that gender is the most important aspect of personhood are called "gender essentialists." For them, maleness or femaleness is an attribute that shapes the fundamental meaning and purpose of life—a view that, sadly, drives gender hierarchy in the world, and also in the church...Our identity is not in our gender, but in our union with Christ, made possible through Calvary. May we glory only in the cross.

  -Mimi Haddad
  Mutuality Magazine
  Vol. 21, Issue 1

- Religion never goes in more danger than when in a crowd of worldly business.

  -William Gurnall
  (CCA, Vol. 2, pg. 325)

♦ History shows us that virtually every major revival of the past has been birthed out of a great awakening of those who thought they were saved, but were not.

-Ray Comfort
(GWP, pg. 100)

***

In interviewing a young Communist, he volunteered this statement, "We Communists do not learn in order to show what a high IQ we have. We learn in order to put into practice what we have learned." (JJ, pg. 25)

Clearly there are no spectators in Communism. Yet how many people sitting in church pews are spectators to the Christian life and have no intention of putting into practice what they know is right. It is a surface commitment that lacks any real heart passion. If we are to be followers of Christ, we need to put into practice the teachings and examples we have been given.

♦ If you're PROUD of being humble...well just maybe there might be a problem.

-Jeannette Haley

♦ People don't change for righteousness and truth; they change because of love.

-Dr. K.P. Yohannan
GFA World Magazine

♦ Using the word "religion" in its classical acceptation, the religion of the Pentateuch is the only divine religion the world has ever known; for in that sense Christianity is not a religion, but a revelation and a faith…But the religion of the nominal Jew was as false as is the religion of the nominal Christian.

-Sir Robert Anderson
(TH, pg.9)

***

Unless we live this cross-bearing life we *cannot* be His disciples. It is not that we "shall not" but "cannot" be. In other words, this is an unalterable law of discipleship. The only possible way by which we can do the will of God, and live out the ideal Christian life, is by absolute surrender of ourselves to our divine Lord.

Without this absolute surrender, which, as we have said, is spread out over the whole of our life, we may come after Christ outwardly, we may be called by His name, but we "*cannot*" be His disciples any more than a bird can fly without wings.

-John Gregory Mantle
(BH, pgs. 156, 157)

♦ The marvelous thing about the commission of our Lord Jesus Christ is that not one of His followers needs to be excluded. Every person is either a missionary or a mission field.

-Corrie ten Boom
(MA, Bk. 1 pg. 44)

♦ We present-day Christians have been misled and brainwashed, at least in a general way, by a generation of soft, pussycat preachers. They would have us believe that to be good Christians we must be able to purr softly and accept everything that come along with Christian tolerance and understanding. Such ministers never mention words like *zeal* and *conviction* and *commitment.* They avoid phrases like "standing for the truth."

-A. W. Tozer
(JG, pg. 66)

♦ When Canaan is made the objective point, two classes of religionists always appear. The spies and the Calebs where their representatives are in every age and clime. The proposal at *once* to go up is always an offense to the one and joy to the other. The one magnifies the hindrances; the other rejoices in the Arm and is almighty. The latter enters the land; the former dies in the wilderness.

-M. L. Haney
(SC, pg. 65)

♦ Religion is what a man does with his own solitariness.

-Professor A. N. Whitehead
(HA, pg. 56)

♦ The urgent need for the Church is to come to grips with the fact that we are living at the twilight period of human history. We must plead with our Lord to light a biblical fire within the present lukewarm Church in America and enable it to understand that current world events are precursors to our King's second coming.

-Marv Rosenthal

♦ There has been a great movement in the last several generations toward external religion and what I refer to as technical Christianity. It is hard for some Christians to put down their religious toys and concentrate on communion with God. yet everything about our regenerated heart is focused in the direction of heaven.

-A.W. Tozer
(MDP, pg. 202)

♦ We cannot receive more from God until we are willing to receive less from the world.

-Jeannette Haley

♦ (In relationship to the work of God.) Gather the work of God in your heart. Dark clouds are covering the world, and who knows how soon you will need this richness.

-Sabrina Wurmbrand
1980 Message

***

They take the flesh that God has condemned and nurse it back to life. They feed it and make it slick and smooth; educate it and call it by nice names. Then the church adopts it and elects it to the board and makes ushers and deacons out of it.

Churches are organized around the flesh now and with the values and standards of the flesh. However, it is the flesh that early Christians believed they left in the waters of baptism. It is that flesh the Early Church said died with Christ when He died on the cross.

-A.W. Tozer
(RCF, pg. 56)

♦ But someone will exclaim; "Why speak of these heresies? Positive truth is what is wanted." Yes, in these days people are intolerant of all denunciations of error. But the seeming triumph of Satan, from the day of the Eden Fall to the present hour, has been largely due to his skill in using "positive truth."

-Sir Robert Anderson
(RT, pg. 128)

♦ We build churches today and wait for the people to come…Too many churches are glorified clubs that have forgotten about the shepherd seeking the sheep.

-Vance Havner
(RG, pg. 103)

♦ (In relationship to entrepreneurial pastors) What these "pastorpreneurs" found was that people would still attend church in a post-Christian culture if it appealed to their felt needs. Rather than viewing the church as simply a means to an end (connecting people with God), they made church an end in itself. But by starting with consumer's desires they were mirroring the shift in passenger shipping away from the liner voyages to cruising.

-How Churches Became Cruise Ships
(Excerpt: SKYJETHANI.COM, 6/19/14)

♦ Evil will come, but I must obey. The world must be shown.

-Elisabeth Elliot
(TGT, pg. 142)

♦ The moment Christians compromise with darkness is the moment the light goes out of their life and darkness reigns

-Jeannette Haley

♦ A cold-heart is an unyielded heart. We are speaking within the language of truth we talk about ice-box churches…I have also been in hot churches, preaching to a crowd of wholly-yielded hearts, and, oh, the delightful heat! What can be worse for the world than to come up against a cold Christian? It is worse than a cold pancake.

-Paul Rader
(GBM, pg. 15)

♦ Let's face it, we were not meant to be Tarzan swinging through the jungle of life with ease; rather, we were designed to walk through the jungles of mundane mire, push back the endless bushes of daily routines in order to advance towards a spiritual prize that we cannot even see.

-RJK

- Dead churches and backslidden preachers, like the *debris* around the avalanche will either be run over or left behind. This glorious doctrine and experience of perfection is nothing but good old-style Holy Ghost religion from the crown of your head to the soles of your feet; purifying your heart, filling you with the love of God, and preparing you to live a hero and die a martyr.

    -W. B. Godbey
    (SC, pg. 36)

- There is a fundamental difference between Christendom and the Church...The Bible teaches that Christendom shall be apostate and shall give up their faith and shall wallow in her own self-righteousness and deny the power of God and shall be totally unprepared for the coming of the Lord Jesus Christ.

    -Unknown

- Every preacher or teacher of the Word of God should have one goal and passion above all else — to exalt Christ and then fade from view. In our daily lives He **must** increase, and we must decrease.

    -Marv Rosenthal

- The church is not the agent God will use to usher in His kingdom of righteousness and justice. That position belongs solely to God's Son, the Messiah. To say otherwise is to deny Jesus the glory ascribed to Him alone.

    -James A. Showers

- There are religions that teach that God is all justice. They live in terror. Others say that God is all love. They become arrogant. Like the philosophers, religionists have concepts and

277

views, ideas and theories. In none of them has mankind found satisfaction.

-A. W. Tozer
(JG, pg. 42)

♦ The spiritual impoverishment of modern preaching can be traced to the bloodless gospel preached. Too many pulpits are silent when it comes to the preaching of the Cross as the only hope for a lost world.

-Herbert Lockyer
(MM, pg. 18)

♦ An air of tranquility, complacency prevails in our houses of worship. What can come out of such an atmosphere? The services are prim, the voice is dry, the temple is clean and tidy, and the soul of prayer lies in agony. You know no one will scream, no one will cry, the words will be still-born.

-Abraham Heschel
(MQG, pg. 50)

♦ In days when the historic apostasy of Christendom has well-nigh captured the National Church, and the new infidel apostasy, hiding under the veil of "the Higher Criticism," is leavening all the churches, it behooves the Christian to "keep himself pure."

-Sir Robert Anderson
(RT, pg. 102)

♦ It is the folly of people who say they believe in God but who in the tenor of their lives and in the whole of their conduct daily forget God and live exactly as if He did not exist.

-Martyn Lloyd-Jones
(SFG, pg. 25)

♦ When a church chooses to obey edicts and mandates is when it confirms it has no god but Caesar.

-Jeannette Haley

♦ False Christians are earthly-minded, and at some point this is shown not only in their teaching (as evident by the prosperity evangelists on television), but also in their lives.

-Rene Malgo
Midnight Call
April 2016

♦ We are serving the Christ of Revelation, not the Christ of some Pollyanna preacher who does not want to offend anybody and believes everything is going to turn out just nice.

-A.W. Tozer
(MDP, pg. 282)

♦ The devil gets his works done today while ministers are asleep; he sows evil in the churches while they are taken up with their own ease. He sows in homes while parents sleep, careless of their children's welfare. He sows abroad in the land while rulers, who should have an eye to the public welfare, look to their own comfort.

-Vance Havner
(RG, pg. 60)

♦ All religions, from the most legalistic to the most liberal to the mystical, have self at the core of one's achieving positive consequences regarding life after death. Only biblical Christianity teaches that *denying self* and turning to Jesus alone for one's salvation is acceptable to God.

-T.A. McMahon
The Berean Call
March 2015

♦ There is a great deal of man-made enthusiasm. This is good so far as it goes, but it is only painted fire, and nothing like the real thing. Man has worked hard to produce this fire, but it is not produced by works but by yielding.

-Paul Rader
(GBM, pg. 13)

♦ Present-day preaching finds little place for repentance, yet without repentance there can be no regeneration. Many have been encouraged to believe that because they have come forward to an appeal or signed a decision card, or prayed to receive Christ, they are saved—whether or not there is any subsequent change in their lives.

-J. Oswald Sanders
(JJ. pg. 19)

♦ The battle is religion versus religion and, to be more precise, it is God's religion versus man's religions: Christianity versus all other religions.

-Bodie Hodge
(TB, pg. 27)

♦ I didn't want to ever leave some bodily print in the pew, while failing to make any spiritual impact in the kingdom of heaven. I observed in the lives of others that such mediocrity will eventually cause individuals to succumb to a willingness to just accept what they already know, ending with them getting by on decayed manna, while trying to squeeze as much water out of empty or stagnant cisterns as they can.

-RJK

♦ We have this habit of trying to put God into our life. We have our own little boundaries, and we think God should fit into them. That is contrary to the very nature of God.

-A.W. Tozer
(MDP, pg. 207)

♦ ...I am almost persuaded that the chief problem today is not the problem of people who say there is no God and who are in the world. It is the problem of people who go to the house of God in a purely mechanical manner. They go there, but why? Because it is the thing to do. They attend a church as a matter of duty.

-Martyn Lloyd-Jones
(SFG, pg.32)

♦ If we look at our present Christianity, we see an increasing spiritual decadence, a Christianity of lives without Christ. Many theological colleges are full of criticism. How many pastors still believe what they preach? We have an increase of lukewarm Christianity, adapted to suit the times, lacking in knowledge and without devotion.

-Samuel Rindlisbacher
Midnight Call
March 2016

Prayer: *Lord, we need to see things from Your perspective: sin, Your Church, the Gospel, grace, and Your glory. We need to rise up out of our religious pews of understanding and seek a place outside of worldly activities, as we discipline the ways of the flesh, while seeking You with all of our heart, trusting You will be found by us. Amen.*

♦ Though our clothes these days may bear the label "Made in China," there is no doubt that the new form of spirituality is "Made in India."

-Ravi Zacharias
(WJ, pg. 96)

♦ The church in the world today is people, those called by the Spirit of God. We are diverse. We are one. The local expression of the church can be in the form of believers who gather in a house in China, under a Banyan tree in India, or in a prison unit in South America—a church certainly does not need a building to be the church.

-Dois I. Rosser Jr.
(GHC, pg. 67)

♦ Sin is nearly always symptomatic of a believer's having distanced himself from Christ. All ministering must therefore begin with where a believer is in his relationship with Jesus— and a recognition of where he needs to be.

-T. A. McMahon
The Berean Call

♦ Modern evangelism has surrendered to the world, excused it, explained it, adopted it and imitated it...We have more liberal morals in evangelical circles than we have biblical.

-A.W. Tozer
(RCF, pg. 58)

♦ The Cross, with its centrality communicates its own attraction to every approaching soul, and by a common energy draws all souls together, making them one in the Savior himself. But somehow the church has missed the blood-red Tree in the center and has created centers of her own, and if men do not travel to such, they suffer expulsion.

-Herbert Lockyer
(MM, pg. 26)

♦ Much of the Church needs to be revived, but it cannot happen unless there is first true brokenness before the Lord. As His people, may we have every ounce of pride broken at its fierce independence and brought low at its self-sufficiency, so that we can once again be revived by His Spirit.

-RJK

♦ There have been preachers who changed the preposition *to* and made it *from*. To preach a salvation with emphasis on what the individual sinner is saved *from*...I do not believe God is concerned at all about where we have come from. He is concerned with where we are going.

-A. W. Tozer
(JG, pgs. 102, 103)

♦ You cannot steer a parked car, and God does not lead passive Christians.

-Marv Rosenthal
(Zion's Magazine)

♦ Prophetic religion may be defined, not as what man does with his ultimate concern, but rather what man does with God's concern.

-Abraham Heschel
(TP, pg. 619)

♦ The man who would force his opinions on others is a bore. He who would die for his opinions is a fool. But Christianity has not to do with *opinions*. It is founded on established facts and

Divine truth; and faith based thereon is the heritage of the Church.

-Sir Robert Anderson
(GAM, Preface)

♦ Racism began to run rampant and even infiltrated the Church because of the rejection of God's Word as the authority, and substitution of man's fallible ideas that humans evolved from lower life forms. In other words, man's ideas were granted greater authority than God's Word.

-Bodie Hodge
(TB, pg. 25)

***

Much of religion has substituted its moral compass with worldly philosophies and practices. The moral standard of the Bible has been readjusted to condone abominable lifestyles, compromised to promote a pseudo peace with the world, and done away with truth in the name of benevolence in order to compete with the world.

The world is spinning out of control as many individuals are calling good evil and evil good as people become more lawless, immoral, and insane.

♦ It has long been understood that a civilization whose citizens are not moral or religious cannot be trusted with freedom. It is impossible to make enough rules or pass enough laws to control a citizenry set on immoral behavior.

-David Wilson

♦ The more I see how Christ builds His church around the world today, the more I realize that it is through ordinary, often slow-growing, organic means. Not through great campaigns designed by the best marketing planners North American has to offer, but through lives changed one by one by one.

-Dois I. Rosser Jr.
(GHC, pg. 179)

♦ There are several unholy religions on earth. The Gospel of Christ is the only holy religion. Its root and ground is holiness. A real genuine witness of Jesus is separated from the world— a gazing stock, a holy man.

-B. S. Taylor
(SC, pg. 112)

♦ There is another privation: the loss of *grace*. Our services have so little charm, so little grace.

-Abraham Heschel
(MQG, pg. 50)

♦ It is to the everlasting shame of the church that we have lost sight of Christ the Healer and stand almost in the place of the Pharisees, ridiculing those who have the gift of healing, plainly taught in the New Testament, and almost ascribing the work of God to Beelzebub.

-Vance Havner
(RG, pg. 47)

♦ Today scoffers are often found in churches where the pastor is either a hireling or an entertainer feathering his own nest. These surely have motives that have nothing to do with preaching the gospel of Christ, but rather a social gospel that neither warns of hell or the way to escape it.

-Bob Glaze
Prophetic Observer
(August 2015)

***

The Church in America is spiritually anemic. I dislike making such an observation. But, unfortunately, it is true. What makes it worse is that there are literally millions of people who call themselves Christians, but there is not a hint of "salvation by grace through faith" found in either their testimony or their lives.

Such people are professors of Christ, but not possessors of Christ. In large measure, this condition can be traced to this one reality: Many churches do not teach that to be a "Christian," one must experience redemption.

-Marvin Rosenthal
Zion's Fire
January-February 2016

♦ The Church, always in danger of pollution by the spirit of the world, begins to choose the proffered alternatives in preference to grace, to replace "I believe" with "I feel."

-Elisabeth Elliot
(TGT, pg. 77, 78)

♦ In the end truth will triumph, whether we like it or not. To sound grand and magnanimous by saying, "I accept all religions," is actually to either violate them all or violate reason, or both.

-Ravi Zacharias
(WJ, pg. 101)

♦ Religion, finally, is a question of knowing God. It is not primarily a matter of living, nor is it just a question of a good life or of doing good. No; the essence of religion is to know God.

-Martyn Lloyd-Jones
(SFG, pg.44)

♦ Keep in mind, if a person lives like the devil, the glory of heaven would be foreign to him or her, while the tormenting darkness of hell would be foreign to a saint. It is for this reason every saint must keep in mind that the middle ground of this present, temporary world is to prepare individuals either to enter into the glory of heaven or fall into the abyss of hell.

-RJK

♦ Arians and Socinians and Unitarians, who deny Jesus, have no soul-saving, soul-stirring testimony. When the testimony meetings die, churches become spiritual refrigerators where religion is kept on ice.

-B. S. Taylor
(SC, pg. 108)

♦ An unfortunate reality today is that the consumer-driven church is becoming increasingly hostage to the dictates of the general culture. Moral authority in the pastorate is succumbing to parishioners who vote with their feet…it may be only a matter of time before the church starts to adjust its theology to accommodate this reality.

-Brad O'Leary
(AWC, pg. 95)

♦ The problem is not *how to attract bodies to enter the space of a temple* but *how to inspire souls to enter an hour of spiritual concentration* in the presence of God. The problem is *time,* not *space.*

-Abraham Heschel
(MQG, pg. 52)

♦ The danger of today is that our pulpits and pews shall lose the testimony of the Holy Ghost, the tongue of fire, the witnessing grace which makes prayer meetings places of power and glory by the presence of God.

-B. S. Taylor
(SC, pg. 108)

♦ Power exerts huge influence, and nobody shows more venom in protection or gaining power than those who invoke religion to defend it...Religion breeds convictions; money and power attract envy; conviction without love leads to heinous abuses justified by sacred talk.

-Ravi Zacharias
(WJ, pg. 122-123)

♦ Prophets are a rare breed and an endangered species.

-Michael C. Catt
(RG, pg. 12)

♦ Men do not want to stand behind the Old Gospel, but want to push something that wins the approval, and gets the money out of the philanthropic and worldly man...Not the methods of men, but only the voice of Jesus can make men walk in newness of life as Lazarus walked. "O God, give us more men and women whose very presence among us is a testimony of Jesus only!"

-Paul Rader
(GBM, pg. 171)

♦ Is it not ironic that while people will applaud and admire the sacrifice, discipline, and self-control of the athlete, they are turned off when it is suggested that there should be a comparable dedication on the part of the disciple of the disciplined Christ?

-J. Oswald Sanders
(JJ, pg. 85)

Prayer: *O God, that I might have towards my God, a heart of flame; Towards my fellow-men a heart of love; Towards myself, a heart of steel.*

-J. Oswald Sanders
(JJ, pg. 85)

♦ God has been talked down and reduced, modified, edited, changed and amended until He is not the God that Isaiah saw "high and lifted up."

-A.W. Tozer
(MDP, pg. 18)

♦ When the church feels it must become like the world to win the world, it has not won the world, the world has won it.

-Paul Powell

***

In reference to a powerless gospel that lacks biblical understanding of fundamental doctrines that leave mankind still doomed in their sins, Mary Danielsen made this statement, "Religiously doing good deeds and finding some gnostic happy place through mystical gymnastics is what many believe it means to find God" (HD, pg. 22).

Oswald Chambers pointed out that we all start out as an agnostic. The truth is, it is only when we begin to truly learn of God that our worldly attitude and agnostic understanding is truly transformed by the Spirit of God.

♦ We have a *cheap church* today because everybody is in it. Anybody can get in and nobody gets out. What started as a sheepfold looks more like a zoo! I am speaking of the professing church.

-Vance Havner
(PD, pg. 10)

♦ No duty can be performed without wrestling. The Christian needs his sword as much as his trowel. He wrestles with a body of flesh; [and] this of the Christian in duty is as the east to the traveler, he cannot go his journey without it, and [has] much ado to go with it.

-William Gurnall
(CCA, Vol. 1 pg. 114)

♦ Sadly, where there is little or no persecution or opposition against Christians, many of the conversions fall into "easy believism" category.

-T. A. McMahon
The Berean Call
June 2021

♦ The problem is not with crusades, but with the methods and message of modern evangelism.

-Ray Comfort
(GWP, pg. 79)

The Highest Call

Many people get defensive about the church. It seems that as people begin to address its impact on the world, they are more apt to see what is wrong with it rather than see the good it is doing. However, if a person is being truthful about what is wrong, it is up to believers to humbly examine the concerns to see if they are true and seek God's face.

It is also true that as humans we can be critical and nitpicky about matters, but we must remember, God did not try to hide the sins of Eli's sons, Saul, King David, or the children of Israel. Paul did not downplay his sins and he openly mourned over Demas going back into the world. Unadulterated truth is what addresses the real problems and allows the light of heaven to reveal the answer or way. In fact, if we are honest, the Bible is full of warnings, but how many preachers skip or soft pedal them?

Our great call is to be conformed to the image of Christ. It is His reflection that gives our life substance, credibility and authority. We can put on our best and draw people to ourselves, but we can't save anyone. We can do great works, and yet on judgment day our Lord will deem us as workers of iniquity because we failed to do the will of God. We can talk about our goodness, but in the end be reminded that our best is filthy rags, that there is no good thing that can come from the flesh, and that outside of Christ it will prove to be all vanity or reprobate.

The problem is we often simply get by, rather than overcome and reach our potential to be conformed to the image of Jesus. Overcoming is not an option. It is true that in our culture we can get by in our Christian walk and be content to call it **nominal** Christianity, because at least there is some semblance there. We can get our feet wet in religion and call it **passable** Christianity because there is a bit of experience there. We can have an outward passion and console ourselves regardless of whether there is character to endure and knowledge of righteousness and call it **zealous** Christianity. We may lack vision and heart when it comes to what is excellent but are religious enough that we can call it **acceptable** Christianity; but to share in His glory we must adhere to our high calling and become those who are chosen by God to fulfill the highest calling of all: TO REFLECT THE GLORY OF OUR LORD, Jesus Christ.

Problem with Man

The Nemesis of My Soul

The world is in constant flux, but there are three things that never change: God, man's sinful plight, and the way to salvation. There are various things that attempt to change God: man, theology, philosophies, man's laws, and religion, but the truths about the Lord will stand when all else crumbles before it.

God is immutable and man's plight remains unchangeable unless he has accepted God's incredible solution of His Son's redemption. In fact, man can only digress into the most incredible cesspool of wickedness, where he begins to drown in it while choking on its wickedness as he gropes in the darkness for something to hold onto, something to brace himself against the storm. For the immutable God to change man, he must be born again, his spirit revived, his mind transformed, and his will humbled before Him.

Since God is unchangeable, man can trust that what God has declared is so and believe it. It is called faith towards the One of trustworthy character, and faith enables the believer to begin an incredible journey to discover who God is as he presses toward the life he has been promised. In the process he becomes more aware of how desperate his plight is, how far away he is from the mark of heaven, and that the greatest enemy of his soul is himself.

His flesh is not only the destructive thorn in his side, but his pride attempts to exalts itself over the true God, as his mind strips God of his glory so that man can believe himself to be self-sufficient outside of God.

When will we see the destruction within that which shipwrecks all faith, causing hope to tumble down into a miry pit of depression? We must know that God is the immovable Rock and that all we need to do is believe, humble ourselves, repent, and look up and the Lord is there to pull us out of the miry filth of this present world.

Prayer: *Lord when I discovered that my life was a hopeless cause, that is when I looked up into the heavens to find the solution. Lord, in my brokenness I could hardly keep my head in an upward position, but out of mercy, You lifted me up so I could look into Your loving face. What joy sprung up, what healing balm ran through my soul, and what hope lifted my spirit up to experience Your glorious heights. Amen.*

♦ Man's sense of injustice is a poor analogy to God's sense of injustice. The exploitation of the poor is to us a misdemeanor; to God, it is a disaster. Our reaction is disapproval; God's reaction is something no language can convey.

-Abraham Heschel
(TP, pg. 365)

♦ Uncrucified love runs to inordinate affection and selfish possessiveness which blights rather than blesses.

-Isobel Kuhn
(IA, pg. 112)

♦ In relationship to the new humanistic, anti-God religion that is being instituted at every level, Ken Connor, chairman of the Center for Just Society made this statement, "Thus the classroom, once a forum for critical thought, analysis, and debate that allowed for many competing points of view, is now used to transform raw human material into a homogenous batch of progressive, enlightened, politically correct,

293

intellectually timed, and spiritually vacant progeny, ready to shape tomorrow's world. We must make our stand now before this new religion amasses so many converts that we find ourselves outnumbered, outmaneuvered, and ultimately irrelevant." (AWC, pg. 83)

♦ Pride is the Satanic mother of all impatience. This is Satan's favorite door, at which he comes and knocks more than any other.

-W. B. Godbey
(SC, pg. 26)

♦ Nothing is easier than self-deception; few things are so difficult as real self-disclosure. We may be claiming and even professing the experience of holiness, and yet know nothing of a total death to the carnal or natural life.

-John Gregory Mantle
(BH, pg. 21)

***

Regardless of how people try to deny the existence of God or make God into a mere conjunction of ideas, sentiments, and imaginations, there is no getting around the fact that even the unbelief of the atheist towards God, in essence declares that some God exists.

For example, how can you hold to unbelief towards something if it does not exist in the first place? How can you make it a cause to get rid of something that does not exist? How can you erect a belief system that rejects the essence of a holy, just God if He does not exist?

-RJK

♦ The more we deny reality, the more mindless our solutions become.

-Ravi Zacharias
(WJ, pg. 245)

♦ Many fail because they shrink back from this entire surrender. They wish to serve Jesus with half their heart, and part of themselves, and part of their possessions. To hold back anything from Jesus means a wretched life of stumbling and failure.

-R. A. Torrey
(BT, pg. 17)

♦ It is very contradictory in human nature that men should love themselves above all the rest of the world, and yet never endure to be alone.

-Abraham Cowley
(HA, pg. 56)

Worldliness

Worldliness is a spirit, a temper. It is not so much an act as an attitude. It is a pose, a posture. It is a certain disposition toward God. It is a certain inclination, a certain aspect of the soul. Worldliness is human activity with God left out.

Worldliness is life without heavenly callings, life without ideals, life without heights. Worldliness recognizes nothing of the high calling of God in Christ Jesus...Worldliness is horizontal life...It has ambition; but it has no aspirations. Its motto is success, not holiness.

-Dr. J. H. Jowett
(BH, pg. 53)

Heavenly Treasures

♦ As human beings, we have ever tried to satisfy ourselves by maintaining a quest, a search. We have not forgotten that God *was*. We have only forgotten what God is like.

-A. W. Tozer
(JG, pg. 41)

♦ Moreover, self-pity invariably exaggerates distresses. Molehills are seen as mountains. Trivialities assume tremendous dimensions in this moaning mind…Self-pity steals a man's courage…It disregards the just place of discipline in this mortal life and assumes that we should spend our days upon a bed of roses.

-W. E. Sangster
(HA, pg. 64)

♦ The deviation of the soul from its God-ward course is caused by the presence of sin, and so long as we remain unbelieving concerning our crucifixion with Christ, we shall be alive to its power and therefore not truly alive for God. There are disturbing forces at work in the unsanctified soul which prevent the hearing of God's voice and the doing of God's will.

-John Gregory Mantle
(BH, pg. 100)

♦ It is important that we invest value in time, but live for eternity. Jesus and His Word constantly remind us to be delivered from the tyranny of the immediate.

-Ravi Zacharias
(WJ, pg. 218)

♦ Indifference and worldliness, neglect of duty and any disobedience of the law of Christ—these are bushels that quench the Spirit and spoil our influence.

-Vance Havner
(RG, pg. 216)

♦ Zeal means full of fire. But without knowledge it ends in fanaticism. Knowledge, however, without zeal terminates in formality.

-L. L. Pickett
(SC, pg. 40)

***

Self is not only the seat and habitation, but the very life of sin; the works of the devil are all wrought in *self*; it is his *peculiar worship;* and therefore Christ is not come as a Saviour from sin, as a destroyer of the works of the devil in any of us, but so far as *self* is beaten down and overcome in us.

Christ's life is not, cannot be, within us, but so far as the spirit of the world, self-love, self-esteem, and self-seeking are renounced and driven out of us.

-William Law
(BH, pg. 33)

♦ The old Adam never changes; no medicine can heal the disease, no ointment can mollify the corruption; it can only be got rid of by death.

-John Gregory Mantle
(BH, pg. 49)

♦ Men and women, intrigued by their sin, did not want the revelation of a living, speaking God. They deliberately ignored the only true God, crowded Him out of their lives. In His place they invented gods of their own; birds and animals and reptiles...When a church begins to think impurely and inadequately about God, decline sets in.

-A. W. Tozer
(JG, pgs. 42, 43)

Cultural War

In relationship to the present world that is based on a shallow pop-culture, there is no real moral compass in which to weigh itself. The fact that the modern generation believes comedian Jon Stewart's disrespectable satire of moral and ethical issues serves as a trustworthy pulse to what is true and right, is frightening.

Brad O'Leary, in his book, *America's War on Christianity* makes this statement, "It's a popular culture in which three times more Americans can name a judge for *American Idol* than can name the U.S. chief justice. And it's a culture in which "irreverent" is actually a compliment. (pg. 86)

♦ A biblical movie is a *visual* interpretation…One of the amazing characteristics of visual media is the power of imagery…A movie-generated catharsis may affect a person *experientially,* but it cannot enrich him *spiritually,* nor can it save anyone who is lost.

-T. A. McMahon
The Berean Call

♦ Every man crucifies Christ as often as he gives way to wrath, pride, envy, jealousy, covetousness, disparagement of others, evil-speaking and kindred sins. Every temper and passion that keeps Christ from being fully formed in the soul, is, in the strictest sense of the words, a murderer and killer of the Lord of life.

-John Gregory Mantle
(BH, pg. 34)

♦ Enthusiasm, which is motivated by striving for personal exaltation, seldom raises man beyond the goals he strives for.
-Abraham Heschel
(TP, pg. 409)

♦ What disservice these propagators of metaphysical medicine perform in an effort to peddle their philosophy! They play god and make gods while denying us our essential humanity. They take the pragmatic and make it the total view. They take the ancient and make it a better view.

-Ravi Zacharias
(WJ, pg. 89)

♦ Sadly, since God called out to Adam and Eve, who were hiding from Him in the garden, His call continues to go forth through each generation, but often falls on ears of unbelief. Individuals with a spiritual hearing problem are those walking around in smug arrogance about their own code of righteousness, along with those who are deluded about the worth of their personal decency, or are simply ignorant about God and His Gospel.

-RJK

♦ So men still chase speculations and vain philosophies. And they will not come unto Him that they might have life.

-Vance Havner
(RG, pg. 211)

♦ Not everyone who professes to be a Christian is actually saved. If sin is the dominating power in someone's life, if he or she lives in sin, there is good reason to doubt that person's conversion. He may be a professor but not a possessor. When Christ comes into a life, he makes a difference.

-William MacDonald
(NAG, pg. 88, 89)

♦ The soulish life longs for ease, for indulgence, for display, for wealth, for position, for popularity, and it is recorded as one of the marks of the grievous times that characterize the last days...

-John Gregory Mantle
(BH, pg. 77)

♦ A heart so occupied with love for others is secure against self-pity. Self-pity is begotten by selfishness out of sensitiveness.

-W. E. Sangster
(HA, pg. 66)

♦ "Know thy God" (1 Chron. 28:9) rather than "Know Thyself" is the categorical imperative of the biblical man. There is no self-understanding without God-understanding.

-Abraham Heschel
(TP, pg. 625)

♦ We live in a part of the world that celebrates the three Bs—beauty, brains, and bucks—and the three Ps—power, perfection, and productivity.

-Ellen Vaughn
(GHC, pg. 67)

♦ If fear is your master, then Satan is your god.

-Jeannette Haley

♦ Giving yourself the privilege of destroying other positions while parking your own position in an unidentifiable location is a form of linguistic terrorism.

-Ravi Zacharias
(WJ, pg. 14)

♦ As long as people are uninformed, they can believe anything, and justify everything.

-RJK

♦ Nothing is more needed among Christians than the lesson of the *decreeing self*. It is an ego-centric age, a day of self-sufficiency. The world's creed is "Glorify Yourself,"" Express Yourself." And just as a penny held close to the eye will hide the sun, so does the penny of self, shut out God.

-Vance Havner
(RG, pg. 198)

♦ Rationalism and Ritualism are great enemies of the cross. A gospel which pays court either to man's reason or man's religion will never fail to be popular.

-Sir Robert Anderson
(GAM, pg. 28)

♦ The Scriptures speak of the *seed* of the flesh, the *will* of the flesh, the *mind* of the flesh, the *wisdom* of the flesh, the *purpose* of the flesh, the *confidence* of the flesh, the *filthiness* of the flesh, the *workings* of the flesh, the *warring* of the flesh, the *glorying* of the flesh.

-John Gregory Mantle
(BH, pg. 50)

♦ Sin and lawlessness are convertible terms. Sin is not an arbitrary conception. It is the assertion of the selfish will against a paramount authority.

-Westcott
(BH, pg. 37)

Prayer: *O my God, selfishness is Thy enemy...Grant me grace not to spare this foe, but to permit Thee to wage war upon it. If it hungers may I never feed it; if it thirsts may I never give it to drink. Undertake for me, O my God, and circumcise my heart with Thy two-edged sword, that I may henceforth be Thine and Thine alone.*

-John Gregory Mantle
(BH, pg. 39)

♦ We live in a love-hungry world, and a pity-provoking world.

-W. E. Sangster
(HA, pg. 71)

♦ We forfeit our dignity when abandoning loyalty to what is sacred; our existence dwindles to trifles.

-Abraham Heschel
(MQG, pg. 18)

♦ If we have to hide behind or defend something, rather than stand on it, it is most likely a biased opinion or a falsehood.

-RJK

♦ People yearn for the mystical and the relational. But at the cost of truth and reality? The vortex that suctions a person down the funnel of falsehood is that people are enamored by material success and want to know how they can get a piece of the pie.

-Ravi Zacharias
(WJ, pg. 64)

♦ I care not what street he lives on, what car he drives or the size of his salary. He may belong to "Who's Who" and "What's What," but God has only one yardstick, and he who does not believe on Christ with a living, saving faith—whether rich man, poor man, beggar man or thief—is condemned already.

-Vance Havner
(RG, pg. 197)

♦ The challenge of the platform of small harassments in the Arena—what is it? It is really the gladiatorial struggle with self-pity, a most unglamorous opponent: so unglamorous that he whispers to us, "I am not important? Just let me be." How many times we have lost the fight just because we *have* left self-pity *be*!

-Isobel Kuhn
(IA, pg. 141)

♦ Hate plays strange tricks with memory. It exaggerates the injury. It opposes time's healing touch. It curdles the milk of human kindness. It strangles the kindlier impulses of nature. It gives one a jaundiced outlook on life until one is shunned by others as a bitter and cynical soul. The men who have lived for naught but vengeance, have made no contribution to the good of humankind.

-W. E. Sangster
(HA, pg. 75)

♦ Racism is Satanism, unmitigated evil. . .You cannot worship God and at the same time look at man as if he were a horse.

-Abraham Heschel
(MQG)

♦ Sin is a state of departure from God, a spending state, a wanting state. The famine always follows the far country.

-Vance Havner
(RG, pg. 172)

♦ (Example of a deadly combination): The best of Western technological advances combined with the best of Eastern ancient divinizing techniques made for the inception of a *nirvanic* world where we could become the new *avatars.*

-Ravi Zacharias
(WJ, pg. 12)

Preference

One of the reasons people prefer the darkness of delusion is the aversion that man's pride has towards being wrong about something. Pride is the last abyss of man that is usually confronted.

It can be found in every layer of the fallen condition from perception (arrogance), emotions (haughtiness), personal standards (elitism), personal intelligence (skepticism), and moral rightness (judgmentalism), to religion (self-righteousness). It can cleverly disguise itself in the forms of fake nobility and self-pity.

Pride represents the big empty dark space between the heart that must be humbled, convicted, and made anew and whole by God's Spirit, and the mind that must be reasoned with according to God's Word and transformed by the truth of His Spirit. It is pride that makes man unmanageable in his mind, undisciplined in his emotions, unyielding in his will, and unruly in his ways.

♦ Man's philosophy, man's power, man's religion—behold their work, the Christ of God upon a gallows!

-Sir Robert Anderson
(GAM, pg. 26)

♦ Oh, how fickle we human beings are! How self-centered and self-serving we can prove to be. It is true; at the door of every unbroken and unrepentant man lays incredible treachery against God.

-RJK

♦ It never does pay to spoil the beauty of character by the love of gold. Money is only a "thing." not all the gold in the world is worth one soul.

-W. E. Sangster
(HA, pg. 101)

♦ Words ceased to be commitments. Our sensitivity to their power is being constantly reduced. And bitter is the fate of those who forfeit completely the sense for their weight, for words when abused take vengeance on the abusers.

-Abraham Heschel
(MQG, pg. 25)

♦ Men pride themselves on business shrewdness and clever management and fail to receive eternal life. Any man who lets Jesus pass by is a fool, however he rates at the bank.

-Vance Havner
(RG, pg. 165)

♦ Action that is clearly right needs no justification.

-Elisabeth Elliot
(TGT, pg. 88)

♦ When we are at the peak of success, we may lead other people to believe that we are God. When we say good-bye, we know we are not.

-Ravi Zacharias
(WJ, pg. 81)

Wicked Systems

We see that for the last five to six decades, certain factions have attempted to strip America of her spiritual foundation, rip from her any real moral compass, and erect a false heretical light by throwing God out of every arena. The halls of justice are now made up of a cesspool of judges who have established oppressive laws and policies, and replaced morality with immorality in light of political correctness.

We see an educational system that is in the business of indoctrinating and not educating. We see a religious system which adheres to worldly philosophies and humanistic gospels. The institution of family has been exploited by those who want to feel good about preferences and lifestyles that have been clearly deemed as abominable by God's Word and cited as already having been judged and condemned by the courts of heaven.

These systems declare they are progressive as far as moving society forward, but it is a lie. It is regressive in the way that it moves the masses towards the abyss while moving the few elites into greater delusion, where greater damnation will take place.

Let us as believers ensure we are standing on the right side of eternity.

♦ We dwell on the edge of mystery and ignore it, wasting our souls, risking our stake in God. We constantly pour our inner light away from Him, setting up the thick screen of self between Him and us, adding more shadows to the darkness that already hovers between Him and our wayward reason.

-Abraham Heschel
(MQG, pg. 4)

♦ It is hard to tell the truth about people we do not like and almost impossible when we envy them. Our little innuendoes and tainted hints will not deceive other people, for they will see the envy in our soul, but they deceive ourselves. Prejudice impairs our judgment and poisons our feeling, and peace and happiness fade out of our life.

-W. E. Sangster
(HA, pg. 113)

♦ Any man is a troublemaker in the church, in the nation, or in the home when he has forsaken the commandment of the Lord.

-Paul Rader
(GBM, pg. 132)

♦ You can't make peace with a wolf if he wants you for dinner.

-Jeannette Haley

♦ The current popular notion that judging others is in itself a sin leads to such inappropriate maxims as "I'm o.k. and you're o.k." It encourages a conspiracy of moral indifference which says "If you never tell me that anything I'm doing is wrong, I'll never tell you that anything you're doing is wrong."

-Elisabeth Elliot
(TGT, pg. 71)

♦ What is it about us that we constantly seek answers? What lies beneath the physical? In country music it is always about a broken vow; in the world of stories it is invariably about a broken world. Where do we go to be mended?

-Ravi Zacharias
(WJ, pg. 7)

♦ Sin has been glossed over; men do not regard themselves sinners and consequently feel no burden of guilt and, of course, no relief in His pardon.

-Vance Havner
(RG, pg. 153)

♦ The doctrine of Agnosticism claims that prayer is rooted in superstition. It is "one of humanity's greatest mistakes," "a desperate effort of bewildered creatures to come to terms with surrounding mystery."

-Abraham Heschel
(MQG, pg. 53)

♦ Disappointed, broken-hearted people I meet everywhere. They are people who always have the blues, because they have so many desires. They cannot all be attained, and therefore their lives are blasted, and life becomes so thin that there is no sturdiness, no real growth, no comeliness or completeness, because of the little cheap desires that are growing in the heart.

-Paul Rader
(GBM, pg. 96)

♦ Such is the immense power of the imagination when it intersects with reality. This is actually how cultures are shaped.

-Ravi Zacharias
(WJ, pg. 5)

♦ There is much shallow repentance today because men have such a shallow sense of sin.

-Vance Havner
(RG, pg. 152)

♦ For many who believe that Christ died for their sins, this event is more mystical than historical...They have imagined that the death of Christ in their place delivered them from their deserved eternal punishment in hell, so that, like Barabbas, they could live as they pleased.

-Dave Hunt
The Berean Call
August 2015

♦ I am more afraid of my own heart than of the Pope and all his cardinals. I have within me that great Pope, Self.

-Martin Luther
(BH, pg. 32)

♦ Pride is a deadly sin; indeed, there is some evidence for believing that it is the most deadly of all the deadly sins.

-W. E. Sangster
(HA, pg. 131)

♦ The most important problem which a human being must face daily is: How to maintain one's integrity in a world where power, success and money are valued above all else? How to remain clean amidst the mud of falsehood and malice that soil our society?

-Abraham Heschel
(MQG, pg. 98)

♦ Of all fools the conceited fool is the worst. Pride makes a man incapable of receiving counsel.

-William Gurnall
(CCA, Vol. 2, pg. 27)

♦ Most men's memories are very treacherous, especially in good things; few men's memories are a holy ark, a heavenly storehouse for their souls.

-Thomas Brooks
(MSR, Dedicatory)

♦ When asked what we, as regular people, can do to prevent sex trafficking, a Minneapolis police officer who works with both victims and perpetrators on a daily basis had only one response: "We need to reinvent what it means to be a man in our society."

♦ It is rather odd that it is necessary to state it, but man's place in the universe is that of a creature.

-W. E. Sangster
(HA, pg. 132)

♦ We have trifled with the name of God. We have taken the ideals in vain. We have called for the Lord. He came. And was ignored. We have preached but eluded Him. We have praised but defied Him.

-Abraham Heschel
(MQG, pg. 148)

♦ Nobody, you see, is a Christian without realizing the immensity and greatness of life, and no one comes to realize that, of course, without thinking. The trouble with all of us, in this world, is that we tend to be absorbed in life, and life sees to it that we never are given a moment to think and to meditate and to ponder.

-Martyn Lloyd-Jones
(SFG, pg.47)

♦ When men refuse to heed the commandments of God and depart from His will and purpose for their lives, then their knowledge and intelligence lead to their own destruction.

-Dr. Noah Hutchings
(GMM, pg. 67)

- There is no mastering of a sinner while unbelief is in power.
>   -William Gurnall
>   (CCA, Vol. 2, pg. 23)

- The deceitful heart finds its friendliest friend in a psychologized gospel, where the sinful nature of man is given free reign and where sinful speaking can be expressed without restriction, questions, or proof.
>   -Dr. Martin & Deidre Bobgan & T.A. McMahon
>   The Berean Call
>   January 2018

- Unabated fantasy proves tormenting, while fantasy played out in reality usually turns into a tormenting nightmare.
>   -RJK

- Often we think that if Jesus were among us today working such miracles, men would believe—but not so. Skeptics would offer their explanations, the magicians would produce their counterfeits, and sinful men would go on their way, loving darkness rather than light.
>   -Vance Havner
>   (RG, pg.149)

- How is it that a culture that once frowned upon certain sexual practices now frowns upon those who frown upon them?
>   -Ravi Zacharias
>   (WJ, pg. XII)

- Self-realization has its counterpart in humanistic psychology where it is termed "self-actualization." ...Psychological concepts and practices can never change an individual's sin nature. Furthermore, the biblical teaching about sin is antithetical as well as offensive to psychological counseling.

-T.A. McMahon
The Berean Call
March 2015

♦ To search out and sort out and "hang out" all the whys and wherefores of what we call our problems (a few of which just might be plain sins) may be one route to the healing of certain kinds of human difficulties, but I suggest that it may be the longest way home.

-Elisabeth Elliot
(TGT, pg. 66)

♦ But is more than a disease. It is a deformity of the spirit, an abnormality in that part of human nature which is most like God's. And sin is a capital crime as well. It is treason against the great God Almighty who made the heavens and the earth. Sin is a crime against the moral order of the universe.

-A. W. Tozer
(JG, pg. 75)

♦ Most sins spring up in the soil of sin, but pride has this peculiarity that is propagates itself in the soil of virtue too. It seduces men and women who are nigh to being saints. It can insinuate itself into the holy places, and catch people out on their knees.

-W. E. Sangster
(HA, pg. 135)

♦ Man's sin is apt to rise with outward prosperity. In the winter, men gird their clothes close about them—but in the summer they let them hang loose. In the *winter of adversity*, many a Christian girds his heart close to God, to Christ, to gospel, to godliness, to ordinances, to duties, etc., who in the *summer of mercy* hangs loose from all.

-Thomas Brooks
(MSR, pg. 99)

♦ First we practice sin, then defend it, then boast of it.

-Thomas Manton
(SWR, pg. 20)

Interesting Admission

Atheist Richard Dawkins surprised other Christians by noting that Christianity was losing its influence for good in the world, creating a vacuum that was giving rise to increasing wickedness. He perceived that the fear of God by those who do believe in a Creator as a welcome deterrent against evil and that once they lose such fear it will give "people a license to do really bad things.

His concerns were valid and we can clearly see evil running amuck in our homes, churches and societies. In our homes it is called rebellion, in our churches it is known as sin, and in our societies, it is called lawlessness.

It is sad to think this admission came from an atheist instead of a broken, repentant church that is aware that it is losing its edge, authority and testimony in this world.

♦ The soul is an active creature. Either it must be employed by us, or it will employ us, though to little purpose.

-William Gurmall
(CCA, Vol. 2, pg. 324)

♦ We do not expect all truth from a teacher; we do not expect all faithfulness from our politicians; and we quickly forgive them when they lie to us, and vote for them again. We do not expect honesty from the merchants, and we do not expect complete trustworthiness from anyone.

-A.W. Tozer
(MDP, pg. 141)

♦ We may feel capable, but we need to have a continuous sense of inadequacy, remember, "I can't do it. The Lord is the one to do it."

-Dr. K.P. Yohannan
GFA World Magazine

♦ Modern man no longer knows how to encounter reality face to face. To him the world of reality is known only through graphs and charts, tools and signs. A wide stream of human callousness separates us from the realm of holiness.

-Abraham Heschel
(MQG, pg. 114)

***

When we stereotype male and female behavior, we alienate those who don't fit; when we stereotype their skill sets, we rob industries, governments, and the church of the diversity they need to flourish.

When we force men and woman into roles based on their sex, we put marriages at risk before they start. When we insist on patriarchy in church leadership, we disfigure the body of Christ.

-Tim Krueger
Editor
Mutuality Magazine

♦ It is imperative that the imagination be healthy, and the thought stream filtered. Success here ensures success all round.

-W. E. Sangster
(HA, pg. 147)

♦ There are three possible lives open to every man's choice: a bad life, in which selfishness or passion or both, either refined or coarse, rule; a good, true, natural life; and a Father-pleasing life.

-Samuel Dickey Gordon
(QT, pg. 27)

♦ We are fallen in all the ways that men can fall, being what they are, and we are all born into a tainted world. We learn from the cradle on to adjust to this. We nurse it in with our mother's milk; we breathe it in the very air. Our education deepens it and our experience confirms it. Evil impurities are everywhere, and everything is dirty.

-A.W. Tozer
(MDP, pg. 141)

♦ Men neglect what they should do, and then are easily persuaded to meddle with what they have nothing to do with.

-William Gurnall
(CCA, Vol. 1, pg. 284)

***

In a world of despair and destruction there is much one can murmur about but according to Thomas Brooks, it is the mother-sin and the first born of the devil. It shows ingratitude, embitters the soul against all mercies, and provokes God to either afflict or destroy.

Murmuring cuts the throat of mercy and stabs all mercies in the heart, setting all mercies to bleed about on a cold, lifeless ground. (MSR, pgs. 70-74)

♦ The moral is that civilization is nowhere and never secure. It is a thin cake of custom overlying a molten mass of wickedness that is always boiling up for an opportunity to burst out.

-Dr. Arnold Toynbee
(ILT, pg. 80)

♦ Pigs need to wallow in mire because they crave the slime to cool their flesh. So it is with the false convert. He never repented, so his flesh is not dead with Christ. It is instead burning with unlawful desire.

-Ray Comfort
(GWP, pg. 86)

***

The extraordinary emphasis on *self* is the common denominator. Eastern mysticism and psychology are two peas in the same pod of self. The supreme goal of Hinduism, Buddhism, and other variants of Eastern mysticism is *self-realization,* i.e., to realize one's ultimate destiny, which is godhood.

Self-actualization is psychology's counterpart, having as its goal "self-fulfillment," i.e., realizing one's self-potential, which leads to self-deification. Neither is scientific; both are *religious* aspirations.

-T.A. McMahon
The Berean Call
December 2919

♦ None find less sweetness and more dissatisfaction in these things, than those who strive most to please themselves with them.

-William Gurnall
(CCA, Vol. 1, pg. 227)

♦ If developments over the last few years in Europe and America are any indicator of what will come about, those who do not wholeheartedly embrace same-sex "marriage" will be: sued, fired, threatened with physical harm, their business boycotted, called names, driven out of the military, considered mean and hateful, singled out for auditing by the IRS and, if they pastor a local church, have their sermons censored.

-Larry Spargimino
Prophetic Observer
August 2015

♦ Introspection is like quicksand: The more you struggle with yourself, the faster you go down.

-K. P. Youhannan

♦ Self-deification attained through sacred rites is found throughout the religions of the East. The Dalai Lama's Tibetan Buddhism teaches initiation rituals to enable one to become a *bodhisattva* or enlightened deity. Shintoism, which is the primary religion of Japan, involves numerous self-purification ceremonies that open the way for followers to become *kami or ancestral gods.*

-T.A. McMahon
The Berean Call
March 2015

♦ People are self-centered instead of God-centered. Their frame of reference is all wrong. Their philosophy, values, and deeds are all directed toward self-gratification and contrary to their Creator and the purpose for which they were created.

-Marvin Rosenthal
Zion's Fire Magazine
Jul/Aug. 2015

♦ As long as you treat God as if He were a man Who cannot look behind your thoughts, read the secret things of your heart, and show you things about yourself that you never even knew of, you will make no progress spiritually.

-Paul Rader
(GBM, pg. 91)

♦ Where God is unacknowledged, the mind is void of judgment. Where God is not worshipped, the heart of man becomes a ruin. The chambers of that dilapidated heart are haunted by places of the reprobate mind and are tenanted by vile lusts and noxious passions, like vermin and reptiles from which we turn with disgust in open daylight.

-Charles Spurgeon
(FJ, pg. 21)

♦ Men judge of sin by its results; and their estimate of its results is coloured by their own interests. But all such conceptions of sin are inadequate.

-Sir Robert Anderson
(RT, pg. 15)

♦ The central concept of multiculturalism is the assertion that there are many versions of truth and no one system of thinking is the "Truth." ...Socialism and multiculturalism need children who have been dependent upon state services from an early age...The fight to save our Christian heritage from not only being expunged from our current lives, but also whitewashed from the history books, begins with teaching our children the truth.

-Brad O'Leary
(AWC, pg. 138, 150)

♦ The spirit that dominates human life everywhere is a spirit of independence.

-Samuel Dickey Gordon
(QT, pg. 22)

♦ It is a great folly to cast your sins upon Satan who tempted you, or upon your neighbor who provoked you; but it is a far greater sin, nay horrid blasphemy, to cast it upon God Himself.

A greater affront than this cannot be offered to the infinite holiness of God.

-Thomas Boston
(SWR, pg. 21)

♦ A man ought to look upon himself as obliged to act in three capacities: as a prophet, to instruct; as a priest, to pray for and with; as a king, to govern, direct and provide for them. (His children).

-George Whitefield
(SWR, pg. 39)

♦ Anticipation is always greater than realization.

-Jeannette Haley

♦ We insanely run at Hell as though it were Heaven, and reject Heaven as though it were Hell itself.

-Ray Comfort
(GWP, pg. 57)

♦ *Forsaken* is surely one of the most tragic words in our language, for is it not the moan of a broken heart? To be *left* is sad enough, but to be *forsaken* is the crown of sorrow.

-Herbert Lockyer
(MM, pg. 60)

♦ A wide stream of human callousness separates us from the realm of holiness.

-Abraham Heschel
(MQG, pg. 112)

The Brocken

Many of our fears have no basis in reality. They are the homemade products of overanxious hearts and as unsubstantial as the Specter on the Brocken. The Brocken is the highest point of the Hartz Mountains in Germany.

For centuries it was a place of dread because of the giant who lived upon its top…The ghostly and terrifying specter which the traveler sees upon the sky is nothing but a magnified and distorted image of himself. He trembles at his own reflection.

-W. E. Sangster
(HA, pgs. 31, 32)

♦ Peter followed first from Galilee in much self-sufficiency; he had to come to the end of himself before at Tiberias, he reached the second "follow Me" (John 21:19). The first time he forsook his nets; the second time he forsook himself. We cannot truly follow our Lord until "afterwards"—after we have been broken in self and have come to Tiberias.

-Vance Havner
(RG, pg. 97)

♦ Our inability to focus or stay the course is reflected in our spirituality in America. It is amazing how jelly-like it is, how it shifts and shapes itself to the individual as truth is remade in his or her image.

-Ravi Zacharias
(WJ, pg. 232-233)

♦ When people turn their back on God, it does not take long to start deviating in many areas, including idolatry.

-Bodie Hodge
(TB, pg. 54)

+ The family is the base of every culture, society, and nation. The family is the brick that holds the entire structure together. If the roof leaks, it can be fixed. If the windows break, they can be replaced. If the bricks crumble, the entire home is lost.

-Dr. Noah Hutchings
(GMM, pg. 43)

+ Authority and power walk hand in hand. For this reason, people who overstep their authority will begin to operate in abusive power that creates chaos, eventually ending in their destruction.

-RJK

+ The reason they cannot believe the doctrine of sin is because they do not know God; it is because they do not understand who and what God is...We are all on very good terms with ourselves, and we can always put up a good case for ourselves. Even if we try to make ourselves feel that we are sinners, we will never do it. There is only one way to know that we are sinners, and that is to have some dim, glimmering conception of God.

-Martyn Lloyd-Jones
(SFG, pg. 34)

+ In these days men have left off faith. The spirit of the martyrs is not in them. Opinions have taken the place of convictions; and the result is liberality which is the offspring, not of humility and love, but of indifference or doubt.

-Sir Robert Anderson
(GAM, Preface)

+ People can twist the sovereignty of God to teach fatalism: what is going to be, is going to be; and there's nothing you can do about it...Sad to say, it is impossible to use the grace of God as an excuse for careless living, for believers to use their freedom as a pretext for launching into all kinds of indulgence.

-William MacDonald
(NAG, pg. 71)

♦ Hypocrisy doubles all the crimes it covers.

-W. E. Sangster
(HA, pg. 177)

♦ Wherever a believer holds to a fleshly, personal right, that is where he or she will remain immature and inexperienced in his or her Christian walk.

-RJK

***

'Twas a sheep, not a lamb that strayed away,
In the parable Jesus told.
A grown-up sheep that had gone astray
From ninety and nine in the fold.

Out on the hillside, out in the cold,
'Twas a sheep that the Good Shepherd sought.
And back to the flock, safe into the fold.
'Twas a sheep the Good Shepherd brought.

And why for the sheep should we earnestly long
And earnestly hope and pray?
Because there is danger if they go wrong.
They may lead the lambs astray.

For the lambs will follow the sheep, you know,
Wherever they sheep may stray.

When the sheep go wrong, it will not be long
'til the lambs are as wrong as they.

And so with the sheep we earnestly plead.
For the sake of the lambs today.
If the lambs are lost, what a terrible cost
Some sheep will have to pay!

-Unknown

♦ This is the day of the common man. We have not only become common, but we have also succeeded in dragging God down to our mediocre level. What is desperately needed today is an elevated concept of God.

-A.W. Tozer
(MDP, pg. 101)

♦ God sent His prophets of old to point us forward, and sent His Son to fulfill what has been declared in the past, and now the Son sends us forth to point upward to what is yet to come.

-RJK

♦ Our opinions have nothing backing them except our high opinions of self.

-Unknown

♦ Poverty doesn't cause instability. Envy does.

-Tucker Carlson
(SOF, pg. 8)

***

We asked a young agnostic lady what did she believe in. She stated that she believed in science. Abraham Heschel pointed out that no matter what we hide our unbelief in, it will in due time fail

323

us and leave us stranded to quickly find either some other veneer to hide behind or some culprit to blame.

Heschel pointed out that people started to suspect that science is a device for exploitation; parliaments pulpits for hypocrisy, and religion a pretext for a bad conscience. He maintained that in the tantalized souls of those who had faith in ideals, suspicion became a dogma and contempt the only solace.

He went on to say, "Mistaking the abortions of their conscience for intellectual heroism, many thinkers employ clever pens to scold and to scorn the reverence for life, the awe for truth, the loyalty to justice. Man, about to hang himself, discovers it is easier to hang others." (MQG, pg. 149, 158)

♦ The last degree of poverty is to be a pauper. Now, the simple truth is that we are all—every last man of us—paupers in everything.

-Samuel Dickey Gordon
(QT, pg. 24)

♦ Now a carnal heart is clean contrary, his zeal is for the world, and his indifference in the things of God; he prays as if he did not pray, etc., he sweats in his shop, but ills and grows cold in his closet.

-William Gurnall
(CCA, Vol. 1 pg. 221)

♦ A truly noble soul will sooner part with all, than the peace of a good conscience.

-Thomas Brooks
(MSR, pg. 53)

♦ We cannot build a highway for God amidst the shanties and hovels of carnality.

-Vance Havner
(ILT, pg. 56)

- Sin is the dare of God's justice, the rape of His mercy, the jeer of His patience, the slight of His power, and the contempt of His love.

-John Bunyan
(NAG, pg. 79)

- When one resorts to taking the low road, he or she will ultimately miss the high road, and fall into ruin.

-RJK

BITS & PIECES

A Mosaic

Life is a mosaic, made up of bits of history and pieces of happenings left behind each day. We juggle to understand the bits of information we gather along the way and wrestle to get by events that disrupt our world and throw it into some chaos.

In the past I have tried to take the bits and use them as stepping stones, while trying to put together a comprehensible picture of the pieces of my life that will give me some gauge as to where I am in my walk with the Lord.

There are times I must let the bits remain and the pieces left about until the Lord brings them together for me. So many times, after He has put certain bits and pieces together, I realize it is a mirror and as He raises it up, I see a bit more of the reflection of His Son in what I thought was a fragmented mosaic.

As I have stated many times, "It is not what you do for God that counts; rather, it is what you allow God to do in and through You." It is the revelation of Christ's life in you that causes the chaotic mosaic to come together, revealing a masterpiece that only the great Creator could have mastered.

♦ Light your lights—because the Babe born in Bethlehem is the Light of the world. Give your gifts to loved ones and friends—because at Christmas God gave us the greatest Gift. Sing your carols—because angels announced the birth of the Son of God with singing and praise.

-Marvin Rosenthal

♦ Right is right, even if everyone is against it, and wrong is wrong, even if everyone is for it.

-William Penn

♦ To us the world is like an eye. The white is everything else. The iris is Israel, Land of the Jews. And the pupil, it is, of course, the Holy City, Jerusalem. But the gleam in the center of the pupil—that gleam is Moriah, the Temple Mount.

-Jewish Rabbi

♦ Christ is the root, and Israel is the olive tree. In other words: Jesus is not here because of Israel, but Israel exists for the sake of Christ. He is the center; He is the zenith to which all Israel's privileges as listed in Romans 9:4-5 are oriented.

-Johannes Pflaum
News From Israel
January 2020

♦ I like your Christ, I do not like your Christians. Your Christians are so unlike your Christ.

-Ghandi

♦ There are 126,000 abortions every day worldwide, and forty-six million annually.

-Happy Ending Magazine

♦ One third of all American pastors who responded to a *Christianity Today* poll admitted to being addicted to internet pornography.

♦ There is a cruelty which pardons, just as there is a pity which punishes. Severity must tame whom love cannot win.

-Abraham Heschel
(TP, pg. 380)

♦ The point is that we never learn from history and that wars have always been the status quo to solve our differences.

-Dr. Bob Glaze

The Truth of A Matter

First of all I want to tell you a story about four people named, EVERYBODY, SOMEBODY, ANYBODY and NOBODY. There was an important job to be done and EVERYBODY was asked to do it. EVERYBODY was sure SOMEBODY would do it, ANYBODY could have done it, but NOBODY did it.

SOMEBODY got very angry about that, because it was EVERYBODY'S job. EVERYBODY thought ANYBODY would do it, but NOBODY realized that EVERYBODY wouldn't do it. It ended up that EVERYBODY blamed SOMEBODY, when NOBODY did what ANYBODY could have done.

♦ When science no longer requires evidence and no longer tolerates scrutiny, it's no longer science. It's dogma.

-Tucker Carlson
(SOF, pg. 235)

- The world has its experts and prophets but the Heavenly Hieroglyphics are too much for them and "if all the wiseacres of earth today were laid in a row they never would reach a conclusion."

-Vance Havner
(RTR, pg. 61)

- If you don't take an interest in the affairs of your government, then you are doomed to live under the rule of fools.

-Plato

- We would rather compromise, bend, hold back on doing the right thing than doing the right thing. We hope problems would go away, and we have adjusted to the fact that they usually don't.

-Pastor Larry Spargimino
Prophetic Observe
August 2020

- 'Evil' and 'unthankful' are the twins that live and die together. As any ceaseth to be evil, he begins to be thankful.

-William Gurnall
(CCA, Vol. 2 pg. 465)

- One must not forget the ancient maxim, "the best medicament is silence. The more you praise a flawless pearl, the more you depreciate it." (MQG, pg. 43)

***

The Extra Mile

They say you will never be lonely,
From the start of each day to its end,

If you walk life's path with God in your heart
And side by side with a friend.

-Unknown

♦ A strong 58 percent majority of Americans say that belief in God is necessary to be moral. Only 6 percent of the national news media share this same belief...The mainstream media believes that America must be delivered from Christianity for the good of us all. They're not about to let profits get in the way of their ideology (no matter how much financial base they lose or how unpopular it proves to be). (Parentheses added.)
-Brad O'Leary
(AWC, pg. 100, 111)

♦ Satan is always waylaying a *loaded* craft. But the very fact that he is after us shows that he has not got us.
-Seth C. Rees
(SC, pg. 120)

♦ People will risk more when they think they will be in control in the end.

-RJK

♦ A word uttered without the fear and love of God does not rise to heaven.

-Abraham Heschel
(MQG, pg. 84)

♦ America and Europe have been blessed with Christian testimony, from the revivals of colonial America to the martyrs in Europe who pressed for a return to New Testament Christianity. But their voices have now been silenced. Hence, apart from revival, only defeat remains. Apart from God's help the West shall go into oblivion with but a whimper.

-Larry Spargimino
Prophetic Observer
December 2015

Thanksgiving Observance

Count your blessings instead of your crosses.
Count your gains instead of your losses.
Count your joys instead of your woes.
Count your friends instead of your foes.
Count your smiles instead of your tears.
Count your courage instead of your fears.
Count your full years instead of your lean ones.
Count your kind deeds instead of your mean ones.
Count your health instead of your wealth.
Count your God instead of yourself.

-Author Unknown

♦ Love precedes discipline.

-John Owens
(SWR, pg. 14)

♦ A pessimist sees the difficulty in every opportunity; an optimist sees the opportunity in every difficulty.

-Winston Churchill

♦ There will come a day where you will cry out for enforcement of the law. There will come a day where you will long for the law to be the foundation of this Republic. So, you be careful what you do with the law today. Because if you weaken it today, you weaken it, forever.

-Trey Gowdy

♦ The Law can only chase a man to Calvary, no further.

-D.L. Moody
(GWP, pg. 47)

♦ The problem with Socialism is that you eventually run out of other people's money.

-Margaret Thatcher

♦ The way to peace is never in retreat. A cancerous tumor needs to be removed. If not, it will destroy the entire body.

-Pastor Larry Spargimino
Prophetic Observe
August 2020

♦ Hypocrisy is a lie with a fair cover over it. An insincere heart is a half heart.

-William Gurnall
(CCA, Vol. 1 pg. 317)

♦ We all know that there are 60 seconds in a minute but a "second" did not become a base unit until the 1800s. It was in 1967 that the precise definition of a second was finally settled. This agreement had to do with the cyclical changes that occur inside a cesium atom when it experiences a certain temperature. The pace of that atomic change is a precise second. (HD, pg. 78)

Communism

I grew up under the ominous threat of Communism. It was the great enemy of freedom, the humanistic religious and philosophical cancer of the day that seemed bent on invading everything. Since then, much has happened including the break-up of the Soviet Union, but Communism is still alive and well. The warnings and concerns remain valid and we must not forget its agenda of total control, and that at the heart of it, tyranny rules because it instills fear with bullying techniques, persecution, and death.

Communism starts out with the idea of **Progressiveness** of going forward but it simply means they are going to be more progressive in getting all of your money through taxes. Then they promote **Socialism** where they push the philosophy that all is equal but they do not tell you it means everyone except the elite will be equally poor regardless of whether someone possesses some type of exceptionalism in a field. As more and more people submit their freedoms for some cause or crises the country will eventually give way to **Nazism** where big corporations are used to dictate to the people while the spirit of entrepreneur and the middle class are done away with, or **Communist,** where the government of a few rules all with an iron fist.

Author Ayn Rand pointed out some simple truths in one of her writings, "There is no difference between Communism and Socialism, except in the same ultimate end: Communism proposes to enslave men by force, Socialism—by the vote. It is merely the difference between murder and suicide."

Ronald Reagan made this statement, "Socialism only works in two places: Heaven where they don't need it and hell where they already have it."

Author Mary Danielsen made this notation about any government that wants total control and say over people, "In order for sovereign humans with free will to be enslaved by a sovereign government, they must surrender themselves to the totalitarian entity, freely and forcibly" (HD, pg. 60).

Vance Havner stated, "There is a weird and sinister movement of the powers of darkness all over the world today...Part of this movement is communism; part of it is paganism; part of it is demonism. Sometimes it wears the robes of religion to deceive, if possible, the very elect and to enlist the support of all clergymen who don't know what time it is" (ILT, pg. 21).

According to *The Black Book of Communism*, "Communist regimes turned mass crime into a full-blown system of government." Communism is Satan's religion, humanism his manifesto, and political correctness his philosophy. The communists are ruthless, godless and void of any real conscience.

In Rudolph Rummel's book, *Death by Government,* he claims that 110 million people were killed by communism from 1900 to 1987. According to Steven Rosefielde in his book *Red Holocaust* the 20th century proved that communism is a failed experiment, and that it needlessly killed approximately 60 million people and perhaps tens of millions more. Life is cheap and that is why Mao admitted that the death of 300 million people by nuclear war was no big deal. (Information in paragraph taken from article by Larry Spargimino in the Prophetic Observer, September 2021.)

Today we are allies with the international Communist countries of Russia and China to bring down the wickedness of the satanic beliefs and practices of the elite Cabal that has been trying to take over the world. Whether it is Communism or freedom-loving countries, neither want to concede their sovereignty or freedom to foreign tyrants, but we must remember the leopard can't change its spots, the Zebra can't do away with its stripes, and the snake his ways. Freedom will always be on a collision course with Communism, darkness will always try to overtake the light, and wrong will be expounded as being right when evil gains the reins of nations. Thankfully, all opposing sides will be silent when Jesus reigns as King of kings from His throne in Jerusalem.

Heavenly Treasures

♦ The human race is being collectivized and homogenized into one faceless mass, one world religion, and one world government.

-Vance Havner
(ILT, pg. 22)

♦ Free speech is the enemy of authoritarian rule. That's why the Framers put it at the top of the Bill of Rights. That's also why our ruling class seeks to crush it.

-Tucker Carlson
(SOF, pg. 121)

♦ When the debate is lost, slander becomes the tool of the losers.

-Socrates

♦ We the people are the rightful masters of both Congress and the courts, not to overthrow the Constitution, but to overthrow the men who pervert the Constitution.

-Abraham Lincoln

♦ The world will not be destroyed by those who do evil, but by those who watch them without doing anything.

-Albert Einstein

♦ In the free world, we have the luxury of speaking about communism as a philosophy. But wherever the Communists are in power, there is no philosophy. It is cruel dictatorship.

-Sabrina Wurmbrand
1980 Message

♦ The world's true man is he that will not wrong man.

-William Gurnall
(CCA, Vol. 1 pg. 323)

♦ Nations do not die from invasion; they die from internal rottenness.

-Abraham Lincoln

♦ Reputation is what people think you are. Character has more to do with what you know you are.

-Marvin J. Rosenthal
Zion's Fire
January-February 2018

♦ I would unite with anybody to do right and with nobody to do wrong.

-Frederick Douglass
(TC, pg. 53)

No Longer Hidden

As two Polish gentile women were dividing the spoils of a large, expensive coat they had roughly taken from a Jewish woman on her way to the Nazi killing centers, they found a secret pocket and hidden inside was a tiny baby girl.

Taken back by their discovery, one woman took pity on the child and since she did not have any children and was too old to do so, she was willing to trade any gold and silver for the child. Her husband was delighted when she brough the child home and they raised her as their own without telling her of her origins.

The girl excelled in her studies and became a doctor, working as a pediatrician in a hospital in Poland. When her mother passed away many years later, a visitor came to pay her respects.

The old woman invited herself in. It was clear she had a mission as she proceeded to tell the young woman about her real origins. At first, the young woman didn't believe her, but the old woman's insistence was backed up by the information that she shared with her that as a baby she was wearing a beautiful gold pendant with strange writing on it, which was Hebrew. The older woman encouraged the younger one to go check it out for herself.

Sure enough, she found the pendant in her deceased mother's jewelry box. She was surprised and struggled with comprehending her Jewish roots, but the proof was there and she realized that it was a connection to the past. From that point on she cherished the necklace and even enlarged it so she could wear it around her neck.

The young woman eventually traveled to Israel and made the necessary contacts in order to find out that the writing on the necklace was Hebrew. She was eventually encouraged to stay on in Israel and work at the hospital. In time, she met her husband there and raised a family.

On August 2001, there was a terrorist attack on a cafe in the center of Jerusalem. The injured were rushed to her hospital. An elderly man was brought in who was in a state of shock and searching for his granddaughter who had become separated from him.

Inquiring how they could recognize her the grandfather gave a description of a pendant she would be wearing. They did find her and when the doctor saw the necklace she froze. "Where did you get that necklace?" she asked.

The man admitted that no one could buy the necklace and then he went on to explain, "I am a goldsmith and I made this necklace. Actually, I made two identical pieces for each of my daughters. This is my granddaughter from one of them, and my other daughter did not survive the war."

Finally, the dots of her life connected. Who would have thought that after 60 years of being hidden in darkness, tucked away in shadows, but brought to the light at the right time that a necklace would reunite her with her lost family?

-Adapted from the book "Heroes of Faith"

- If government is big enough to give everything you want, it is strong enough to take everything you have.

  -Thomas Jefferson

- This country cannot afford to be materially rich and spiritually poor.

  -John F. Kennedy

- Freedom of speech is vital, not just because it's inherently gratifying to say what you think, but because speech is the foundational right of an open society. Free speech makes free thought possible.

  -Tucker Carlson
  (SOF, pg. 124)

- The word "Hebrew" which means "passing over" finds it origins in Eber, a grandson son of Shem. (TB, pg. 68)

- Scriptures like Ephesians 6:12, John 8:43-45 and 1 Peter 5:8 helps us to realize why the evil in the world is an orchestrated, systematic attack on godly values coming from the same source: same-sex marriage, political correctness that restricts Christian testimony and prayer, transgenderism, radical social engineering, anti-Semitism and anti-Zionism, all suggest that this is warfare—spiritual warfare—aimed at unseating God from His rightful place.

  -Larry Spargimino
  Prophetic Observer
  January 2016

- It takes more than knowing the Constitution to make one an American, and it takes more than knowing theology to be a Christian.

  -Vance Havner
  (RG, pg. 192)

- Force may make hypocrites, but it can make no converts.

  -William Penn

- Today's complacency is tomorrow's captivity.

  -Rodriquez

- We who have not crossed the stream must beware lest we burn the bridge.

  -Abraham Heschel
  (MQG, pg. 113)

- A nation can survive its fools, and even the ambitious. But it cannot survive treason from within.

  -Jesse Lee Pertson

- Politicians and diapers must be changed often and for the same reason.

  -Mark Twain

- The sacrifices that are demanded of Americans today may be necessary, but they must never become customary. The purpose of our government is to keep us alive, yea, but also to keep us living and working, as is our right.

  -Larry P. Arnn

The Tipping Point of Freedom

According to authors Chris and Ted Stewart in their book, "7 Tipping Points that Saved the World", it is estimated that fewer than five billion of the earth's total inhabitants have ever lived under conditions that we consider free. This means something like 4.5 percent of the people who have ever lived have tasted true freedom proving that freedom and democracy are extraordinarily rare events in human history.

Yale professor Robert Dahl identified only 22 nations with a democracy older than fifty years. It is for this reason that the Stewarts put this forth, "freedom is a relatively unstable marvel."

America was an experiment to see if a nation of people could and would govern themselves and found it worked, but to maintain self-governing the people must be moral to govern, just towards others to encourage it, and ensure strong family units to maintain healthy societies.

♦ Culture is not neutral. American culture is downright hostile to godliness. Make sure you have more than Christian beliefs (that's only a starting point); make sure you have a Christian worldview. People with Christian beliefs are easily duped; people with a Christian worldview still stand strong.

-Larry Spargimino
Prophetic Observer
April 2016

♦ We have to break free from this mindset in today's generation that we can disregard God and do whatever we want because it's "my life" and then expect Him to simply go along with our plans and bless them.

-Daniel Punnose
Gospel for Asia's Magazine
March 2016

♦ Here are the different names, meanings and work of Satan that were given in an article in Zion's Magazines by Marvin Rosenthal.

Dragon, which means "crafty."
Serpent, which means "subtle."

Devil, which means "accuser."
Satan, which means "adversary."

♦ Any nation that neglects the teaching the sacredness of life and the family does so at its own peril. Any nation that sanctions the removal of God's boundaries will destroy its own.
-Ravi Zacharias
(WJ, pg. 188)

♦ An estimated thirty thousand of today's North Korean Christians are living out their faith in concentration camps. (TG, pg. 114)

♦ (A nation) is poor precisely because it has been ruled by a narrow elite that has organized society for their own benefit at the expense of the vast mass of people. Political power has been narrowly concentrated, and has been used to create great wealth for those who possess it...
-Daron Acemoglu & James Robinson
(Why Nations Fail: the Origins of Power,
Prosperity and Poverty)

♦ A wide stream of human callousness separates us from the realm of holiness.

-Abraham Heschel
(MQG, pg. 112)

♦ The President's behavior is akin to a father who abandons his own family to care for another. He's a deadbeat dad to American children.

-Jesse Lee Peterson
Founder/President of BOND
Prophetic Observer

♦ The Book of Genesis spans nearly one-third of world history. (TB, pgs. 203)

♦ Too many friends are like shadows; they follow us only on sunny days.

-Vance Havner
(RG, pg.48)

♦ Four words that are easy to grasp to capture the medium of television: *induction, seduction, deduction,* and *reduction.*

-Ravi Zacharias
(WJ, pg. 29)

♦ Rabbit trails have nothing to do with anything and never come back to anything of significance.

-Jeannette Haley

♦ Without some central authority, society will disintegrate into chaos and anarchy. Every ship must have a captain, every kingdom a king, and every home a head if they are to function aright.

-J. Oswald Sanders
(JJ, pg. 41)

Definitions

I deal with lots of words and I can assume I know what they mean but assumption is a poor substitute for knowing and having the ability of keeping a word in perspective in your studies. Below are some interesting words that would behoove us as Christians to know.

Humanism is a subtle worldview that demotes God to not being God! It describes a philosophy that rejects the supernatural and relies on human reason as the ultimate authority—collectively or individually. (TB, pg. 25)

Atheism is but one form of humanism where man is elevated to a position of being greater than God. (TB, pg. 245)

Evolution did not take place at all; it is a religious concept. It actually supports a humanistic outlook which is a religious concept in its primary doctrinal dogma. (Dr. Carl Baugh, FST, pg.5)

Docetism is a belief that Jesus was truly God, but not truly human—he only *appeared* to be human. (MIC, pg. 24, 25)

Gnosticism is a belief that salvation comes through a secret knowledge that only an elite few could obtain. It also believes in *dualism,* which is the idea that what is spirit is, by definition, good, and what is material is, by definition, evil. Dualism was necessary to deny the incarnation of Jesus. (MIC, pg. 35, 39)

Materialism denies the supernatural and looks to redeeming society by concentrating its energies on ameliorating the outward conditions of human life. (BT, pg. 130)

Pessimism is the offspring of materialism. It proclaims that the balance of life is always toward suffering, that misery is the law of our being, and that there is no other gospel for men than the gospel of despair. (BT, pg. 130)

Arianism claimed that Christ was not fully God, but rather a created being. It is also known as *subordinationism.* (MIC, pg. 95)

Apollinarianism claimed that Christ was not fully human. He had a human body, but the rest was deity. (MIC, pg. 95)

Nestorianism claimed that Christ was two persons: Jesus was the human person and Christ was the divine person. (MIC, pg. 95)

Manichaeism is a philosophy/religion that assumed two eternal and equal principles? of good and evil in constant struggle with one another. (MIC, pg. 102)

Deism is the belief that the universe was created by God to operate on its own, much like a machine. They ignore or reject the doctrines of the Trinity and the deity of Jesus Christ and classify it as being irrational. They basically stripped historic Christianity of everything supernatural. (MIC, pg. 207, 216)

Socinian was a theological movement in the 16th and 17th centuries that professed belief in God and adherence to the Christian Scriptures, but denied the divinity of Christ. (BT, pg. 130)

Liberal Theology was thoroughly entrenched in German universities in the nineteenth century. It entered the North American scene as the "New Theology" through pastors and scholars who received their graduate theological training in these European universities. It has inspired the "social gospel" (salvation through good works) and sees American capitalism as a societal sin because it appears to repress the poor and the workers. It is best described in this way by H. Richard Niebuhr, "A God without wrath brought men without sin into a kingdom without judgment through ministration of a Christ without a cross." (MIC, pg. 226, 227)

Liberation Theologies focus the specific form of oppression that is being addressed. For example, black theology focuses on racism in the United States and feminist liberation theology focuses on the repression of women wherever it occurs. (MIC, pg. 271)

Rationalism operated according to the intellect and would not accept anything but that which harmonized with the depraved and imperfect reason of man. (BT, pg. 130)

Sacerdotalism is the exaltation of priestcraft, its substitution of the sensuous for the spiritual, and it subtle attempt to lead men back to the "beggarly elements" of externalism.

Adoptionism: The belief that Jesus was only human until John baptized Him. After that He was "adopted" by God to become a

Son of God. This was the teaching of some early Gnostics who pretended to be Christians.

Dialectics: A term for negotiation where opposing sides can "meet in the middle." It carries the idea everyone wins, but we all know in such a setting everyone compromises to get along, while truth is sacrificed in the process.

Exponential Curve: This is an acceleration in time such as what happens during the birth pains or travailing of a woman in childbirth. Time may seem to stand still when in fact, when it is over it appears as if it actually accelerates. This possibly describes the times we are living in. It seems time has stopped when in essence everything (events) seems to be accelerating towards Jesus' coming.

♦ Religion *begins* with the sense of the ineffable; philosophy *ends* with the sense of the ineffable. Religion begins where philosophy ends.

-Abraham Heschel
(MQG, pg. 141)

♦ At this rate, it is obvious that the America we once knew will soon become a vestige of the past. The once prosperous and peaceful nation that drew many to its shores by American exceptionalism will be turned into an American disgrace, a whimpering third-rate nation that can neither care for its own, nor those who come here for refuge. The nation that was once a beacon of hope for the oppressed will have the flame of liberty snuffed out.

-Larry Spargimino
Prophetic Observer

♦ Blowing out someone else's candle doesn't make yours shine any brighter.

-Unknown
(Internet)

Eternity

Are you living in light of eternity? Everyone is preparing for eternity, but not everyone lives in light of eternity. The way to life and heaven is narrow and hard, but the way to death and hell is broad and will prove to be hard for the transgressor. People who live for this present world do so because it is the only life they know. They pursue the idea of life based on the lusts of the flesh, the ideas of life according to culture, and the promise of life according to the world. Such a life is about creating or finding a lifestyle that will fit a person's unrealistic concept of it, but the truth is there is no life in any of it.

As a believer in Jesus Christ, I try to live the life I was entrusted with according to the eternal promises of heaven. I fight battles with the flesh to advance forward, run the race to put the terrain of this age behind me, stand on the Rock when hell is shaking my world, and choose to remember that my real heritage started at the cross of Christ and my real inheritance is not only before me but it is eternal.

I have dealt with people who are facing death. As one man was walking through the valley of the shadow of death, I told him he had to let go of this present world to take the hand of the Lord. I told believers who were about to lose a spouse to let them know it was alright to cease from trying to exist in their present state so they could enter the glorious promises of the next. I have talked to my Christian friends who were about to enter glory, and the one thing we discussed was their preparedness to meet Jesus.

Heavenly Treasures

As I walked through the valley of the shadow of death with my cousin, LeNita. Her main concern was whether she was ready to stand before Jesus without fear or shame. All of her Christian walk she had been a diamond, ever being prepared by the faithful hand of God. When she wrestled with her own status in God's kingdom, I would remind her that she had entrusted her soul to Jesus and that He was the One who held her.

One day we discussed how members of our family just before their death had shared how some family member who had previously entered through the door of death, would come to them in a dream or vision just before their departure. Then she shared how her mother had just come to her and that she sensed her departure was close at hand.

Less than a week later her daughter called me with the inevitable news that her mother's departure was close at hand. I knew for the daughter's sake she had to make sure she was at peace in letting her mother go. Even though LeNita was in a comatose state, there were unspoken words that needed to be articulated by her daughter that I knew would reach the spirit and soul of her mother. The daughter spoke the words.

She told me that there was a peace that settled upon her mother and then shortly afterwards her mother's eyes suddenly opened wide as if she had been awakened by someone, possibly speaking her name, and then her eyes closed, and her body slumped back as her spirit and soul entered into glory.

The Bible tells us Jesus will call His sheep by name, and in my mind when my cousin's eyes opened, it was to see the Shepherd of her soul reaching for her hand to take her home.

In another situation we were ministering to our friend, Vickie Brown, whose body had been ravished. She had been in a car accident that ended with the doctors reconstructing her face. Her body had been scared by various surgeries, she had a pacemaker, her kidneys were failing and she was living on dialysis. She was imprisoned in a body that challenged her in every way, but through it all, she kept her sense of humor.

As we were ministering to her, I mentioned that one day we would receive new, glorified bodies. I will never forget how Vickie's face lit up as she marveled at the very thought. I can still hear her voice as she repeated, "I'm going to have new body!" At that moment heaven came down, transforming her face with a glow that made her wrinkles flee, leaving her looking young. Needless to say, she left our home with such great expectancy. That night she left the prison of her body behind as she went home to be with the Lord.

As believers, we have nothing here of any value except the spiritual investments we make of Christ's life into souls. We have little that we can leave behind except the precious nuggets of truth. We have no lasting legacy except our example of a godly life, and we have no real inheritance to leave behind except the testimony of the impact made on our souls by an old rugged cross, upon which God's sacrifice became the means of lifting up our sin-laden souls above the condemnation of the present age.

Psalm 116:15 states, "Precious in the sight of the LORD is the death of his saints." It is bittersweet to walk with a Christian on the last leg of their journey. It is bitter because their physical absence will leave behind a great sense of loss, but it is sweet because there is such confidence of the great promise that awaits their soul. That is why Paul made this declaration about death, "Where is thy sting?" King David was able to declare that even though he walked through the valley of the shadow of death, he feared no evil.

The song writer of "Rock of Ages", Augustus Toplady, who lived only two more years after his famous song was published in 1776, found consolations of God during his final illness. Near his last waking hours from a sleep, he made this statement, "Oh, what delights! Who can fathom the joy of the third heaven? The sky is clear, there is no cloud; come Lord Jesus, come quickly!" He died saying, "No mortal man can live after the glories which God has manifested to my soul."

But what about the other side of the coin when it comes to eternity? That of death, damnation, hell, and the lake of fire. This is a side of the coin that is kept face down so man can skirt around it with a quasi-take on Universalism as a way to make everyone's departure tolerable to any fragile, struggling mind regardless of the person's spiritual state.

There was a heretical preacher that prepared for his death. As he was dying, he began to mumble, "Open the door, open the door." His wife perceived he was talking to her, and as I heard the story, I thought of a couple of scriptures. The first one is found in Revelation 3:7, "And to the angel of the church in Philadelphia write; These things saith he that is holy, he that is true, he that hath the key of David, he that OPENETH, and no man shutteth and SHUTTETH, and no man openeth." (Caps added.)

The second scripture is found in Matthew 7:21, "Not every one that saith unto me, Lord, Lord, shall enter into the kingdom of heaven, but he that doeth the will of my Father which is in heaven."

When I heard this preacher's story, I trembled. He assumed he was okay, but the door to glory was closed to him. It reminded me of the parable of the ten virgins in Matthew 25:1-13. Five were ready for the Bridegroom, and five were not and when the Bridegroom came he shut the five who were ready in with him and when the other five came up to the door, it remained closed to them regardless of their knocking and cries.

This brings us to what the Bible refers to as "fools." Calamity can quickly fall on the wicked, leaving no place for repentance, but what about those who know death is coming? Do they sense that their rejection and mocking was foolish? Do they realize that there is a God and eternity? Although I read much of this in a book called, VOICES FROM THE EDGE OF ETERNITY, the following information was summarized quite nicely on the internet. See for yourself.

1. **CAESAR BORGIA**—Italian nobleman, politician, and cardinal: "While I lived, I provided for everything but death; now I must die, and am unprepared to die."
2. **THOMAS HOBBS**—Political philosopher: "I say again, if I had the whole world at my disposal, I would give it to live one day. I am about to take a leap into the dark."
3. **THOMAS PAYNE**—The leading atheistic writer in American colonies: "Stay with me, for God's sake; I cannot bear to be left alone, O Lord, help me! O God, what have I done to suffer so much? What will become of me hereafter? I would give worlds if I had them, that The Age of Reason had never been published. 0 Lord, help me! Christ, help me! No, don't leave; stay with me! Send even a child to stay with me; for I am on the edge of hell here alone. If ever the Devil had an agent, I have been that one."
4. **SIR THOMAS SCOTT**—Chancellor of England: "Until this moment I thought there was neither a God nor a hell. Now I know and feel that there are both, and I am doomed to perdition by the just judgment of the Almighty."
5. **VOLTAIRE**—famous anti-Christian atheist: "I have swallowed nothing but smoke. I have intoxicated myself with the incense that turned my head. I am abandoned by God and man." He said to his physician, Dr. Fochin: "I will give you half of what I am worth if you will give me six months of life." When he was told this was not possible, he said "Then I shall die and go to hell!" His nurse said: "For all the money in Europe I wouldn't want to see another unbeliever die! All night long he cried for forgiveness."
6. **ROBERT INGERSOLL**—American writer and orator during the Golden Age of Free Thought: "O God, if there be a God, save

my soul, if I have a soul!" Some say it was said this way: "Oh God, if there be a God, save my soul, if I have a soul, from hell, if there be a hell!"

7. **DAVID HUME**—Atheist philosopher famous for his philosophy of empiricism and skepticism of religion: He cried loud on his death bed "I am in flames!" It is said his desperation was a horrible scene.

8. **NAPOLEON BONAPARTE**—French emperor who, like Adolf Hitler, brought death to millions to satisfy his greedy, power-mad, selfish ambitions for world conquest: "I die before my time, and my body will be given back to the earth. Such is the fate of him who has been called the great Napoleon. What an abyss between my deep misery and the eternal kingdom of Christ!"

9. **SIR FRANCIS NEWPORT**—Head of an English Atheist club, to those gathered around his deathbed: "You need not tell me there is no God, for I know there is one, and that I am in his presence! You need not tell me there is no hell. I feel myself already slipping. Wretches, cease your idle talk about there being hope for me! I know I am lost forever! Oh, that fire! Oh, the insufferable pangs of hell! Oh, that I could lie for a thousand years upon the fire that is never quenched, to purchase the favor of God and be united to Him again. But it is a fruitless wish. Millions and millions of years will bring me no nearer the end of my torments than one poor hour. Oh, eternity, eternity forever and forever! Oh, the insufferable pangs of Hell!"

10. **CHARLES IX**—The French king. Urged on by his mother, he gave the order for the massacre of the French Huguenots, in which 15,000 souls were slaughtered in Paris alone and 100,000 in other sections of France, for no other reason than that they loved Christ. The guilty king suffered miserably for years after that event. He finally died, bathed in blood bursting from his veins. To his physicians, he said in his last hours:

"Asleep or awake, I see the mangled forms of the Huguenots passing before me. They drop with blood. They point at their open wounds. Oh! That I had spared at least the little infants at the bosom! What blood! I know not where I am. How will all this end? What shall I do? I am lost forever! I know it. Oh, I have done wrong."

11. **DAVID STRAUSS**—Leading representative of German rationalism, after spending a lifetime erasing belief in God from the minds of others: "My philosophy leaves me utterly forlorn! I feel like one caught in the merciless jaws of an automatic machine, not knowing at what time one of its great hammers may crush me!"

12. **JOSEF STALIN**—Soviet Georgian revolutionary and politician. In a Newsweek interview with Svetlana Stalin, the daughter of Josef Stalin, she told of her father's death: "My father died a difficult and terrible death. . .God grants an easy death only to the just. At what seemed the very last moment, he suddenly opened his eyes and cast a glance over everyone in the room. It was a terrible glance, insane or perhaps angry. His left hand was raised, as though he were pointing to something above and bringing down a curse on us all. The gesture was full of menace. . .the next moment he was dead."

13. **ANTON LEVEY**—Author of the Satanic Bible and high priest of the religion dedicated to the worship of Satan. One of his famous quotes was: "There is a beast in man that needs to be exercised, not exorcised". His dying words were: "Oh my, oh my, what have I done, there is something very wrong. . . there is something very wrong."

14. **GANDHI**—At his death, he said, "For the first time in 50 years, I find myself in the slough of despond. All about me is darkness. . .I am praying for light."

> **Notation:** *God will always have the last say in all matters and His Word clearly states, "Only fools say in their hearts, there is no God" (Psalm 14:1). (KJV – "The fool hath said in his heart,…")*

- Those who deny freedom to others deserve it not for themselves.

  -Abraham Lincoln

- We must be ready to dare all for our country. For history does not long entrust the care of freedom to the weak or the timid.

  -Dwight D. Eisenhower

- In the truest sense, freedom cannot be bestowed; it must be achieved.

  -Franklin D. Roosevelt

- This nation will remain the land of the free only so long as it is the home of the brave.

  -Elmer Davis

- I must study politics and war, that our sons may have liberty to study mathematics and philosophy.

  -John Adams

- Those who expect to reap the blessings of freedom must, like men undergo the fatigue of supporting it.

  -Thomas Paine

A Bit of Humor

Man in his imperfect state can add bits of humor to innocent measures. It is not what is said that makes a matter humorous;

rather, it is the type of connotations individuals can put to something that can create laugher. This is true when it comes to signs, billboards, and church bulletins.

Consider the following statements that found their way in church bulletins. We call them BLOOPERS. And, perhaps you have already read some of these, but allow them to once again tickle your funny bone. The Bible tells us that laughter is good for the soul. (KJV – "A merry heart doeth good like a medicine.")

- The Fasting & Prayer Conference includes meals.
- The sermon this morning: Jesus Walks on the Water. The sermon tonight: Searching for Jesus.
- Ladies, don't forget the rummage sale. It's a chance to get rid of those things not worth keeping around the house. Bring your husbands.
- Don't let worry kill you off – let the Church help.
- Next Thursday there will be tryouts for the choir. They need all the help they can get.
- At the evening service tonight, the sermon topic will be "What is Hell?" Come early and listen to our choir practice.
- Eight new choir robes are currently needed due to the addition of several new members and to the deterioration of some older ones.
- The ladies of the Church have a case of clothing of every kind. They may be seen in the basement on Friday afternoon.
- This evening at 7 PM there will be a hymn sing in the park across from the Church. Bring a blanket and come prepared to sin.
- Low Self Esteem Support Group will meet Thursday at 7 PM. Please use the back door.
- Weight Watchers will meet a 7 PM at the First Presbyterian Church. Please use large double door at the side entrance.

Can You Solve It?

A friend gave us the following riddle to see if we could figure it out. It took two heads, two days and much summation before Jeannette and I figured out the answer. Apparently, this riddle was prepared after a challenge went out by a particular individual that if anyone could present him with a riddle that he could not solve that he would pay that person $1,000.00. This particular riddle was one he could not solve and he had to pay the money.

The answer is found in the Bible. If you have not already been challenged with this riddle and know the answer, see if you can solve it. The answer of the riddle can be found on page 361.

Adam, God made out of dust,
    But thought it best to make me first,
So I was made before now,
    To answer God's most holy plan,
A living being I became,
    And Adam gave to me my name,
I from his presence then withdrew,
    And more of Adam I never knew.
I did my Maker's law obey,
    Nor never went from it astray,
Thousands of miles I go in fear,
    But seldom on earth appear,
For purpose wise which God did see,
    He put a living soul in me,
A soul from me God did claim,
    And took from me the soul had fled,
I was the same as when first made,
    And without hands or feet or soul,
I traveled on from pole to pole.
    I labor hard by day, by night,

To fallen man I give great light,
    Thousands of people, young and old,
Will by my death great light behold,
    No right or wrong can I conceive,
The Scripture I cannot believe
    Although my name there is found,
They are to me an empty sound,
    No fear of death doth trouble me,
Real happiness I'll never see,
    To Heaven I shall never go, or to Hell below.
Now when these lines you slowly read
    Go search your Bible with all speed,
For that my name is written there,
    I do honestly to you declare,
"The answer is ONE word."

Who Am I?

1. This man obtained seven million four hundred dollars by prayer.
2. This revivalist not only authored nearly forty books, but he is considered by many to be the most quoted preacher of the 20th century.
3. This pastor and author lived from 1828-1917. He humorously once described himself in this manner when preparing a message, "that he was like a hen about to hatch an egg; he was restless and unhappy until he got the burden of the message off his mind."
4. He was a brilliant young Cambridge scholar who at the age of 20 after gaining the highest award in mathematics, threw away his prospects for seven years of missionary work. In those seven years he gave the world the New Testament in three of the major languages in the East.

5. He was head of the criminal investigation department of Scotland Yard and the political crime advisor to the British Home Office.

6. This individual lived during the 17th century and his book sold more than 100,000 copies within his lifetime and has never been out of print. Even today it is the second most widely distributed book in the world and only has been surpassed by the Bible, and it has been translated into over two hundred languages.

7. Without his approval, this man was nominated for vice president of the United States on the Equal Rights Party ticket in 1872.

8. This famous author wrote the book, "The Life of Our Lord," to read it to his children every Christmas season. He had no intention of publishing it, and it was not until after his son's death that he bequeathed the original manuscript to his wife to do as she will with it that it was finally published in 1934, sixty-four years after the author's death.

9. This missionary labored in India for forty years and established forty-five schools, founded a leper hospital, and published a newspaper.

10. He was a poor sightless musician born in Ireland, who felt he could do very little for the Master he loved, but in spite of his challenges became a missionary to India where his first convert was a Muslim.

11. He and his wife spent over 50 years on the mission field in Africa. His daughter Mary, married another famous missionary of Africa by the name of David Livingstone.

12. He was known as the Apostle of Prayer.

13. This missionary had to appeal to President Tyler for a treaty to push back the colonization of the Hudson Bay Company in the territory of Oregon to secure it for the United States of America.

The answers are found on the next page: **358**

Answer to the Riddle

Whale (Genesis 1:21)

Answers to Who Am I.

1. George Mueller
2. Vance Havner
3. Andrew Murray
4. Henry Martyn
5. Sir Robert Anderson
6. John Bunyan
   Pilgrim's Progress
7. Frederick Douglass
8. Charles Dickens
9. William Carey
10. William Butler
11. Robert Moffat
12. John Hyde
13. Marcus Whitman, M.D

Bibliography

(HA) He Is Able, W. E. Sangster, © 1937 by Whitmore & Smith

(BT) The Best of R. A. Torrey, third printing, March 1992, Baker Book House

(MM) The Man Who Died for Me, Herbert Lockyer, © 1979 by Word Inc.

(TP): The Prophets, © by Abraham J. Heschel, Harper Perennia Modern Classics

(CCA) The Christians in Complete Armour, William Gurnall; Hendrickson Publishers Marketing, LLC; The first edition of this work was published in Scotland in 1865.

(MQG) Man's Quest For God, Abraham Joshua Heschel, © 1996 by Sylvia Heschel, Aurora Press

(TG) These Are the Generations, Mr. & Mrs. Bae, as told to the Rev. Eric Foley, © 2012 Seoul USA, W. Publishing, Colorado Springs, Co.

(GHC) The God Who Hung on the Cross, Dois I. Rosser Jr. & Ellen Vaughn, © 2003 by International Cooperating Ministries. Zondervan

(IA) In the Arena, Isobel Kuhn, OMF International

(AWC) America's War on Christianity, © 2010 by Brad O'Leary, WND Books

(NAG) Now That Is Amazing Grace, © 2001 by William MacDonald, Gospel Folio Press

(CS) Choosing to See, © by Mary Beth Chapman, Published by Revell, a division of Baker Publishing Group

(TH) Types In Hebrews, Sir Robert Anderson, © 1978 by Kregel Publications

(SC) Sunrise in Canaan, © 2000 by Schmul Publishing Co.

(BH) Beyond Humiliation (The Way of the Cross), John Gregory Mantle, 1974, Testimony Book Ministry

(MA) Messages of God's Abundance, Corrie ten Boom, © 2002 by Stichting Trans World Radio Voor Nederland en Belgie

(JG) Jesus, Our Man in Glory, A. W. Tozer, © 1987 by Zur Ltd.

(WC) With Christ in the School of Prayer, Andrew Murray, © 1981 by Whitaker House

(RG) Reflections on the Gospels, Devotional Thoughts From the Pen of Vance Havner, © 1994 by Michael C. Catt, published by CLC * Publications

Captive In Iran; Maryam Rostampour & Marziyeh Amirizadeh, with John Perry, © 2013, Tyndale House Publishers. Inc..

(HC) Hebrews: An Ironside Expository Commentary, published in 1932. Reprinted in 2008 by Kregel Publicaitons.

(TGT) Trusting God in a Twisted World, Elisabeth Elliot, © 1989, Fleming H. Revell Company.

(WJ) Why Jesus? Ravi Zacharias, © 2012, FaithWords, Hachette Book Group

(GBM) God's Blessed Man, Paul Rader, © 1922, Georg M. Doran Company

(FJ) The Fullness of Joy, Charles Spurgeon, © 1997 by Whitaker House

(SBB) Stories of the Book of Books, Grace W. McGavran, © 1947 by Friendship Press, Inc.

(JJ) The Joy of Following Jesus, J. Oswald Sanders, © 1990, 1994 by The Moody Bible Institute of Chicago

(TB) Tower of Babel, Bodie Hodge, © 2012, Master Books

(FST) Footprints and the Stones of Time, Dr. Carl Baugh & Dr. Clifford Wilson, © 1992

(GMM) God the Master Mathematician, © 2012 by Dr. N. W. Hutchings, Bible Belt Publishing.

(RT) Redemption Truths, Sir Robert Anderson, © 1980 by Kregel Publications

(SFG) Seeking the Face of God, Martyn Lloyd-Jones, © 1991 by Elizabeth Catherwood and Ann Desmond, Published by Crossway

(GAM) The Gospel and Its Ministry, Sir Robert Anderson, © 1978 by Kregel Publications.

(TG) 199 Treasures of Wisdom on Talking with God, Andrew Murray, © 2007 by Barbour Publishing, Inc.

(MDP) My Daily Pursuit, A.W. Tozer, © by James L. Snyder, Published by Regal from Gospel Light

(SWR) Susanna Wesley Her Remarkable Life, Ray Comfort with Trisha Ramos, © 2014 Bridge-Logos, In.

(HSC) How to Succeed in the Christians Life, R.A. Torrey, © 1984 by Whitaker House

(KC) The Kneeling Christians, An Unknown Christian, © 1945, 1971, 1986 by Zondervan.

(GWP) God Has A Wonderful Plan For Your Life, © 2010 by Ray Comfort, Living Waters Publications

(TC) They Were Christians, © 2016 by Cristobal Krusen, published by Baker Books

(SL) Spiritual Leadership, J. Oswald Sanders, © 1967, 1980, 1994, 2007 by the Moody Bible Institute of Chicago.

(SOF) Ship of Fools, © 2018 by Tucker Carlson, published by Free Press

(PH) Praying Hyde, Edited by Captain E. G. Carré, © 1982 by Bridge-Logos

(The Miracle of Freedom) 7 Tipping Points that Saved the World, Chris Stewart and Ted Stewart, © 2011 The Shipley Group Inc. and Brian T. Stewart.

(RCF) Reclaiming Christianity, A.W. Tozer, © 2009 James L. Snyder, Regal from Gospel Light Ventura, California

(HD) Home Before Dark, Mary Danielsen © 2019

(MSR) The Mute Christian Under the Smarting Rod, Thomas Brooks 1659, London; Sovereign Grace Treasures, August 2006

(PD) Playing Marbles With Diamonds, Vance Havner, © 1985, 1989 by Baker Book House

(ILT) In Times Like These, Vance Havner, © 1969 by Fleming H. Revell Company

(RTR) Road to Revival, Vance Havner, © 1940, 1968 by Fleming H. Revell, a division of Baker Book House Company

(QT) Quiet Talks on Following the Christ, Samuel Dickey Gordon, Published in 1913, Cosimo Classics, New York

(VOV) The Valley of Vision; © The Banner of Truth Trust; Last reprint 2015

Other books by Rayola Kelley

Hidden Manna
Battle for the Soul
Stories of the Heart
Transforming Love & Beyond
The Great Debate
Post to Post: (1) Establishing the Way
Post to Post: (2) Walking in the Way

Volume One: Establishing Our Life in Christ
My Words are Spirit and Life
The Anatomy of Sin
The Principles of the Abundant Life
The Place of Covenant
Unmasking the Cult Mentality

Volume Two: Putting on the Life of Christ
He Actually Thought It Not Robbery
Revelation of the Cross
In Search of Real Faith
Think on These Things
Follow the Pattern

Volume Three: Developing a Godly Environment
Godly Discipline
Prayer and Worship
Don't Touch That Dial
Face of Thankfulness
ABC's of Christianity

Volume Four: Issues of the Heart
Hidden Manna (Revised)
Bring Down the Sacred Cows
The Manual for the Single Christian Life
Parents are People Too

Volume Five: Challenging the Christian Life
The Issues of Life
Presentation of the Gospel
For the Purpose of Edification
Whatever Happened to the Church?
Women's Place in the Kingdom of God

www.ingramcontent.com/pod-product-compliance
Lightning Source LLC
Chambersburg PA
CBHW071156020726
47502CB00002B/438